The Sacred and the Secular

Prentice-Hall International, Inc., *London*
Prentice-Hall of Australia, Pty. Ltd., *Sydney*
Prentice-Hall of Canada, Ltd., *Toronto*
Prentice-Hall of India Private Ltd., *New Delhi*
Prentice-Hall of Japan, Inc., *Tokyo*

The Sacred and the Secular

MICHAEL J. TAYLOR, S.J.
Seattle University

Prentice-Hall, Inc. *Englewood Cliffs, New Jersey*

Imprimi potest:
John J. Kelley, S.J.
Provincial of the Oregon Province

Nihil obstat:
William F. Hogan, S.T.D.
Censor Librorum

Imprimatur:
✠ Thomas A. Boland, S.T.D.
Archbishop of Newark

Library of Congress Catalog Card Number: 68:21291

Printed in the United States of America

Current Printing (last digit):

10 9 8 7 6 5 4 3 2

Contents

The Sacred
and
the Secular

Introduction

Michael J. Taylor, S.J.

Most men have seen life on earth as containing both sacred and secular elements. In the past these two factors were not always easy to identify. But now, because of the process of secularization, they are more easily distinguished. The Christian may be suspicious of the term "secularization," but he need not consider it a threat to his faith. In a commonly accepted sense, secularization simply means that that which is secular, the natural world, is understandable in itself; for the most part it is autonomous and man can know and penetrate its meaning without referring to God or the supernatural; nothing extrinsic to the world and nothing beyond man's mind and experience are necessary to discover how the universe works.

Of course, some carry this view too far. Secularists who do not believe in God claim that the day will come when even the supposed sacred elements of life will yield their mystery to human intelligence. There are, however, "secularists" who do believe in God and who therefore see things differently. With the discovery of a world that runs by itself, they give more respect to both the sacred and the secular. Whereas the ancients confused these two elements, believing secularists now clearly distinguish the two. Christianity, in fact, has done more toward liberating the secular from the sacred than any of the older religions. This new faith had such a unique regard for God and the supernatural that it would not permit the sacred to be identified with the secular. In this sense Christianity *desacralized* the world and permitted man to investigate it fully without fear of violating the territory of the gods.

The science of the world, indeed the science of politics and social living, have hereby been desacralized; they are no longer what ancient men thought them to be, that is, essentially religious matters. It was primarily Christianity that distinguished between the church and the state. The state's mission was limited to the human welfare of man in the secular city; the church's mission was concerned with a higher welfare, with man's spiritual status in this world and his salvation in the next. The state had often assumed authority over man's entire life, but the church insisted that the state had no power over matters that were spiritual and eternal.

What is this spiritual or sacred element in man's life? Admitting that we still have much to learn about the sacred, this much we can say. It is the presence and self-communication of God, who, though transcendent, has revealed and communicated himself to man in the world. The sacred, then, is concerned with God; anything and everything that is properly called sacred comes from him. When God created the universe and gave it its autonomous nature, he never intended to remain apart from it, a distant figure only to be worshiped. He always wanted to share himself with man, and if Christianity means anything, it means that God has come to us through grace; we can now share his life and love, his kind of knowing and happiness. In brief, life is sacred because God has brought us into personal union with himself.

But how does this personal union affect man's secular life? This is an important question because the Christian lives his life with God *in* the world and, in a real sense, *for* the world. When he becomes indwelt by grace, the human and secular elements of his life, the social, the cultural, the political—in fact all elements of human living —take on a deeper significance. Man's secular activity remains autonomous, but it is now given a new value and direction. Affected by grace, it is not only an activity worthy of his efforts as a man; it can become a work of Christian commitment, undertaken to promote a fuller humanization of man and the world.

Nevertheless, we still tend to separate grace from ordinary life and work, to show only a pragmatic interest in the secular as such. For many believers the purely secular has little Christian significance; only activity that explicitly centers around the sacred deserves to be called Christian. This attitude greatly minimizes the importance and value of secular activity as something good in itself, as a worthy vocation for the Christian, indeed as the work which should command his best energies during this life.

In order to relate the sacred to the secular in a way that does credit to both, we should distinguish between that which is sacred in itself and that which, though secular, can and should be affected or sanctified by the sacred. The Christian is concerned with bringing Christ's redemptive love to bear on all secular activity, on every phase of human life. In doing this, however, he seeks to *sanctify* the secular, not to sacralize it.

For a secular reality to become sacred it must be somehow changed; it must be consecrated or set aside for a spiritual or supernatural purpose, as, for example, the consecration of a church, an altar, or, in some ways, a priest. The church, the altar, and the priest would then in some sense be withdrawn from worldly purposes and set aside for spiritual activities, such as the worship and service of God. If the task of Christianity were to make secular activity sacred in this sense, it would indeed entail sacralization. The strictly secular life of man would disappear; everything would be sacred. But if as Christians we seek to sanctify the world, perhaps we can establish a more meaningful relationship between the sacred and the secular.

Christians accept the secular character of the world and view man's life as good and filled with meaning. They seek not to deny the intrinsic worth and meaning of the world, but only to sanctify it so that they might deepen and fully exploit its meaning for man. Christians respect the world and work for it because it is good. They want to sanctify it to insure its goodness, to make it less apt to compromise its goodness. They desire to make scientific investigation of the world and every human pursuit something that always redounds to the good of man, his further perfection and humanization.

Respect for secular values demands a new vision of the world different from the one the church has often shown. The church must put aside its past suspicions of the world and see again that the universe is good because it comes from God. The church must also accept the secular city for what it is and give itself in love and service to the city as the "light among the nations." The world as such is not an obstacle to salvation, a "vale of tears" or place of exile. The church must see the natural world as something given to man to develop and fulfill; it is his responsibility to discover its deepest meaning, to find for it a place before God.

Finally, the church must see that grace is present and working in all men of good will. The former view of the world as a reality without grace and opposed to the church is no longer valid; Vatican II in its Constitution on the *Church in the Modern World* has made that clear. It is true that Christ has visibly manifested his sacred presence in the church and the sacraments, but in subtle and hidden ways he is influencing the consciences of all men. Granted that much of secular reality seems to have nothing to do with grace, secular history in its totality is never untouched by it. From God's intervention in history, grace has been working a sanctifying effect on all men. Despite sin and evil Christ leads all of us to his love and grace. There is, for example, a growing awareness of the dignity of the human person with his own freedoms and rights. Men are slowly beginning to accept their neighbors as brothers even though they do not yet see their fraternity as flowing from the common fatherhood of God. Surely this change in attitude must be seen as a result of the universal influence of grace and not just the product of man's unaided reason.

We need not worry, as some suggest, that the presence of universal grace will create religious indifference or dampen the Christian's missionary effort; for the grace that is hidden within man needs the constant exemplary influence of the grace that is visible in the church and the sacraments. To accomplish its perfective purpose, grace must be seen to exist and to exercise a decisive influence on man's human development. Only when we see that grace helps man to become more human will others come to appreciate its higher and more sacred purposes.

The church must concern itself with grace, with the sacred itself. It must clearly proclaim the message of God-with-us and the availability of his saving grace to all men. The church is God's instrument through which he gives himself to men; it is the visible community whose members are united in love through faith, baptism, and the celebration of the Eucharist. The church's very visibility indicates that it has a mission in the world. It can win explicit acceptance for Christ and the sacred by directly preaching about him and salvation, but each Christian must also aid in less direct ways by his committed service to the world. By working to solve the great human problems that confront men in the secular city, he can also bring the humanizing, sanctifying Christ to the world. Christians can and must work together for brotherhood, for social and racial justice, for the care and protection of the old, the poor, the oppressed, for the humanization of cities, for peace among the nations—these are the great secular tasks of our day and, a fortiori, the important Christian projects. The mission to serve the world's needs is the common task of all men, and it is consoling to know that in our portion we can all bring to it the grace of Christ.

Many look at the lack of genuine faith today and blame its disappearance on a secular spirit, which they say has overtaken us. It might be closer to the truth to say that faith has become weak because Christian culture no longer supports it. In the past, too many embraced Christianity because it was a cultural condition of life; too few worried about the depth and quality of their faith. Now, however, the cultural atmosphere of the age is not Christian; it is secular or neutral, and true faith, if it is to survive, must be deep and personal. A pluralist society need not prevent us from developing such a faith. Our society more and more respects the dignity and freedom of man; it works to develop human values; it endeavors to create citizens who are mature, just, honest, and concerned about their fellows, especially the less fortunate; in such a world man's faith *can* become strong, personal, and less self-centered.

The following essays speak of Christian faith in a time of ever-increasing secularization. In one way or another they are concerned with forming a contemporary theology of the secular; they also seek to talk about God in terms meaningful to modern man.

What does the reality of a rapidly changing world mean for the Christian? Does the new secular society offer more opportunities for finding God or does it hinder the quest? How does God and his grace enter into the secular life of modern man? Does a world that is increasingly more autonomous mean that Christ's dominion over it is coming to an end? Or is this new world in a way more receptive to Christ's gospel of love and grace and more able to live its precepts?

Whatever the answers, these questions demand frank discussion and a desire to search honestly for relevant solutions. The modern Christian cannot shrink from such investigations because it is in this world that he must experience Christ and communicate him to others. And these questions cannot be met by repeating solutions that satisfied an earlier generation; they demand answers modern Christians can understand.

The contributors to this volume have sought to give thoughtful answers to these questions. It is hoped that these essays will provide some general guidelines for the formation of a theoretical and practical theology of the secular. It is also hoped that they will help us see that our faith cannot live and grow in isolation from the world or from our fellow man, but must find daily expression in full service to the world that God created and redeemed in love.

Christian Secularity

Thomas E. Clarke, S.J.

Thomas E. Clarke, S.J., is Professor of Systematic Theology at Woodstock College in Maryland. He received his doctorate in theology in 1954 from the Gregorian University in Rome. He is co-author of two Christological anthologies, *Christ and His Mission* and *Word and Redeemer, Christology in the Fathers.* He is also an associate editor of *America* magazine.

Ecumenical Councils tend to survive in popular history in some word or phrase that encapsules their contribution to the ongoing life of the Church. The mention of Nicaea evokes the famous *homoousios;* Florence, reconciliation; Trent, justification; Vatican I, papal infallibility. And Vatican II? Will the world be *ecumenism?* Or *collegiality? Religious freedom? The people of God?* Or the triad of *self-realization, self-reform, dialogue,* with which the two Popes of the Council designated its goals? I would venture the guess that, important as all these aspects are, Vatican II may well live in history as the Council in which the Church inaugurated the age of *Christian secularity.*

The very suggestion may be startling to some. Apart from communism, has not secularism been the chief target of Popes and bishops during the past several decades? Are we not confronted today, particularly in the United States, with a progressive and almost systematic effort to exclude religion from significant influence on our national life, specifically in the area of education?

Yet pure error without at least a dash of profound truth is rare,

Reprinted with permission from *America,* The National Catholic Weekly Review, Vol. 12, No. 22 (May 29, 1965). The original title was "The World Is Already Christic."

and it has frequently happened in the Church that a period of rejection of heresy is quickly followed by the gradual assimilation of the truth embedded in the error. May we not interpret the warnings against secularism of earlier years as a necessary preparation for the eventual endorsement of Christian secularity?

At this point the reader may quite legitimately be asking for a distinction between secularism and secularity. Later in this article I hope to oblige (at least to some degree). But for an initial image of Christian secularity and its opposite, I would propose the following rather oversimplified example. Over a decade ago, like countless visitors in Rome, I was startled by the sign "*Banco di Spirito Santo.*" My first reaction was one of amusement: "Isn't this just like the Italians?" There quickly followed, as I recall, a feeling of approval: "Finding God in all things," "a thoroughly Christian atmosphere in the whole of life," were a few of the comments that came to mind. Today, however, the memory of the sign and of my reaction to it somewhat embarrasses and chagrins me. Today I feel: A bank is a bank is a bank. It is not a church. It is a place for money and finance, not for devotion. There are surely enough churches in Rome whose names may honor the Holy Spirit.

However homely and even trivial, the example may serve to raise the issue: Is my present attitude secularistic? Or does it represent a legitimate Christian secularity? And if banks are to be stripped of Christian labels, why not political parties and (to be trivial again and closer to America) breads and wines and hotels and aspirins and cough medicines? But then—what of hospitals and welfare organizations? More delicately still, what of schools and learning? Should we not also say: A poem is a poem is a poem; or, an atom is an atom is an atom, and leave the non-religious aspects of education and scholarship unembarrassed by religious preoccupations?

One of the most deeply rooted attitudes of modern man is his refusal to see his cherished human values captured or manipulated by forces and institutions he considers extraneous, whether it be by party-line communism or party-line Christianity. To what extent should the Church accommodate herself to this tenacious mentality? And to what extent is it a matter not merely of pragmatic accommodation (which frequently breeds even deeper resentment), but of a real exigency of the gospel, that human institutions be permitted a larger autonomy in Christian thought and action than they have enjoyed in the past?

The dilemma confronting Christian man today may be expressed as follows: He is, on the one hand, deeply convinced that the Incarnation profoundly touches human (and cosmic) life in all its aspects; for him it is inconceivable that any area of human endeavor should be unaffected by the gospel. On the other hand, he knows from history and perhaps from his own life that a too facile or imperialistic "baptizing" of human values ultimately serves neither these values nor Christianity. Is there not some way the world can be fully Christ's world without violence being done to its very *Weltlichkeit?*

It is curious and doubtless providential that two movements of modern Christian thought, at first glance contradictory, are today coming into vital confrontation in our effort to adopt a new Christian posture before the world and its values. For the sake of a name, we may identify these currents with the labels of *immanence* and *secularity.*

The first movement, reaching back to Maurice Blondel at the turn of the century, was a reaction against a certain dichotomy between natural and supernatural, between the human and the Christian. For over half a century now, through the sometimes risky and always tentative gropings of such thinkers as De Lubac, Von Balthasar and Karl Rahner, the insistence has been on the *unity* (rather than the distinction) of natural and supernatural orders, the *immanence* of the Christian in the human (rather than its transcendence of the human). The openness of nature to grace, a certain exigency in existential man for the gift of grace, a radical orientation of all men to the vision of God—such are the key affirmations of this current of ideas. It has more than a merely technical theological importance. For, in a very profound way, it strikes at the very roots of secularism, by maintaining the orientation of all human values not merely to God but to the Christian supernatural. It is one of the principal reasons why the Christian of tomorrow will find it impossible to thing of his Christianity as a glossy finish sprayed on the natural surface of human life. *Nil humanum alienum* and *ta panta en to Christo*—will be inseparable from his vision of Christ.

But the movement of immanence, if it answered a real need, also ran a real risk—the risk of a regression to a certain Augustinianism, which would so enclose natural and temporal structures within the Christian destiny of man as to deprive them of their inherent autonomy and consistency. The danger was perceived by many, and has been met by a movement of quite a different tenor, which still needs to be better integrated with the movement of immanence. This is the movement of Christian secularity. It has been gaining momentum in the last few decades.

Secularity is by no means new in modern Christian thought. Three decades ago, Jacques Maritain gave it powerful and distinctive expression in his remarkable *True Humanism.* He held up for the coming age the ideal of a Christendom (a term that today is expendable) that would not represent, as did the Middle Ages, a *consecration* of the temporal order and its *instrumentalization* for spiritual goals, but would rather aim at a refraction of the gospel in the world that would be secular in character, i.e., that would leave to the created and the temporal a certain status of autonomy that they lacked in the Middle Ages.

Much of what Maritain said may need revision today, but the basic insights were truly prophetic and are now finding many echoes in Christian thought. It is noteworthy that Karl Rahner, whose conception of the "supernatural existential" is the most prominent contemporary formulation of the movement of immanence stemming from Blondel, has also been in the forefront of those calling upon the Church to recognize that her medieval stance toward the world is no longer possible. He and many others have pointed out, for example, that it was Christianity that denuminized the forum and the market place, so that men might pursue their human tasks without being haunted by intruders from the upper world. His insistence on the "diaspora" situation of Christians today is too well known to need elaboration here.

Other Catholic thinkers have been writing in this vein. The Dominican Père Chenu has recently asked whether and in what sense the phrase *consecratio mundi,* despite its occurrence in modern papal documents, is an appropriate one to describe the layman's function with respect to the world. Another prominent Dominican, Fr. E. Schillebeeckx, in his essay "The Church and Mankind" moves in a similar direction [see pp. 14–40 in this volume]. On one specific aspect of the Church-world confrontation, that of religious freedom and Church-State relationships, it has been the effect of the contribution of Fr. John Courtney Murray to show that we are *not* reduced to choosing between a sacralistic and a secularistic solution.

Among Protestants a very influential movement, which stems from the writings of Dietrich Bonhoeffer (executed by the Nazis in 1945) and finds its chief popularizer in Bishop John Robinson, whose *Honest to God* and other publications currently have English Christians excited, has called for a secular version of Christianity in tones that have shocked many people. More recently, Paul Van Buren's *The Secular Meaning of the Gospel* and Harvey Cox's *The Secular City* show that the movement is by no means confined to the other side of the Atlantic. One of the tantalizing things about evaluating such writings is the difficulty of discerning where pastoral and apologetic adaptation stop and doctrinal innovation begins.

But enough of mere description of current theological trends. What is being proposed here under the rubric of Christian secularity? And how does it differ from secularism? Let me say at once that the following remarks are not intended as a definition of secularity. Probably we are in need of a few more decades of experience of it in actual life before we can adequately define it. Nevertheless, a few points of a descriptive nature may render the idea less vague.

First, Christian secularity excludes *instrumentalization.* The goodness of the creature (and not merely its non-evilness), of the world, of time and temporal institutions, is a central conviction of Christian secularity. Any *purely* instrumental approach to the world—that is, any attitude that would see in it merely a tool for Christian evangelization, that would neglect its innate values, its own immanent dynamisms and finalities—is incompatible with Christian secularity. The world is to be taken seriously. As Fr. Robert Johann has put it: "Whatever ultimate meaning life many have . . . life is a call to share in the world's making" (*America* 2/27, p. 287).

Secondly, Christian secularity excludes *sacralization.* This must not be misunderstood. The distinction betwen the *sacred* and the *secular* is beyond question. There is an area of man's life that is necessarily withdrawn (though not isolated) from his temporal concerns. In heaven the distinction will cease; God will be all in all, and the tension between man's commitments to the world and to God will have ceased. But as long as he is in this life, Christian man will need to express and confirm his transcendence of the temporal and the worldly by creating a realm of the sacred. Liturgy, or, to use Josef Pieper's term, celebration, is the heart of this realm of the sacred.

But it is one thing to affirm the distinction of the sacred and the secular, and something else again to deny all Christian and salvific value to the non-sacral areas of human life, or to approach the secular with the attitude that unless it is sacralized it is somehow lost or at least irrelevant to the Christian destiny of man. It is here that modern theology gives us an immense advantage over the man of the Middle Ages. For him, it was only the presence of the institutional and sacramental Church that rescued the world from its sinful condition, or at least brought the world, conceived as a neutral reality, within the sphere of the holy. For Francis Xavier, the ancestors of the pagans he evangelized were lost, because only the presence of the baptizing Church made salvation possible. More broadly, only the formal consecration (not to speak of exorcism) of the temporal gave it salvific status.

Today, we realize that the theology underlying such convictions, though correct in its insistence on the universal necessity of Christ and the Church for salvation, was not correct in some of the inferences it drew. Today, while we still realize that there is no salvation *apart from* Christ and the Church in the full scope of their presence and activity, we are aware that there is salvation for men and institutions *outside* the institutional, sacramental Church. We realize, too, that the world, as set over against the Church, is not necessarily to be conceived as a hostile or merely neutral force. By the Incarnation, by the cross and resurrection, the world is already Christic and ecclesial in its dynamic orientation. Its Christianity is, in Rahner's now famous term, *anonymous,* but it is real. To quote Fr. Schillebeeckx: "In the plan of salvation, the concrete world, by definition, is an *implicit Christianity;* it is an objective, non-sacral but saintly and sanctified expression of mankind's communion with the living God; whereas the Church, *qua* institution of salvation, with her explicit creed, her worship and sacraments, is the direct and sacral expression of that identical communion." [1]

Even from this sketchy presentation, one may see the implications of such a theology for the Christian's attitude toward the world—and toward the Church. The world is not so much to be consecrated, captured, given meaning and salvific relevance. Rather it is to be recognized, endorsed, brought to fulfillment. Also, if the world is, in a true sense, the undisclosed Church, the Church in her turn is the world fulfilled and manifested. In St. Augustine's beautiful phrase: "The Church *is* the world reconciled." She is not only the sign of Christ but the sign of the world—*sacramentum mundi.*

[1] *The Church and Mankind* (New Jersey: Paulist Press, 1965), p. 84.

From all this it may be seen that Christian secularity is not merely to be distinguished from secularism; it is at the opposite pole from it. Where secularism maintains that religion and Christianity are irrelevant for the world, Christian secularity insists that the world itself, even prior to its contact with institutional Christianity, is inescapably religious and Christian. Indeed, Christian secularity may run a greater risk of being a neo-sacralism than of being secularistic. The balance between these two extremes is a most delicate one. Even in such a champion of the world as Teilhard de Chardin there are passages (such as the one in which he says that the only reason he came to China was that he might preach the "great Christ" in Paris) that could appear to succumb to instrumentalism and sacralization.

Of the many possible ramifications of this view of the Church and the world, only one may be touched on here: the role of the laity in an era of Christian secularity. Among many others, Maritain, Rahner and, in a more pragmatic way, John Cogley, have warned against conceiving the lay apostolate as merely the secular arm of the institutional Church. Certainly there is in the Church a variety of instrumental roles—from parish catechist to member of a secular institute—for those of the laity who wish to participate in the hierarchy's task of formal evangelization. But the layman's primary role as Christian and therefore as apostle must be simply his active, Christian, witnessing presence in and to the world through his performance of the tasks of the world.

A host of other questions are raised by this idea of Christian secularity: Does it throw a theoretical light on the current debates over Catholic schools and over the presence of the Church on secular campuses? Will it reduce our emphasis across the board on Catholic organizations in favor of greater participation by Catholics in the secular counterparts of these organizations? One thinks, for example, of some recent differences of opinion regarding the Peace Corps as compared with Catholic lay missionary organizations. What of the nature and role of religious men and women in a Church characterized by secularity? Should religious (who, as religious, are not members of the clergy) reinterpret their embracing of the evangelical counsels in such a way that, while still to be distinguished from the members of secular institutes, they are less removed from the world and the secular quest? Or, on the contrary, in an era in which the Christian role of the laity and of the secular institutes in the world will be stressed, should religious withdraw from some of the active roles they have assumed in the modern Church?

It would be a mistake, I feel, to seek a solution to such questions merely in terms of theology. Actual Christian experience in the years ahead will help to disclose what is possible and valuable, and what is not. But, in turn, this experience needs to be guided and stimulated by the fruits of theological reflection. In any case, the likelihood is that Catholics—and many other Christians as well—will long look back to Vatican II's Constitution on the *Church in the Modern World* as a stirring invitation to all of Christ's disciples to enter boldly into the dawning era of Christian secularity.

The Church and Mankind

Edward Schillebeeckx, O.P.

Edward Schillebeeckx, O.P., internationally known theologian, studied at Le Saulchoir in Etiolles, France, and at the Sorbonne in Paris, where he became a Master and Doctor of Theology. From 1943 to 1957 he taught at the Dominican Studium in Louvain, Belgium, and has been, since 1958, Professor of Dogmatic Theology at the University of Nijmegen, Holland. He was an advisor to the Dutch hierarchy during Vatican II. Among his many published works are *The Sacramental Economy of Salvation; Mary, Mother of the Redemption; Christ, the Sacrament of the Encounter with God;* and *Marriage, Human Reality and Saving Mystery.*

The Problem

In our age we have become aware, more than in the past, that our salvation comes about within the one reality that is ours, within the scope of our own life in this world. Everywhere there is evidence of a reaction against any kind of religious practice which is alien to this world. Christianity had come to be regarded as something added on to life here on earth with its sorrow and joy, its fear and hope, its activities and moments of recollection. Many Christians used to practice their Christianity as a superstructure erected on top of their normal lives. Frequently they would look upon this life as merely matter, without religious significance in itself, for the occasional exercise of Christian virtues. Life's own significance had, in their eyes, nothing to do with Christianity.

Reprinted from Edward Schillebeeckx, O.P., *Concilium,* Vol. I, *The Church and Mankind* (Glen Rock, N.J.: Paulist Press, 1965), pp. 69–101, with the permission of the publisher.

Real religion, they held, was only practiced within a church edifice or by saying a few prayers at home—in other words, at the periphery of life. As a result, many Christians gave the impression that Christianity was an ideological superstructure, or a special department where people talked about forgiveness, redemption, the cross and resurrection, while life in this world waited outside. The human problems of life on this earth failed to get from them the attention they received from non-believers to the benefit of mankind.

At present, there is a strong emerging realization that adherence to faith is not a mere structure superimposed upon human and secular relationships, which would in fact be what they are, with or without Christianity, and so would be unaffected by faith. Consequently, reaction against ghetto-Catholicism and ghetto-Christianity is characteristic of present-day religious awareness among both Catholics and Reformed Christians. Service to a world which is growing into a closer unity; the ethical commitment imposed upon Western man by the advanced position which the West enjoys in contrast to the rest of the world, particularly the underdeveloped countries; the plans for a dynamic blueprint to set up a society upon earth that shall be worthy of men—all this is seen, also by the religious man of today, as the concrete, even the principal way in which he purposes to give form to his religion and to Christianity.

Hand in hand with this new religious awareness there is opposition to an exotic religious vocabulary. Religious ideas have to be couched in "profane" words, in language that springs from the profound realities of human existence. People want their Christianity to be less explicit and prefer it to work implicitly, almost incognito, toward salvation within their secular human relationships.

This current phenomenon, however, has one drawback. Many believers are at a loss as to what to do about the Church as an objective reality. Sociological researches draw attention to the fact that some kind of faith in God as the basis of all existence, and faith, too, in the Man Jesus, who by his life has shown the meaning of God's love for men, actually exist in persons who had "practiced" earlier in their lives but do not belong at present to any Church: they also show that precisely these persons no longer find any room in their belief for the "Church."

They could only accept the Church—and with enthusiasm—if Church meant no more than the establishment of a community among men, the real expression of the community that human fellowship ought to build up in the world. There is talk of "Christianity without a Church," a Christianity in which fellowship and brotherhood appear as the essence of Church.

The lines of our essay take two directions. We inquire first into the increasingly "ecclesial" tendency in the world, or rather in mankind; and secondly, we inquire into the tendency within the Church to sanctify the secular. On the one hand, the human fellowship in Christ is surely the heart of the Church as a phenomenon: St. Thomas calls sanctifying grace *gratia fraterna,* the grace that establishes brotherhood. On the other hand, as believers, we cannot help admitting that the Church is a community *sui juris,* or rather, *juris Christi.* But *ipso facto* we then create a certain distance between the Church and mankind. There are boundaries between the Church and humanity, and yet they are fluid, not hard and fast. Into the implications of this we now propose to inquire, for the sake of a mankind that grows away from the Church and for the sake of faith in the Church as founded by Christ.

I

The Unity of Mankind and the Communion of Saints

Mankind's specific unity from an anthropological viewpoint must formally (*formaliter*) be based, not on its biological substratum, but, by its very nature, on a community of *persons,* a *communio.* It can only be built on a value-appeal, the community-building force of truly human values. This means simply that human unity has its origin in oneness of vocation and destiny.

Communio among all men is the immanent human expression of this single vocation. Human unity in its essence is not a mere datum: it is a task to be carried out. This task, we know from revelation, is in fact the response to a free and gracious act of God. The *koinonía* or community which he wills is also his gift. By his absolute self-communication to men he at once reveals himself as their highest value and reveals mankind to itself as his People, the People of God. By the granting of his grace God constitutes mankind "the People of God." Communion among men is the reflection, immanent in mankind's history, of man's transcending communion with the living God: the God-willed unity of mankind is therefore nothing less than the *communio Sanctorum,* the community of mankind sanctified.

Not only is the fact of this community an undue gift to men, but the manner of producing it also has its origin in a sovereign, free act of God. This history of salvation in both the Old and the New Testaments, even though the outlook of the ancient Near Eastern peoples plays its role in them, makes this fact clear: God did not intend "abstract" fundamental values to be the basis on which human unity was to be realized. He intends to gather all men into a holy community of persons on the basis of values that were expressed in living persons as in prototypes.

Time and again someone is chosen from among ourselves to be the means of salvation in forming the "great gathering" of men from the diaspora, the People of God.[1] The manner, not due to men, in which God establishes a community among them is that of representative or vicarious mediation: for the sake of one man, whom God freely calls for the purpose, salvation—or destruction—is brought to many. In the Old and the New Testaments, time and again, the representative function whether of one man or of a limited collectivity is essential for salvation or destruction: Adam, Noah, Moses, the twelve Patriarchs, "Israel," the "King," the Servant of Yahweh, Jesus.

In the Bible the establishment of a community through mediation implies that election and universal mission coalesce into one. Thus, however gradually and hesitantly, Israel did at last become aware of her election to be an example to all peoples—of her election for the service of all men. In the Old Testament conception it is to Yahweh's redemptive covenant with Noah after the Flood that the totality of mankind throughout history owes its existence. And in connection with that covenant a catalogue is drawn up of all the nations existing in the world as conceived by the ancients (Gen. 10).[2] Again, in Abraham "shall all nations be blessed" (Gen. 12, 3; 18, 18; 22, 18). His election, too, is God's ratification of universal salvation.

The notion of mediatorship shows us that men are dependent upon one another and that God in bringing his transcendent salvation means to preserve the structure of human fellowship. Through men he wants to bring salvation to men. The notions of "the first-born among many brethren" (Rom. 8, 29), which embraces prototypical

[1] See J. Scharbert, *Heilsmittler im Alten Testament und im Alten Orient* (*Quaest. Disp.* 23, 24, Freiburg im Br., 1964).

[2] See G. von Rad, "Das z. erste Buch Mose," in *Das Alte Testament Deutsch,* 2 (Göttingen, 1949), pp. 119ff.

religious fellowship, and of "God's first-born son" (Ex. 4, 22), in which divine choice and service to the neighbor are united, are led up to throughout the Old Testament. They suggest the fundamental notion that salvation is a gift conveyed through man's fraternal service to others according to God's election. Even Israel, the People of God, is, when chosen, "God's first-born son" (*loc. cit.*): Israel is personified, initially, in the vicarious figure of the King, who is therefore eponymously called "Son of God" (*e.g.*, 2 Sam. 7, 14; Ps. 2, 7), and ultimately in the figure of the coming Messiah and Son of Man, "the Son of God" *par excellence.*

Jesus is not merely one of us—he represents "Israel, the Son of God," but in an incomparably deeper sense: in a uniquely transcendent manner he is "the Son of the Father." Nevertheless, he is our fellowman "taken from among men" (Heb. 5, 1), "born of a woman" (Gal. 4, 4). Election and fraternal service, "Son of God," servant of God and men—these ideas find their highest fulfillment in Jesus. And so it is in him that the "great gathering" of all men around God, *he ekklesia toû Theoû* (1 Cor. 11, 22; 15, 9) is formed into a mutual *communio* of men with Christ as their center—a "Church of Christ," *hai ekklesiai toû Christoû* (Rom. 16, 16). Scattered mankind becomes in Christ unified mankind (Eph. 2, 15) founded on the "eschatological Man,"[3] the *eschatos Adam* (1 Cor. 15, 45). He is a vivifying Spirit (*loc. cit.*), not merely man, but a man who "gives life" to his fellowmen.

Mankind, then, has received salvation through the fraternal service of one chosen from among ourselves—Jesus Christ, the Elect of God, the Son of the Father. This fact of Christ, which took place in our history and in our secular and human affairs, has had a real effect on human history. Mankind's new fundamental but real unity and new structure as a community rests upon God's universal saving will. This will is not an actuality that is simply beyond history; it has manifested itself visibly within history in the "objective redemption," that is, in the personal life of Jesus, representative man, Son of God, appearing among us in our history.

In one Man—the *homo principalis*, as Irenaeus says,[4] *i.e.*, he who

[3] See among others E. Peterson, "Die Kirche," *Theologische Traktate* (Munich, 1951), pp. 409–28.

[4] Irenaeus, *Adv. Haereses* V.21.1 (*PG* 7.1179). *Principalis* (*archaios*) in *Adv. Haer*. means "standing at the point of," and is used in connection with Irenaeus' theory of Recapitulation. Christ stands at the new beginning of all things.

stands at the wellspring of the new mankind, which *ipso facto* he has gathered into a community—in this one Man all men have already ascended through the passion to the glory with the Father.

Thus the history of Israel, which is a component of, and imbedded in, human history, takes on a new meaning. For human history, wherever it is made, has in this manner found grace with the Father and is already conclusively accepted by the Father in the *Eschaton,* Jesus Christ. For the Father has established Jesus who humbled himself, as the glorified Christ, the "Son of God in power" (Rom. 1, 4) at his own right hand. Consequently Christ is at once the Alpha and Omega of human history in its entirety (Apoc. 1, 8; 21, 6; 22, 13). As such, he is the key to history, not only in an exclusively transcendent manner beyond time and space, but his humanity now glorified is a truly historical humanity that has reached its consummation at a real point in history. In Jesus, history is finally and conclusively perfected with that kind of perfect achievement that persists in eternity. As representative, first of Israel, and so of mankind, he is the prototypical moment of mankind's history; this moment has already been inserted in eternal glory. And so our Lord, although in a dimension that exceeds our experience, gives our human history its final immanent meaning. Every historical human event wherever occurring, even in areas called "profane," can thus be understood only through the eschatological Man, Jesus Christ.

II

Dialectical Tension Between "Mankind" and the Church

Christ has bestowed a new religious meaning upon mankind in principle and in the concrete (*i.e.,* integrated in our own history). Nevertheless, between mankind "gathered" into a collectivity in principle and its actual manifestation in Christ there exists a certain distance. This distance and tension are embodied in Christ's Church. For it is in the Church, by free assent to the grace of justification, by acceptance of God's Word in faith, and by admission to baptism in the name of the Holy Trinity, that mankind's new religious meaning takes on the form that establishes an historical, visible, concrete community. When a man is incorporated into the Church, Christ's triumphant grace becomes a plain, historical, recognizable fact.[5]

[5] See among others K. Rahner, "Kirche und Parusie Christi," in *Catholica* 17, (1963), pp. 113–28.

The result is that, at least from the ascension until the Second Coming, there is a certain distinction and dialectical tension between humanity redeemed in principle, at its source, and the Church.

In a series of articles of progressive subtlety, A. Vögtle, a Catholic biblical exegete, has demonstrated that Jesus, at least in his public teaching, nowhere manifests an intention of selecting from Israel a specific group of persons in order to form them into a separate community.[6] By his public preaching of God's dominion and by his call to repentance he plainly intended to gather not a remnant only but all of Israel and make of it the new Israel, the eschatological People of *God.* Sectarianism was alien to him. Radically he pursues the path of the history of salvation as Paul will afterward copy it: salvation is announced first to Israel, and then, according to the divine design, *via* Israel to the whole world.

Jesus' call of "the twelve" from among the group of disciples is clearly explained as a parable in action that his contemporaries could not mistake: [7] in "the twelve," the twelve Patriarchs of Israel are represented—a further proof of Jesus' purpose to win all Israel for the kingdom of heaven. Actually, however, all Israel does not adhere to his doctrine, but on the contrary, opposition to his activities grows ever stronger. Chiefly because of the massive dimensions the opposition assumed and as he sees the historical event of his death approaching and the violent form it is to take, Jesus begins within the limited circle of the disciples to interpret its meaning and to explain it in the light of the prophecy in Deutero-Isaiah: his death is to be an expiation "for the many"—that is, for all—and God has arranged it so beforehand. Not before his death and resurrection,[8]

[6] A. Vögtle, *Das öffentliche Wirken Jesu auf dem Hintergrund der Qumranbewegung* (Freiburger Universitätsreden, N.F., 27, Freiburg im Br., 1958), pp. 5–20, esp. pp. 15ff; "Ekklesiologische Auftragsworte des Auferstandenen," in *Actes du Congrès internationale catholique des sciences bibliques à Bruxelles* (1959), pp. 892–906; "Jesus und die Kirche," in *Begenung der Christen,* ed. Hoesle-Cullman (Frankfurt am Main, 1960), pp. 54, 82; "Der Einzelne und die Gemeinschaft in der Stufenfolge der Christusoffenbarung," in *Sentire Ecclesiam,* ed. Daniélou and Vorgrimler, (Freiburg im Br., 1961), pp. 50–91; see also "Die Adam-Christus Typologie und der Menschensohn," in *Trierer Theol. Zeitschrift* (1951), pp. 209–28. See also footnote 7 below.

[7] See A. Vögtle, *Das öffentliche Wirken Jesu,* p. 15; F. Braun, *Neues Licht auf die Kirche* (Einsiedeln, 1946), p. 71; A. Fridrichsen, "Messias und Kirche," in *Ein Buch von der Kirche* (Göttingen, 1951), p. 33; see K. Rengstorf, *Theol. Wörterb. z. N.T.* (Teil 2), pp. 321–28, s.v. *dodeka.*

[8] See A. Vögtle, "Messiasbekenntnis und Petrusverheissung," in *Biblische Zeitschrift,* N.F. 1 (1957), pp. 257–72 and 2 (1958), pp. 85–103. The connec-

and only in connection with them, is he to speak to his disciples of "the Church which he is going to build upon the Rock" (Peter) (Matt. 16, 18f.; see John 21, 15–17).

This implies that the redeemed People of God will become after Jesus' death and resurrection an *Ecclesia Christi*—an historical, visible gathering or congregation of men around Christ, in visible communion with the "Rock" and the twelve apostles. This situation gives Jesus' community a special ecclesiastico-social structure, which as such does not coincide with the social structure of secular society.

We see, then, that on the one hand, in his public preaching Jesus never speaks of a Church with forms of organization, and that he lays down obedient acceptance of his message of salvation, here and now, in the *kairos* of the present moment, as the sole condition for entering the kingdom of God. And on the other hand, it is in the light of his death as an expiation for all men that he speaks of the founding of his Church. This he presents as a post-paschal event: "I *shall* build my Church." Holy Scripture, then, clearly connects the messianic suffering—Jesus' "going away"—with the post-paschal realization of the Church.

The Church is God's People with a special qualification: the People of God who through Jesus' death and resurrection become through the Spirit the Body of Christ—*soma Christoû*—the Body of the *Lord*. On earth this Body is built as "the Church" upon Peter, the Rock. The return to the Father—the vertical theme of Jesus' public preaching—becomes in the light of his death, explained to his apostles as reconciliation, after Easter and Pentecost also a horizontal theme: the building of a mutual community around the Rock. It becomes, consequently, a clear theme of a mankind redeemed with the purpose of an ecclesial brotherhood, a communal Church with its own initiation, its own cult, especially the sharing of the eucharistic table, a community guided and accompanied by a ministering office. Thus the death and glorification of Jesus, the Christ, have made access to this brotherhood, the sacramentally and historically visible Church, a condition for entrance into the kingdom of God.[9] The *communio* of believers gathered about its bishop (in communion with the Rock)—this *is* salvation, the Church of Christ. Precisely

---

tion between Peter's confession at Caesarea and Christ's promise of the *Ecclesia* is called secondary, *i.e.*, it is an "arrangement" of Matthew or of the Matthew tradition.

[9] Mark 10, 40 and Matthew 20, 20–23; Mark 14, 25; see Luke 22, 16, 18.

in this *koinonía* must the Father's absolute self-communication through the Son in the Holy Spirit find that historically visible realization, which is in truth the sign of all mankind's vocation. Hence the Church is not just a *koinonía,* a communion or sharing of grace with Christ, the fruit of his redemptive work, but it is also an institution for salvation to which the keys that make entrance possible into the kingdom of God have been entrusted. In contrast to Jesus' "Woe unto you, scribes and Pharisees," who bar the entrance to the kingdom (Matt. 23, 13), Christ gives Peter the keys that open the gates.

III

The Basis of the Dialectical Tension

There is, then, a distance or interval between mankind, fundamentally and historically redeemed, and the community of Jesus built upon the Rock, which is the Church or body of "practicing Christians." To understand this distance we must first remember the connection laid by Holy Scripture between the messianic death —Jesus' "going away"—and the Church, which is only post-paschal and therefore a new reality, new even in comparison with that universal reality which is the People of God.

From our point of view the death of Jesus is mankind's rejection of him: Israel's rejection through its representative, the Sanhedrin; the Gentiles' rejection of him in the person of Pilate, and even the rejection by the hierarchy of the future Church in the persons of the apostles who ran away, and of Peter, who denied him. In his death Jesus stands alone, crushed by "the sins of the world"; alone in his surrender to the Father for the service of his fellowmen. That which achieved this reconciliation was, therefore, also the cause of Jesus' factual absence—the absence, in other words, of the source of grace. From our point of view, the breach of the covenant of grace was made complete by his death: mankind has banished from the world "the coming of God's kingdom" in Christ and so has expelled it from the *communio* of men.

Every death, of course, means bodily absence and the breaking off of relations with the dead as fellowmen. In the case of Jesus, however, it is a matter of the death of the only one who could bring redemption. From our point of view, this removal of Christ, the Man of grace, is therefore irrevocable. For the renewal of his relations with us through the resurrection is certainly not owing to us, not even to Christ's humanity as such. Only by understanding the profound importance of his death can we fully appreciate the basic saving significance of his resurrection, which, on account of the sacrifice that had been offered, made possible the sending of the Holy Spirit and the building of the Church. In the resurrection, which was a grace of the Father, the redemptive work of Jesus triumphed. But this triumph implies that henceforth our salvation depends upon someone who is absent from our experience, Jesus Christ.

We may justly conclude from this that the final state of our condition as it was created by original sin is "a situation in which the *privation* of supernatural grace can *only be removed sacramentally,* a situation in which man found himself ever since, and, because of the breach of the covenant with God, was made complete through man's rejection of Christ." [10]

Jesus himself connects his going away with the coming of the Spirit and the building of his Church. In his Body, the Church, wherein the Holy Spirit dwells, he intends to remain as the source of all grace. Hence, this Body, the Church, becomes the condition or the embodiment of our restored relationship with Christ and our entrance into the kingdom of God. Christ, absent from the universal human community, is made present again through the resurrection in the Church, his Body on earth.

The weighty consequence of this fact is significantly expressed by St. Thomas: "The grace of Christ comes to us not through human nature but through the *personal action* of Christ himself." [11] In present-day terms this means that the source of Christ's grace is not fellow-creaturehood in and by itself, but fellow-creaturehood with Christ, who, while absent since his death from the horizon of our experience, means to remain present among us, but post-paschally, in virtue of the Spirit of God, in his Body, the Church.

As the Body of our Lord, the Church forms the living link with Christ—horizontally, with the Jesus of history, who arose and appeared to the apostles; vertically, with the Lord of glory, thanks to the Spirit that dwells in the whole community of the Church in its hierarchical function, its preaching, its sacraments. Because of

[10] P. Schoonenberg, "Natuur en zondenval," in *Tijdschr. v. Theol.* 2 (1962), pp. 199–200; see also E. Schillebeeckx, *Christ, the Sacrament of the Encounter with God* (New York, 1963), pp. 40–46.

[11] *Summa Theologiae,* III, q.8, a.2, ad 1.

Christ's fellowship with us the universal human fellowship, too, takes on a deepened meaning, and the boundaries between mankind and the Church begin to blur.

IV

Fluidity of the Boundaries Between the Church and Mankind

The history of salvation, then, deals with one covenant that has passed through two phases, or a twofold *dispositio*. An absolutely new situation has been created in the plan of salvation by Christ's death and resurrection. Now the further question arises: What is the relationship between the universal People of God, coextensive with mankind, and the Church, in which the People of God has become the Body of our Lord?

The *locus theologicus* of all reflection on the faith and, consequently, of the theology of the relationships between the Church and the world, is the historical advent of salvation in Jesus Christ: the Man Jesus who is to us the absolute and gratuitous presence of God. In Christ and through him, human existence has become the objective expression of God's absolute communication of himself to man and, by the same token, the objective expression of the human response to that total divine gift. As a corollary of that fact, the human condition in its historical setting has become the concrete matter and space of the historical manifestation of man's God-related life in Christ. The human existence of Christ, taken with all its determinisms and all its human implications, is the *personal* life of God, the Son.

This means that the entire temporal dimension and the unabridged reality we call profane can be assumed into a God-related life, given that in the Son the eternal has presented itself personally within temporal and terrestrial realities. The very definition of the hypostatic union is exactly that. This also reveals the fact that thanks to Christ all of human history is swathed in God's love; it is assumed into the absolute and gratuitous presence of the mystery of God. The worldly and the temporal remain worldly and temporal; they are not sacralized but sanctified by that presence, that is, by the God-centered life of Christ and of his faithful.

Everyone will agree that our human existence is immersed in unfathomable mystery, although the way of saying so may vary infinitely. In her revelation-through-the-Word, the Church merely clarifies for the benefit of all mankind the reality of the mystery's absolute presence in Christ; it proclaims that this mystery has drawn closer to us, not only in some mystical and interior intimacy, but also through the medium of a palpable and visible historical reality. The whole kerygma and all of Christian dogma can be summarized in that fundamental affirmation: beginning with the Trinity, the incarnation, the life of grace, but also including the Church with her ministry, worship, preaching, sacraments as well as collective and individual eschatology.

Word-revelation, of which the Church is the herald, only unfolds the implications of that absolute and gratuitous presence which, as revelations-reality, is already present in the lives of men, even prior to their historical encounter with the phenomenon "Church." Moreover, the free acceptance of the mystery's absolute and gratuitous presence is the very substance of what we call theologal or God-related faith. To believe is to have confidence in this mystery thus present; it means trusting in him in spite of everything and under all circumstances. That affirmation strikes me as of the utmost importance because what is implied is that the acceptance of real human existence, concretely taken with all its responsibilities, is in truth an act of God-centered faith: for Christ has shown us, by living it, that human existence taken concretely—not in the abstract—was for him, precisely in his human condition steeped as it was in the mystery, the objective expression of his communion with the Father in the *Dynamis* of the Holy Spirit and for the benefit of his fellowmen.

Here is what this brief analysis shows us:

1. Within the Church of Christ the absolute and gratuitous presence of the mystery becomes an explicit epiphany, historically and humanly observable—both as a reality and as a task to be accomplished.

2. This concentrated ecclesial manifestation of God merely explicates that which in fact and at its own level is going on in all of human existence, even if the subject is not aware of it, namely, the gratuitous presence of the mystery, which is an active, an operative presence.

From this viewpoint, the incarnation teaches us that the entire human reality may ferry divine grace and can be assumed into a God-centered life. Day-to-day human life with its worldly concerns for human advancement is the area wherein normal Christian life must develop; the explicit and ecclesial expression of that selfsame communion with God shall indeed be the fountainhead and the driving force of the expression of Christian life in the world. St. Paul told us as much in a masterful though negative manner: "Neither death, nor life, nor angels, nor principalities, nor things present, nor things to come, nor powers, nor height, nor depth, nor any other creature will be able to separate us from the love of God, which is in Christ Jesus our Lord" (Rom. 8, 38–39). What does it all mean if not that Christianity is upheld by faith in the absolute and gratuitous presence of God within Christ as well as by the fact that we must accept human history and our entire earthly life as a reality steeped and swaddled in God's love? Improving the world whenever we improve ourselves, we are always in the presence of and beneath the wings of the mystery who gives himself freely.

While respecting the worldly and earthly significance of the reality we call the world, this outlook gives it a profoundly theological meaning. This is what the world is: the profane, earthly and temporal reality with structures all its own, with its special and immediate end, but which, in Christ, is assumed into the absolute and gratuitous presence of God. In saying this one should beware of imagining the world as some static, immobile reality. Planet earth is the material given to man with which to fashion a human world, a dwelling-place worthy of man. Of course man's world has the mark of the creature upon it; moreover, as everything else common to man, it is a world wrought by sin. The construction of the world and the promotion of peoples remain a finite task, the work of men, and as such it shares in the ambiguity of all that is human. This world is creature, non-God. To say this is to affirm the secularity of earthly tasks. Indeed, creation is a divine act that situates realities within their respective spheres; and contrary to the mythological legends held by the contemporaries of ancient Israel, the Bible refers to that divine act, in Genesis, as desacralizing and unmystifying the world, handing it over to itself, into the hands of man for God's glory. This means that as a result of the divine act of sustained creation, the history of mankind will assert itself as the progressive and prolonged desacralization of earthly structures and functions.

But that is only one facet of a far richer and more profound reality: since God created so as to bestow himself to man and to be, he himself, present in a gratuitous and redemptive manner, in our brother, Jesus the Anointed. This means that in the plan of salvation the concrete world, by definition, is an *implicit Christianity;* it is an objective, non-sacral but saintly and sanctified expression of mankind's communion with the living God; whereas the Church *qua* institution of salvation, with her explicit creed, her worship and sacraments, is the direct and sacral expression of that identical communion—she is the *separata a mundo.*

To speak of the relationships between the Church and the world does not mean therefore that a dialogue is to be launched between the strictly Christian dimension of our human life and its distinctly non-Christian dimension; nor is it a question of conductng a dialogue between the religious and the profane, between the supernatural and the natural or intra-worldly—it is rather a dialogue between *two complementary, authentically Christian expressions* of one and the same God-related life concealed in the mystery of Christ, namely, the *ecclesial* expression (in the strict sense of the word) and the *worldly* expression of that identically same life, internalized within human life through man's free acceptance of grace. In other words, the *implicitly* Christian and the *explicitly* Christian dimension of the same God-related life, that is, of human life hidden in God's absolute and gratuitous presence.[12] In that context, this is what is meant by implicit Christianity; it is the human, earthly and profane reality assumed in its secularity into the God-related life which it proceeds to express objectively, even when that God-related life remains anonymous and implicit. Earthly reality will at the same time share in the fruits of eschatological grace and in the advent of the kingdom of God. Within that God-centered life, albeit anonymous, the construction of the world and the promotion of peoples, those two great hopes of mankind on earth, become an activity which is not only intentionally but intrinsically relevant to the kingdom of God.

It is evident that the ultimate eschatological perfection of all earthly values completely transcends the temporal construction of this world, precisely because it is an absolute and gratuitous perfection; but nevertheless, by virtue of its assumption into God-related life, harbinger of the *vita venturi saeculi,* the world of earthly values

[12] It is obvious that in so saying I speak of the state of implicit Christianity as such, realizing that the individual can shut himself away from grace. God is the sole judge of man's conscience. One does not therefore affirm that all non-Christians are by the mere fact implicitly Christians, just as one does not maintain that every member of the Church is an authentic Christian. Nevertheless the redemptive grace of "Christus Victor" is more powerful than the fragility of human freedom.

will participate in that mystery of eternal life, as we are told by the dogma of the resurrection of the flesh and by the kerygma of the new earth.

Unequivocally, God loves man; and the being called man is not some abstract "human nature" but a flesh-and-blood being who, together with his fellowmen, takes the fate of the world and of mankind into his own hands; he is a being who, by humanizing the world humanizes himself. It is this historical, real being whom God loves. Every single human and worldly reality is therefore implied in God's absolute and gratuitous presence. This conveys a sense of the eternal and, therefore, of the irrevocable to the construction of the world and the promotion of the advancement of peoples.

Although it is solely due to his *capacitas gratiae* that man is the object of grace, the very being who, upon transcending his own self is assumed into theologal intimacy with God and shares in the eternal life—that being is none other than man, all of man as he really and historically exists, committed to this world.

In the past, a dualistic anthropological conception misled Christians into considering grace and redemption as a matter for God and the soul of man to deal with, so much so that the whole range of earthly life and of human responsibility for the terrestrial future of mankind seemed to be relegated to the fringe of Christianity; one ran the risk of disregarding the truly Christian value of building the world and of promoting the advancement of peoples, thereby relinquishing the chore to those who called themselves non-Christians. How easy it is to discern in that behavior one of the many factors through which the institutional Church alienated men from herself.

When we connect now the things which were said about the one signification of the Church with that which is called "implicit Christianity," we arrive at new explicitations concerning the relation "Church and World."

The acts of Christ in glory are the acts of the whole Christ, the integral Christ in and with his Body, the Church. Hence, what the Church as such does, is done also by the glorified Christ together with the Spirit, his Spirit. What is Christian, therefore, is also ecclesial: the qualifications are inseparably and organically united.

However much Jesus, as the Lord, transcends his Body, the Church, his immanence in the Church is coextensive with his transcendence. He transcends the Church through his immanence in it. That he transcends the boundaries of his Body, the Church, means that his free self-giving reaches out from within the Church to all who are not yet visible members of the Church. This implies that he is active among those who have not yet been historically confronted with the Church, but also that this activity of his is equally an activity of his Body, the Church. The bond with Christ, forged by this activity is, even when not explicitly seen as such, *ipso facto* an equally strong bond with the Church. Consequently, the Church represents the source of redemption also for that portion of mankind that has not yet experienced and availed itself of her in her peculiar historical form.

Seen in this perspective, the real interval separating the Church as such from mankind becomes less pronounced. The Church is actively present even where her adequate ecclesial form has not yet appeared. The contrast between the Church and mankind cannot be equated with an opposition between Church and non-Church. There is, moreover, much in her own life that is "non-ecclesial," just as in the collective life of mankind there is much that is ecclesial. In the strict sense, of course, the Church is mankind insofar as it willingly places itself under Christ's influence through faith and baptism, and "helps its unbelief" at the common table of the eucharist.

Perhaps it is better not to give the name "Church" to that portion of mankind that is anonymously Christian and in which the Church is anonymously present. This phenomenon might be called a "pre-Church"; but even against this, various objections might be brought. In the proper sense of the word, the Church is the saving revelation, the explicitly Christian realization of our Lord's activity among all mankind—the *koinonía* of men with one another in the acceptance of God and baptism in Christ, which is the efficacious sign of the call of those not yet in the Church.

On the other hand, anonymous Christianity—and its existence must be taken as a fact—not least because of its hopeful trust in the triumphant grace of Christ's redemption ("I have overcome the world") inwardly demands a fitting sacramental visibility. Because the worldwide activity of Christ's grace is carried out in and through the Church, since his "going away" is related to the Church's post-paschal reality as the Body of our Lord, in virtue of the Spirit of God, this very grace is essentially "Church founding." Where the Church is at work as grace—and as such it is coextensive with mankind and therefore with universal fellowship—something of the *Corpus Mysticum* is brought to visible realization, though in a veiled manner. Because this grace takes on particular, historical, visible forms in the Church, its appearance bears witness to the fact that wherever it is operative (and that is wherever human history is in process of realization), it has an inward leaning toward historical manifestation, *i.e.*, toward ecclesial explicitness.

This process can be observed in human history. Beyond the pale of the concretely situated, real Church, this grace will express itself, as a result of the unrecognized bond with Christ and his Church, in widely varying human interpretations—whether in other religious forms, or in so-called "secular" institutions, whose explicit form is inadequate to express their true purpose. Failure to grasp the proper meaning of this deepest feeling latent in the restless life of mankind is no indication that the difference between mankind and the Church is merely one of "knowing explicitly" and "knowing implicitly." For it is only in self-expression that man reaches full self-consciousness. Whatever is experienced without being recognized is a fragile datum until it finds its way to authentic self-expression. And this is more than a question of mere knowledge.

Without the God-given ecclesial form and expression of this deepest core of life in Christ, this experience remains a "light hidden under a bushel," a flickering flame ready to be quenched by the weakest draught. The properly ecclesial milieu is where the word of God's forgiveness is heard, where baptism is administered and the eucharist celebrated, where there is the faith that nothing can separate us from the Lord and that for men there is no absolute solitude because God is with us. This milieu, which believers, the faithful, jointly constitute, is vitally necessary for the breakthrough of what grace effects silently and anonymously in human life. But the Church's special importance as a sign and revelation demands that she return again and again to the sources of biblical authenticity and show herself in forms that clearly and simply manifest her authenticity.

Thanks, therefore, to Christ's historical coming there is in living humanity a kind of built-in compass pointing to the Church. Her missionary activity is merely the counterpart of this. This pointing to the Church, or mankind's need of her in the concrete, and, on the other hand, her going out to mankind, are both visible forms of the one operative salvation which our Lord is in the Spirit of God, *Pneuma Theoû*. In both, Jesus the Christ visits his messianic community that he acquired upon the cross to prepare for himself his eschatological bride without spot unto the glory of God the Father.

The anonymous Church that is the work of Christ's Spirit and of his Body, the explicit Church vitally joined to him, will become manifest through the Spirit, as his Body, incorporated through baptism into his death and resurrection, as a visible sign both of the eschatological Man, Jesus Christ, and of what human life is concretely—namely, a deep and painful suffering, an existence ending in death, coupled with the unquenchable hope that this is not the last word about mankind. In Christ's *kenôsis* and *hypsôsis,* in his final humiliation and his exultation, the destiny of human life is exemplified. The enduring struggle for life in mankind, hoping against all hope, is the nameless echo of this fact: there is here more than mere secularity, even though it is expressed perhaps in a purely secular fashion.

The boundaries between the Church and mankind are fluid not merely in the Church's direction, but also, it may be said, in the direction of mankind and the world. The present-day process toward desacralization and secularization points to the fact that what was earlier felt to be a specialty of the Church—helping those of slender means, works of charity and the like—has nowadays become "desacralized" as state relief measures for humanity within a secular vision, and is now an accepted feature of mankind at large. What had earlier taken the form of specific activities of the Church, in its precise sense, has now become in many ways an accepted expression of man's life in and for the world.

This osmosis from the Church to the world knows no final point on earth because here below the old aeon and the new continue to co-exist. The fact that the communion of men coincides with the communion of saints is, when manifest, a heavenly, not an earthly fact. The blurring of the boundaries between the Church and mankind can never abolish the dialectical tension between the two. This tension, however, does not destroy either the dynamic of the world's tendency to become ecclesial or the Church's tendency to sanctify the secular. The latter process, however, is a holy secularization arising from the transcendent community with God in Christ. Whoever forgets this would have the Church in the long run dissolve into something like UNO or UNESCO.

All this has been expressed by St. Paul in his own way and in the framework of his ancient world picture. Christ by his death and glorification has fulfilled "all things"—"all things in heaven and on earth," "visible and invisible," all created reality (Eph. 1, 10; Col. 1, 16–20). H. Schlier, the biblical exegete, in his commentary on Ephesians comments rightly upon this point: "There is no sphere of being that is not also the Church's sphere. The Church is fundamentally directed to the universe. Her boundaries are those of the universe. There is no realization of Christ's dominion without the Church or outside her, no 'fulfillment' apart from her. The way in which the universe grows toward Christ is the way the Church grows. There are areas, to be sure, that are opposed to 'fulfillment' through the Church; but ultimately the reason is that they are filled with themselves." [13]

St. Paul says this plainly: "God has placed all things under his feet, and has given him, exalted above all, as Head to the Church, which is his Body, the fullness of him who fulfills all in all" (Eph. 1, 22f.). It is through the Church that the fulfillment of all existence and all reality is achieved.[14] Eschatologically, Church and mankind coincide fully.

V

Unity of Creation, Redemption and Growth of the Church

The Church and mankind, then, are coming closer together; and yet the undeniable boundary remains between them because of Christ's post-paschal "building of the Church upon the Rock." [15] It now remains to clarify a dogmatic insight in which creation and the bestowal of grace, redemption and the building of the Church are all seen together in the sublime unity of God's covenant with men.

Grace is God's absolute self-communication to men; it is the personal sharing of life with God—Father, Son, and Holy Spirit. That even in the pre-Christian era grace could only be trinitarian, we only know in the light of the historical mystery of Christ. It is in him that this fundamental aspect of the whole life of grace first

[13] H. Schlier, "Die Kirche nach dem Briefe an die Epheser," in *Die Zeit der Kirche* (Freiburg im Br., 1956), p. 69.

[14] Schlier has the following acute comment on this passage in Saint Paul: "The Church is the *Pleroma* of Christ. This means the plenitude, fulfilled by him and in its turn fulfilling, of him who has fulfilled all things and continues to do so. In her (the Church's) plenitude, all is enclosed and so this all becomes itself that plenitude which is the Church" (*ibid.*, p. 170).

[15] The thought of this article will be taken up again in *Concilium* and applied to the problem of membership in the Churches, in connection with the pluralism of the Christian Church communities.

becomes explicit. There is a close connection between him and grace. The fact that the trinitarian character of grace, imparted before his coming, remained implicit and anonymous leads to the question whether the anonymous character of this trinitarian grace is not due to the fact that man's existence was originally oriented to Christ, and that this obviously had to remain implicit. An analysis of the trinitarian character of grace as well as of its postponed revelation in Christ shows that its original conferment and God's establishment of mankind as his People were the consequence of man's creation in view of Christ. "Adam's" creation was implicitly directed toward Christ, and because of this, grace was bestowed upon him.[16] In other words, human existence in the concrete is itself a messianic prophecy pointing to him who is to come. The task to form a true *communio* among men as the essential task of a community of *persons* is a prophecy of the coming of Christ's Mystical Body, the Church. Thus, by another and perhaps more radical way we come to a conclusion at least materially the same as Karl Rahner's who speaks of mankind in its entirety as the (faithful or unfaithful) People of God, and considers membership of this People a constitutive element of our concrete humanity.[17] Therefore, in the concrete, every free human act is one that works toward salvation or perdition. But it seems to me that the manner in which we arrive at this insight sheds a clearer light on mankind's objectively new situation since the death and resurrection of Christ.

Surely this new situation makes it obvious that salvation is conferred upon the People of God, not as such, but insofar as it has become the Body of Christ. This implies that since the appearance of the mystery of Christ in history at least the faithful People of God, in virtue of his sole saving power at work in his Body, the Church, becomes the expression of a *desiderium ecclesiae.* The basis of this should be clear from what has been thus far presented here, but it may help to clarify it further.

Creation in view of Christ, which includes the gift of grace, means that since creation all mankind carries within itself and anonymously this ecclesial orientation as a grace that is accepted or rejected. We

[16] I have attempted to develop this in detail in "Die Heiligung des Namen Gottes durch die Menschenliebe Jesu des Christus," in *Gott in Welt* (Festgabe für K. Rahner, Freiburg, 1964), esp. pp. 73–90.

[17] K. Rahner, "Die Gliedschaft in der Kirche nach der Lehre de Enzyklika Pius XII, *Mystici Corporis,*" in *Schr. z. Theol.* 2 (Einsiedeln, 1955), pp. 7–94.

may say, then, that it is always within and for a People of God that man's religious life is fulfilled, whether this People be mankind as yet unspecified or Israel, in which messianic humanity began to manifest itself more clearly, or the People of God redeemed by Christ, with its features sharply drawn and constituted as the Church.[18] The human community, insofar as it is created with this orientation toward Christ is an early rough-draft of the Church that is to come. But it is no more than that. For the appearance of Jesus in history and his exclusion from the human community created a completely new situation. It is as the Risen One that he built his Church and set it visibly among men as a community with its peculiar sacramental community structure, with its hierarchical function, with its service of the Word.

This absolutely new fact in salvation history restricts the universal application of this reality of God's People as coextensive with mankind. On the other hand, this new fact lifts that reality into a new dimension and turns its implicit acceptance into a *votum ecclesiae*. The anonymously Christian portion of mankind now becomes for the first time a true *votum ecclesiae,* precisely because of Christ's universally operative action *in* the Church to the benefit of all mankind.[19]

Christ's Church, then, is not so much the last phase of the interior development of God's People as it comes into ever clearer view in visible form, although this aspect cannot be denied. Rather, Christ's historical redemptive work with its post-paschal fruit, the Church, recapitulates in his death and resurrection the People of God created from of old in view of him, and *constitutes* that People as the *votum ecclesiae*. Hence, we can say: *Extra ecclesiam nulla salus:* apart from Christ and his Body there is no salvation.

At the same time we must say that the Church here on earth has not yet reached the perfection of what she ought to be. This was acutely formulated by Origen: *"Ho kosmos tou kosmou he ekklesia"*:

[18] E. Schillebeeckx, *Personale Begegnung mit Gott: Eine Antwort an John A. T. Robinson* (Mainz, 1964), pp. 78f.

[19] Be it noted that I do not claim that *all* those who do not belong to a church are *per se* anonymous Christians, just as we do not maintain that all church members are authentic Christians. I only say that such an anonymous Christianity is a genuine possibility, and, considering the abounding power of grace, a reality in the case of many. We do not wish, nor are we able, to affirm their number. We know well the essential ambiguity of human freedom: it is a potentiality for good and for evil. But our confidence in God is greater than that ambiguity!

man's world brought to actual perfection, to order—to peace and *communio*—this is the Church.[20] The Church carries within herself the principles and the incipient reality of this peace in virtue of the fact that she, the fruit of Christ's redemption, is his Body in this world.

In and through that Body he, now in glory, carries on his universal activity in the Spirit. The Church in human history, then, is, as token for all the world, the forerunner of eschatological salvation. Hence, her apostolic duty; hence, the constant demand daily to orientate herself anew at the wellsprings of Holy Scripture, especially at this time when the face of the world and of man is fundamentally altering.

VI

The Church as Fellowship to Be Realized

The blurring of the enduring boundaries between the Church and mankind can also be explained more clearly through the Church's inner structure. In the one Church of Christ we may distinguish two different, though not opposed, dialectical aspects: the one, of the Church as a community guided by the Spirit of God active in the apostolic office of the episcopacy throughout the world; the other, of the same Church guided by the Spirit of God active in every individual's conscience.

This latter activity of the Spirit, and hence of individual Christians, also effects the building of the Church, especially in the midst of the world and of ordinary everyday things. This is where they are to be found who have not yet joined the Church community explicitly. Here, too, the building of the Church retains a kind of hidden character. Because this is a non-hierarchical activity, which is just as much the work of the Holy Spirit in Christian consciences, there really is an active building of the Church by her members in the midst of the so-called "profane" world, where the hierarchical Church is not present. A genuine, but even more veiled manifestation of this reality, moreover, is the genesis of the Church in the world that is Christian without the name. It can be recognized for what it is only in the light of Christ and the visible Church.

If, therefore, we would inquire into the pregnant characteristics that mark out the anonymously Christian Church which, because

[20] See A. Auer, "Kirche und Welt," in *Mysterium Kirche* II (Salzburg, 1962), pp. 492f.

of what she is, longs for the moment when she can appear in her own ecclesial manifestation, we should not consider the fellowship or brotherhood among men in general, but with the special qualification which Jesus himself indicated. This qualification is love, a love that reaches out to the *mikroi,* the little ones, and to the *elachistoi,* the least of men, to help them for the reason that Jesus calls them "My brethren" (Matt. 25, 31–36). It is in respect to their practice of this love that Church members and non-Church members alike are to be judged at the end of time (Matt. 25, 35–45): "What you have done to the least of my brethren, you have done to me" (Matt. 25, 40). "I was hungry and you gave me to eat; I was thirsty and you gave me to drink; I was a stranger and you welcomed me" (Matt. 25, 35f.). "What you have failed to do for the least of these, you have failed to do for me" (Matt. 25, 45).

In modern terms this might be expressed thus: Your failure to help the underdeveloped countries is failing Christ himself. The help you extend to them, not from political motives, but out of pure brotherhood and fellowship, is authentic Christianity. Self-sacrifice to the extreme was the messianic act by which Christ founded his Church. Where men follow in his footsteps on the way of self-sacrifice, without even knowing perhaps whose steps they are, they are working to establish the Church, the community in Christ. The parable of the Good Samaritan teaches us, with a certain amount of sarcasm directed at those who are "in the Church," that everyone who assists anyone whom he finds in need and helps him superabundantly, with the luxury of extravagant love, is actively establishing the *koinonía.* He makes of the man he helps, his neighbor and brother.

The activity that establishes the Church which is, even without the name, Christian, goes outside and beyond the limits of the official Church, which is sociologically situated and clearly visible in history —the Church of those who acknowledge Christ and share the table of the eucharist. This activity exceeds the official Church's limits even in such a way that this superabundant love, however clearly visible in the Church's saints, is not, historically and *per se,* necessarily realized by practicing Christians. And yet the Church is truly established only where love makes men brothers, because the active love that establishes her is the core of her being. It was to preserve that core that Christ established an official hierarchy, which he assists in a special manner in order to preserve his People in one community of love and hope founded upon one faith in him. Ultimately, however, the Church is not a matter of this hierarchy but of the People of God and the active love that establishes her. And for her, the hierarchy, although in the *modus* of Christian authority, has a function of service.

Outside the visible community of Jesus, then, the establishment of the Church is accomplished primarily by surrender to one's fellowmen in unselfish love. Concretely, our fellow-creatures are a token of God's grace, a sacramental sign of his saving will. Such they are only because created in Christ and for the sake of him who is the constitutive sign of God's saving will. The universal sacramentality of fellow-creaturehood is not destroyed because of the perfect sacramental form of Christ's fellow-creaturehood, nor is it, so to say, translated into the formal structure of the visible Church. On the contrary, because of the appearance of the Man, Jesus Christ the Son of God, in history, the sacramental power of the grace of fellowship can be realized in its full meaning now for the first time. It is realized in him and for him. The general sacramental feature of fellowship is made concrete only in the community that is called the Church. And the seven sacraments, the preaching, the worship, the hierarchy's guidance—all these are but the highest point of crystallization of the stake the Church has in our fellowmen.

The Church, therefore, will appear as a sign among men, actually drawing and inviting them, only when the love of her members for humankind becomes concretely and historically visible here and now, and is no longer confined to those particular climactic moments in which at present Christ places his grace in a concentrated manner. It is just during the Second Vatican Council that out of the deliberations on the nature of the Church there has come a desire to include in the schema a consideration of the active presence of church members in the world. The schema which is shortly to become the Constitution, *De Ecclesia,* cries out from the heart for schema xvii.

On all these grounds we cannot relegate the Church's significance for the unchurched to some kind of "representative function" that would dispense them from the superabundant love and redeem them by "substitution," that is, by the overflowing love which is at least present in Christ's Church. In an authentically Christian perspective, vicariousness and mediation never stand for substitution, but for a prototypical reality which gives of its abundance *in order that* others, by virtue of the grace they have received, may be enabled themselves to achieve what had already been done by the prototype. In this sense the Church exists in the strength of Christ's Spirit for the good of all men. But equally, the operation of Christ's grace among men through the Church must retain a visible form, especially in its apostolic activity. In the Church's confrontation with mankind in history her members must be living examples and "types" of this overflowing love and manifest their willingness to give up their personal lives in the service of others.

VII

Secular and Sacral Realization of the Church's Holiness

The problem posed at the beginning of this essay has found some answer, it is hoped, in the course of our investigation. There is obviously going on throughout mankind a process of bringing things into the Church, and in the Church, correspondingly, there is a process of secularization that conveys sanctity. Within the inviolable limits set by the Word, the sacrament, and the office—and all those are forms of *service*—the boundaries between the Church and mankind are blurred. It is in the positive encounter with Christ in his Church that the most complete form of Christianity that may be realized is objectively offered to us.

The Church, then, must be a really habitable home, and her mission is to bring this to pass in every age in ever differing ways. Complete religion has an explicitly Christian and ecclesial practical expression. Because of this, Christianity, however involved it is in our everyday cares and tasks and all our secular activity, has a special sacral space set apart from secular developments and from culture, within which we grow in intimacy with God. Here we are simply together with God in Christ. Now, on a merely human level silence forms a part of discourse and social intercourse, though in and for itself it has no meaning; it has meaning only as a function of fellowship. It is necessary in order to make contact between men human and to keep it so—to humanize it. It is silence that makes speech personal. Without it, dialogue is impossible. But in a revealed religion, silence with God has a value in itself and for its own sake, just because God is God. Failure to recognize the value of mere being with God, as the Beloved, without doing anything, is to gouge the heart out of Christianity.

Our whole immersion in the world of men and things penetrates also into our communion with God, not as mere distraction, but essentially. We cannot tell God that we love or desire to love him except with words, concepts and pictures taken from our human environment. Moreover, our communion with God is not individualism, for our prayer would be insincere—not prayer at all—if we did not pray: "Our Father, . . ." or if in our prayer we forgot God's kingdom and our fellowman.

Christianity means not only communion with God in the concrete milieu of Christ in his Church, but also *working* with the living God, with the Father "who is ever active" (John 5, 17) both in the Church and in the world. Religion is primarily personal intercourse with God—the living God, who is the Creator of men and things, all of which he offers to us for humanization. Therefore, our living relationship with our neighbor and with the world is not only cultural, but also religious.

Agape embraces God and men. Love of God cannot and must not be separated from love of men. Christian love for the neighbor means that we—God and I—love *my* fellowman. While in natural human love, God is present only in silence as the transcendent Third, my Christian *caritas* toward my fellows is just as much love, but a love lived in communion with God. And so the Christian loves his fellowman with the same love as that with which he loves God and with which both he and his fellowmen are loved by God. In Christ alone do we learn the proper meaning of "being a man for the sake of others," although secular and human experience will teach us how we must express this fellowship in concrete situations.

But, however ecclesial the explicit expression of religion and Christianity may be, the working out of our Christian character must needs take shape in the ordinary daily dealings in and with the world and our fellowmen. The sincerity of our personal dealings with God, of our Christianity and ecclesial status must therefore be tested constantly by the authenticity of our fellowship, our genuine love of men. The source of this Christian love of the neighbor, however, lies in our personal assimilation of those ways of dealing with God which Christ himself has given us: hearing the Word of God, familiarity with Holy Scripture, the common celebration of the Church's sacramental liturgy. In our world, then, authentic Christianity has both a *sacred* and a corresponding *secular* milieu. In everything he does, by acceptance or refusal, man brings about salvation or perdition.

We must be close to God, not merely in church, in prayer and the sacraments, in Scripture reading—in a word, in the sacred forms of religion—but also in our secular and human relationships and in our everyday tasks. Then we may say with serenity that there are different ways of being Christian. Some will bring their interior relationship with God to fulfillment chiefly in sacral forms, thereby stressing the fact that the Church is "not of this world." Others will express their Christianity particularly in secular activities, in "secular sanctity," and so will stress the fact that the Christian faith is not an ideological structure superimposed upon human life.

But these are emphases of the one Christian life which is immanent in this world precisely because it is transcendent. For what has been said here about the universal relationship between mankind and the Church is also valid for the individual Christian. The unrecognized genuine witness of the Christian in this profane world finds the source of its strength in that explicit Christianity which is shaped by active participation in the life of the Word and of the Sacrament of "Christ's Church."

The Changing Character of the Christian Understanding of the World

Alfons Auer

Alfons Auer is professor of moral theology at the University of Würzburg. In his lectures and books he has given special attention to lay spirituality, marital problems, and a Christocentric basis for moral theology. His books include *Der Weltoffener Christ, Theologie des Berufs und der Arbeit,* and *Open to the World.*

I

The Medieval Understanding of the World

A. *The Concept of World*

The Middle Ages would not recognize our modern inquiry into the world as world, the world per se. We may no more expect a direct statement of this issue from the medieval mind than we may from the New Testament. The problem of the worldliness of the world can really come into perspective only when the "horizon of the world's nothingness with this horizon's origin and claims" [1] has been surmounted. On this point we must agree with H. R. Schlette.

But Schlette traces the absence of a theological treatment of this question in medieval theology to the fact that "the world as world, because of the ever-valid belief in creation, could not at all be cate-

Reprinted from "The Christian and the World," *Readings in Theology* (New York: P. J. Kenedy & Sons, 1965), pp. 3–44. Translated from the German original, "Gestaltwandel des christlichen Weltverständnisses," in *Gott in Welt* (West Germany: Verlag Herder, 1964). Reprinted by permission of Verlag Herder.

[1] H. R. Schlette, *Die Nichtigkeit der Welt. Der philosophische Horizont des Hugo von St. Viktor* (Munich: 1961), p. 9.

gorized."[2] This is true only of the specifically medieval form and vitality of belief in creation, but not of the belief in creation as such. Otherwise, one would have to maintain that the man who believes in creation could not possibly comprehend the world as it is in itself. We would prefer, rather, to arrive at such an understanding in the scholastic spirit, which recognized that the self-subsistence of creatures and yet their total dependence on God were not mutually exclusive concepts.[3]

Since the Middle Ages did not reflect on the problem of the world in the modern sense of the term, it is hardly surprising that the concept of "world" was not clearly determined. In the theological and spiritual literature of this period, "world" means the God-created totality of visible and invisible realities—the creation of God, the goodness and beauty of which are so often enthusiastically praised.

In the spiritual literature, however, this doctrinal concept of the world is considerably overlapped by a one-sided emphasis on its evanescence and frailty, which have experienced an extreme intensification in the sinful disordering of the world. The text of 1 John 2:15–16, in which the world appears as the embodiment of evil, as a triad of possessions, pomp and inordinate desire, acquires an almost canonical status in the *De contemptu mundi* literature from Ambrose to Erasmus. Very often we come across a view of the world as life outside the cloister, life amidst the allurements and temptations of earthly goods.[4] In this stratification of the medieval understanding of the world, we can expect to find both positive and negative factors.

B. Positive Factors in the Medieval Understanding of the World

The truths of revelation form an obvious foundation for the medieval understanding of the world: God, the supreme Lord, has created the world out of nothing and keeps it in existence through

[2] H. R. Schlette, "Welt" in: *Handbuch Theologischer Grundbegriffe II* (Munich: 1963), p. 826.

[3] Cf. H. Conrad-Martius, *Metaphysische Gespräche* (Halle: 1921), p. 113; A. Auer, *Weltoffener Christ* (3rd ed.; Düsseldorf: 1963), p. 43.

[4] Cf. the not-yet-published work of H. Hergenröther, *Die christliche Weltverachtung nach der De-contemptu-mundi Literatur von Ambrosius bis Erasmus*, pp. 59–89, where much material on this subject has been compiled; also, H. R. Schlette, *Die Nichtigkeit der Welt*, pp. 163f.

his creative presence. The disaster resulting from the sin of man was fundamentally overcome when God, through his Son, embraced the fallen world in grace. At the end of history, by the power of God, the world will be brought home into his glory. These truths of revelation no doubt were sometimes watered down in a spiritualistic sense; by and large they were not able to develop their full spiritual import. This situation is especially true of the early Christian centuries, when the Christian will to realization pursued a primarily introspective course.

The picture changed at the beginning of the Middle Ages, when a new dynamism poured into Christianity from the Germanic realm. The Christian learned to understand the world as a gift and assignment from God. He actively sensed his profession as a calling; this received its first recognizable form among the leading classes of society—the princes and knights—but at an early date began to appeal to all ranks, down to the merchants, horse dealers and innkeepers. This sense of profession was being cultivated in guilds and crafts long before Thomas Aquinas pondered over his theological teaching on vocation.

Christian mysticism saw in every creature the realization of a divine thought; it taught man to look for the traces of God in the world in order to find the creator. Medieval symbolism is likewise unthinkable without a candid respect for creatures, even though, on the other hand, it frightened man away far too quickly from their intrinsic value. Since the Renaissance and the Age of Humanism, not a few authors have praised the *dignitas hominis.* The theological motives had been at hand since patristic times: man's origin from God, his destiny to be an image of God and to rule in the world, his calling to communion with Christ and his final fulfilment in the glory of heaven.

This theological evaluation of man was, in principle at least, the common property of the entire Middle Ages. Man appeared as the center of the world, created in order that through him the world might be brought back to God. In general, however, God's image appeared founded not in the whole man, but rather in his spirituality and freedom. Also, the place of man in the world was explained not so much from his own make-up as from divine ordinance. Man's value lay in his function as God's trustee in the world.

In the twelfth century we hear the first faint suggestions of our modern problem regarding the worldliness of the world. An attempt was made to recognize the inherent value in the realms of earthly realities and to obtain a clearer view of the true relation between the orders of creation and salvation. Thomas Aquinas forcefully demonstrated that despite contingency and creative dependence there was still room for the genuine reality of the world as such. The French Dominican R. A. Gauthier asserts that it was to St. Thomas's credit that "he made possible the formation of a typically lay mentality" alongside the monastic spirituality directly aligned to God. This typically lay mentality was "made available for men who continue to have obligations toward the world which has returned to its worldliness [*profanité*]." [5]

We find in the Middle Ages only the beginnings of the kind of inquiry into the world pursued by modern science. But man's knowledge of the world and his understanding of the basic aspects of human existence were viewed together in the bold systems of medieval philosophy and theology. The great *Summas* not only uniformly recapitulated the total learning of the time, but above all offered an ultimate interpretation by integrating this learning with the statements of revelation as reflected upon in theology.[6]

C. Negative Factors in the Medieval Understanding of the World

The positive factors we have just considered never came to the fore historically as we might have expected. The basic attitude of the Middle Ages was one-sidedly that of flight from the world. The monastic, ascetical ideal prevailed also in the world; medieval Christianity was predominantly shaped by monks. Its ideal of life had a fascinating effect also upon laymen; one thought he could serve God best and most uncompromisingly when he bade farewell to

[5] "Magnanimité. L'idéal de la grandeur dans la philosophie païenne et dans la théologie chrétienne," *Bibliothèque thomiste* 28 (Paris: 1951), p. 496. For a treatment of the whole problem, cf. A. Auer, *op. cit.*, pp. 30–42.

[6] R. Guardini, *Das Ende der Neuzeit* (3rd ed.; Würzburg: 1951), p. 27. (Eng. tr.: *The End of the Modern World:* New York.) The medieval *Summas* seem strange to the modern spirit "until this spirit grasps what the medieval *Summas* really wanted to do: not an empirical research or rational elucidation of the world, but rather a construction of the 'world' from the content of revelation on the one hand, and from the principles and insights of ancient philosophy on the other. The *Summas* contain a world which has been erected in the mind, the whole of which can be compared with the endless differentiation and splendid unity of a cathedral . . ."

the world. Numerous writings bear the title: *De contemptu mundi, De miseria conditionis humanae* and *Ars morendi.*[7]

Unquestionably the "divinistical mentality of the Fathers" (Y. Congar) had lasting repercussions in the Middle Ages. One properly adhered to the dogmatic assertions, but in the area of Christian living many an escapist tendency of Stoic, Manichaean and Neo-Platonistic origin crept in. It was an easy matter to give such tendencies a biblical garb and thereby create the impression of a kind of super-Christianity. The Bible was held in great esteem; but its interpretation was attempted in a quite arbitrary manner. Qoheleth 1:2[8] and 1 John 2:15–16[9] were the most frequently quoted passages in the *De contemptu mundi* literature. These passages were interpreted to maintain simply that Sacred Scripture in its totality demanded a contempt for the world.

Undoubtedly the attitude of many authors toward the world was aggravated by a certain decadence of the time, a gloomy estimation of their own religious situation, severe catastrophes such as famine, plague, devastation and war, and a bitter personal fortune. Perhaps the strongest motive for adopting an attitude of contempt for the world, however, was the need for peace and security. Possessions, pomp and inordinate desire cause man a plethora of troubles; contempt for them would free him from many worldly hardships and burdens and would open to him a more reliable path to salvation.[10]

What H. R. Schlette states about Hugo of St. Victor holds for almost the entire output of medieval ascetical literature. According to the religious consciousness and experience of the time, goodness of creatures was overshadowed by the reality of man's fallen nature. This outlook "often awakened a harsh dualistic impression."[11] Beginning with its composition of matter and form, the world presented a danger which reached extreme acuteness in the disaster of sin; sinfulness appeared to be the ruling characteristic of the contemporary situation in salvation history. This conception of the

[7] Cf. A. Auer, *op. cit.*, pp. 44–48; and for what follows, H. Hergenröther, *op. cit.*

[8] "All is vanity."

[9] "Do not love the world or the things that are in the world . . . because all that is in the world is the lust of the flesh, and the lust of the eyes, and the pride of life; which is not from the Father, but from the world."

[10] H. Hergenröther, *op. cit.*, pp. 287–320, convincingly shows that this attitude was the strongest motive of the medieval contempt for the world.

[11] H. R. Schlette, *Die Nichtigkeit der Welt,* p. 35.

world as materiality (corporeality, sexuality) and especially as the domain of evil clearly pushed into the background of religious consciousness the doctrinally held belief in the world as creation. Man must be protected from the fascination of the world. And the best way to do this was to concentrate on the darker side of the world, to screen one's eyes from the allurement of the world and to fix them squarely on God.

D. An Appraisal of the Medieval Understanding of the World

In appraising the Middle Ages, we should not be content with the declaration that, thanks to the fidelity to dogmatic teachings, false principles were time and again clearly and resolutely averted. The far-reaching pedagogical and moral depreciation of the world opened the door, and kept it open for too long, to many a tendency stemming from pre- and non-Christian sources to disavow the world.[12]

Yet we should not assess the Middle Ages solely from the modern viewpoint. In contrast to the Middle Ages, modern times have certainly much more clearly seen the intrinsic nature of the world and the obligation inherent in it. The medieval understanding of the world appears to many to be primitive, barbaric and unenlightened. But we cannot consider history in this way. "The sole criterion by which an age can be rightly measured is the question: How far in it does the fullness of human existence expand to and attain a genuine meaningfulness? This occurred in the Middle Ages in a manner which associates it with the greatest periods of history." [13]

[12] *Ibid.*, p. 103. For Hugo of St. Victor, "the result of this practical understanding of the world is formally and materially equivalent to a basic dualism."

[13] R. Guardini, *op. cit.*, p. 34. H. R. Schlette, *Die Nichtigkeit der Welt*, pp. 80, 100, 160, in reference to K. Rahner on the "phenomenon of oblivion in the philosophy of religion," explains that the Middle Ages, epsecially Hugo of St. Victor, was permeated by an overwhelmingly dualistic conception of the world; this was so despite the fact that it could have come to a more positive outlook as a result of the theological groundwork (creation, redemption, consummation of the world). It is a fact that important theological truths are sometimes misunderstood or forgotten, although they are still handed on in dogma. "Despite the dogmatic correctness of the content of the Christian faith, in practical life and in the world-understanding an existential way of life may prevail, which—under Gnostic or Neo-Platonic influence—may totally deny this life and world and prefer that they did not exist at all." The question is this: whether the basic theological truths were ever held so lively in consciousness that one looking back at the Middle Ages can speak of "oblivion."

In the greatness of the Middle Ages, its very limitations become all the more apparent. No other age was able to achieve to the same degree a blending of the terrestrial and heavenly kingdoms into a single universal order in which the temporal realms were directly ordered to the spiritual reality of the Church, and even—in order to maintain this order—directly or at least indirectly subjugated to ecclesiastical regulation. This unitary order necessarily resulted in a situation in which temporal matters were not adequately considered with respect to their inherent value nor sufficiently seen as fashioned according to their own laws. In the long run, the sacred order of the Middle Ages amounted to the same thing as Monophysitism. This point will be dealt with later in this article.

II

The Modern Profane Understanding of the World

A. The Phenomenon of Modern Profaneness

"To the question of in what way those things that have being exist, the modern consciousness answers: as nature, as the subject of personality, and as culture. These three phenomena are interrelated; they mutually limit and perfect one another. Their framework signifies a final entity beyond which nothing can further be referred. It needs no foundation from anywhere else, nor does it tolerate a higher norm." [14]

The modern view of the world no longer sees nature as the creation of God, but rather as an autonomous universe standing on its own two feet and needing no other basis or standard from without. The modern man wrenches himself, as well as nature, from the authority of God and enthrones himself as the autonomous master of his own life. He is no longer the subordinate who receives the world as a fief from God and, against his own will, fashions it in obedience. The modern man sees only himself. Astonished, man discovers himself as an individual and suddenly becomes self-important.[15] He now represents only himself in civilization; he comes

[14] R. Guardini, *op. cit.,* p. 55; cf. for what follows from pp. 48 ff.; see also R. Guardini, *Welt und Person* (5th ed.; Würzburg: 1962), pp. 19–22.

[15] This turning point is visible in Petrarch, "the first modern man." Man no longer relates his experiences to God or mankind around him, but rather to himself; he is satisfied with the experience of himself. The starting point for the interpretation of life is no longer salvation history but the psychic experience. Regarding this self-experience of man according to Petrarch, cf. B. Groetuysen, *Philosophische Anthropologie* (Munich-Berlin: 1928), pp. 99–107.

to envisage himself as creator, and thereby also frees his work in the world from obedience to God. This autonomy is the pith of modern secularism: world and man stand by themselves, having their value, law and goal in themselves; there are no references to the transcendent. The voice of the Church, which strives toward an understanding of the world and life from revelation, is rejected as that of a foreign intruder (heteronomy).

The increasingly conscious "autonomous reason" of his own power further induces man gradually to understand and shape all earthly spheres according to an immanent set of laws. The sheer rules of the game prevail: power determines politics; mere profit, economics; pure form, art; possible disposability, technology. The Middle Ages had bound up all these spheres into its whole temporal-spiritual order, whose purpose and end it believed to be found in revelation. The way to freedom and salvation proceeded through the acknowledgment of these factors. In modern secularism there is a "self-liberation through knowledge." [16]

Reason finds the objective laws of order; reason verifies its ethical obligation; reason sees the individual orders in an over-all interpretation of man and world together. The statements and claims of a self-revealing God wishing to speak to man no longer have any place here. One concedes to earlier generations that they had to resort to such notions. But one is sure that it was a question only of a veiled kind of human self-assertion: man simply projected outwardly his own longings and needs. There was no basis at all in reality for these concepts, and it was therefore incumbent upon an enlightened age finally to break through to the truth.

Profaneness or secularism thus means a general intellectual attitude in which reality is accounted for from a purely inner-worldly mode of thinking. The truths of revelation and their interpretation by churches and theologians remain not only *de facto*, but also con-

[16] Cf. K. Popper, "Selbstbefreiung durch Wissen," in: *Der Sinn der Geschichte*, ed. L. Reinisch (2nd ed.; Munich: 1961), pp. 100–116. Instead of looking for a hidden meaning in history, we must give a meaning to history. We must agree with K. Popper, inasmuch as he is opposed to a prognosis of progress, a cyclic prognosis, one of destruction, and so forth. The fact that we ourselves give a meaning to history can imply that we ask ourselves: "What goals of political world history are worthy of man as well as politically possible?" (p. 102). Here also we must agree with the author. But he does not pose the question whether a meaning for salvation history unfolds itself behind everything in world history. This is the author's perfect right, but theology has a right and a duty to pursue this inquiry.

sciously and intentionally excluded from consideration, because the truth ascertained by reason alone is denied them. Religion can still be allowed a private and interior place of its own, so long as no objections against state, society, technology, art, or science ensue from it. In the pure, absolute profaneness, every outlet to the transcendent is excluded.

By the terms "secularizing" or "making worldly," we understand the historical process which led to the mentality of profaneness or secularism. This historical process is judged within the profaneness itself as a liberation, the coming of man to himself. From the standpoint of religion, it is characterized as the culpable, or in any case fatal, breaking-away from the coordination of the mundane orders with religion as its center, a coordination prescribed and expressed by the order of creation and salvation.[17]

B. *The Crisis of Modern Profaneness*

In his book *The End of the Modern World,* R. Guardini offers not only a phenomenological view of modern profaneness, but also points to the elements which have led to its crisis.[18] For several decades now man's relationship to nature has been in transition. Nature is no longer the kind, all-protecting "Mother Nature"; rather it is the medium within which man's work is set out. In technology man experiences the dimensions of this potentiality, but also the converging dangers. The more he scientifically investigates and technically masters nature, the more unfamiliar and hostile it appears to him.

The autonomous individual, who a short time ago so emphatically extolled personality as the "greatest boon of mortal men," suddenly finds himself constrained by the very forces of those structures which a perfected technology has developed in all areas of life and which now relentlessly regulate his freedom and his whole way of living. Man comes to learn that the more he organizes all spheres of life, the more he is treated as an object, a functionary. He no longer sees himself on the lonely summit of a unique and creative self-experience; rather, in the phenomenon of the masses, he feels himself restricted by the structures around him, which penetrate to his

[17] C. H. Ratschow, "Säkularismus," in: *Die Religion in Geschichte und Gegenwart V* (Tübingen: 1961), p. 1288.

[18] R. Guardini, *Das Ende der Neuzeit,* pp. 67–105.

innermost being. He is afraid of what appears to him to be the heart of his human existence.

A final peril for him arises from the very civilization he created: his hope for a never-ending progress, a life of prosperity, freedom and peace is dampened. He sees the development of undreamed-of potentialities as an accomplished fact, but a profound skepticism overcomes him as to whether every growth in technical might is really an enrichment of his person and of his solidarity with the community.

Because he is not used to the power so quickly devolved upon him, he loses his feeling of security in his control over technology. His ever-prodigious technical works seem to have detached themselves from him and set themselves up as an independent power opposed to him. Much to his dismay he discovers that the chaos of nature, which he had harnessed and against which he had safeguarded himself, might with its sinister force overtake him, and that the final situation might become much worse than the first.

Modern profaneness finds itself in its ultimate intensification. In contrast, its earlier forms—the autonomy of the state, of science, of art, and so forth—appear as harmless child's play. Natural science and technology in the last one hundred years have invested pristine worldliness with an importance which it did not have (at least not recognizably for most people) so long as it concerned itself with reality in a purely speculative or artistic manner. Technocratic profaneness with the full impetus of its economic, technical, social and political structures has taken the wind out of the sails of the human person. The inquiry into the meaning of the world and of human existence is thereby silenced. "Vitalism and existentialism express the self-understanding of this secularism. They base themselves insistently on the grounds of a pure vitality and existential receptivity that precede and are outside reason; they then converge in mystical solipsism." [19]

[19] C. H. Ratschow, *op. cit.*, p. 1294. On p. 1293 the author ascertains that the specific point about this technocratic form of secularism is the "autonomy of an objective and calculable set of laws all its own . . . which comprise and have the last word on everything about life as world and self and as nature and history." Cf. also J. Hommes, "Naturrecht, Person, Materie—das Anliegen der Dialektik," in: *Gesellschaft, Staat, Wirtschaft,* ed. J. Höffner, A. Verdross, F. Vito (Innsbruck-Vienna-Munich: 1961), esp. pp. 65–69, where it is philosophically shown how, at the apex of the modern profaneness, in the "absolute dialectic" not only the reality of nature, but also the reality of man in control of nature falls apart and disappears.

C. An Appraisal of Modern Profaneness

It was stated that modern profaneness has reached a crisis, but this does not necessarily mean it has foundered, for every genuine crisis has within itself the possibility of a good denouement. Later it will become more evident how far this is true of modern profaneness. Here is not the place for any premature assertions as to whether the crisis of modern profaneness can be mastered either in a *pure* inner-worldly, or *only* in a Christian sense. In any case, the mere fact that modern profaneness has reached a crisis still does not absolve Christianity from its historical complicity in the secularization of the modern world; nor does it at all mean an approval of the present state of secularism.

We might be able to throw light on the whole situation by posing the concise question: What is the evaluation of modern profaneness from a theological viewpoint? From outright rejection, that is, the relentless indictment of modern profaneness because of the world's disavowal of God's acceptance of it in Christ, the appraisal passes to the express welcome of this evolution by those who see therein the new possibilities for the realization of Christianity. Before we turn to some opinions from Catholic and Protestant Evangelical theology, we should first briefly describe the religious-psychological approach to the problem. (We pass over a purely negative appraisal of this modern development, especially since it is nowadays scarcely treated in theological writings.)

1. A religious-psychological appraisal. C. H. Ratschow,[20] following P. Radin, holds that profaneness or, as he calls it, secularism, is a latent pitfall for every religion. His argument runs something like this: There are men everywhere who have no religious convictions or experiences; they tend to be a thoughtful, rational type of people. Because religion as the center of man's existence remains foreign to them, in their search for the meaning of existence they are compelled, so to speak, to set out in a purely worldly, secular and immanent manner and thus to depend upon their power of reason alone. These skeptics are a constant hidden danger to all religions.

But as the occasion presents itself, their rationalistic interpretation of world and life gains a considerable foothold and then in violent eruptions of "enlightenment" becomes historically actual, as in the

[20] C. H. Ratschow, *op. cit.*, pp. 1288–96.

case of Averroism and Nominalism during the Middle Ages, the Renaissance and Humanism at the beginning of modern times and most visibly—picking up increasingly more momentum—since the Enlightenment of the seventeenth and eighteenth centuries.[21] This way of thinking undoubtedly plays an important part in the appreciation of modern profaneness.

Man, with his deep-rooted and lively experience of the absolute, always has the inclination to depreciate and reject what is finite and temporal precisely because it is not absolute. The absolute becomes the only thing; any truth the finite realities may have is thereby lost. One could say it is the function of profane thought to counteract such a neglect of the world and in that way also to help discover the full truth about God.

2. *An appraisal from Catholic theology.* With all due respect for the Middle Ages, Catholic theology has not let the positive elements of modern profaneness go unnoticed. We know that in the Middle Ages the absolute was often so one-sidedly emphasized that earthly realities could not fully unfold their genuine meaning. The modern age, on the contrary, has shoved the absolute *so far* into the background, even completely denying it, that the creatureliness of the world has been more and more obscured and sometimes totally impugned. Nevertheless, the created universe with its own existence and its own dignity stands out more clearly. The world has been seen as a reality, and explored and molded with great candor and objectivity. Modern man takes the world more seriously than his medieval counterpart could. R. Guardini characterizes this development in the modern relationship of man to the world as a "coming of age."[22]

[21] C. H. Ratschow is of the opinion that the Reformers' systematic clarification of the Middle Ages resulted in "a positive conclusion and faithful recapitulation." Through the teachings of the three classes, the two kingdoms and the *usus politicus legis*—thought patterns which have since become foreign to us—Luther determined the relationship of faith and the worldliness of the world in a novel and positive way. He could stress the worldliness of the world without impairing the majesty of God.

[22] R. Guardini, *Welt und Person,* p. 35: "The term 'coming of age' [*Mündigkeit*] does not mean anything ethical, but refers rather to the fact of advanced time, of greater age. A man is of age [*mündig*] in comparison to a boy. This does not mean that he is morally better, but that he sees the world more penetratingly, feels its reality more keenly, has a better idea of the potentialities and limits of his power, and a more distinct consciousness of his responsibility . . . A corresponding phenomenon is found here. The modern man is of age in comparison to his medieval forebear." Cf. *ibid.*, pp. 24–26, 86.

According to J. B. Metz, modern profaneness originated not in opposition to, but on account of Christianity. It is initially a Christian event brought on by Christian impulses. The pantheism of the ancients never allowed the world to become entirely worldly, because it never let God become entirely divine. It was lacking the notion of a transcendent creator; the divine seemed to be an element of the world. A Christianity which rightly understands itself must appear "not as increasing divinization but precisely as a mounting removal of divinity from the world, and in this sense as a profanation of the world." [23] To the pagans of old, the Christians were the real "atheists."

If only Christianity had taken more seriously its belief in creation with all the ensuing consequences, it would not then have fallen so deeply into theological and religious embarrassment as a result of the modern secularization of the world. Certainly the Christian believed that God created the world and constantly kept it in existence. But the believer did not see clearly enough that precisely through the mysteries of creation and Christ, through the creation and adoption of the world in grace, there occurred "the original and radical liberation of the world to its own character and properties, to the undisguised reality of its non-divinity." [24] It is one of the tragic events in the history of Christianity that the secularization of the world, to which it gave the impetus, *de facto* has prevailed contrary to Christianity's concrete historical understanding of the world. And not least of all because of the opposition of Christians, this secularization of the world has taken on such militantly secular features.

Modern profaneness, however, implies a protest not only against the pantheistic undoing of the world as it is in itself (through a merging with God), but also against its Monophysitic undoing, which happened in the Middle Ages through the merging of the world with the church. A conscious intention to respect and safeguard the world and the church as they are in themselves should in no way, at least not generally, be imputed to the supporters of the secular movement. But in their protest against the expropriation of the world by the church, they have brought to bear the right of the world, and its true nature, in the face of illegitimate ecclesiastical claims. And right here there is something of theological significance.

[23] J. B. Metz, "Weltverständnis im Glauben. Christliche Orientierung in der Weltlichkeit der Welt heute," in: *Geist und Leben* 35 (1962), p. 175.
[24] *Ibid.*, p. 175.

Not only is there the charism of *agape*, through which the world is brought home to Christ, there is also the charism of *eros*, which recognizes and loves the truth and beauty of the world. How could something not recognized and loved be brought home to Christ?

Certainly men on the road to modern profaneness are at fault for having spurned God, their Creator and Saviour. But no one can say whether there are many or few who proceed against the clear dictate of their conscience. On the other hand, the one-sided exaggeration of the absoluteness of God and the more or less Monophysitic interpretation of the relationship of church and world have in no small way contributed to the fact that the self-subsistence of the world has been so overshadowed. Since man is seldom a master of moderation, it is not surprising that the reaction to such developments took the radical form of an autonomous profaneness.[25] Modern profaneness has in fact helped—and perhaps even given the decisive impulses—to rectify the one-sided constructions of the Christian understanding of the world. Modern profaneness has also suggested to Christianity new and legitimate factors in man's relationship to the world that can be integrated into the actuality of salvation.

3. *An appraisal from Evangelical Protestant theology.* We can sketch just a few opinions—and these only very hastily—from Evangelical Protestant theology, which comes to terms in a frank and penetrating way with the phenomenon of modern profaneness.[26]

D. Bonhoeffer has expounded the relationship between Christian faith and the modern lack of religion. On the one hand, the church is to blame for the modern process of secularization; on the other, this process of secularization is only possible within a Christian background and should for that reason be assessed as "a historical execution of what is already founded in the Christian faith itself in its relation to the world: namely, the removal of divinity from the world." [27]

[25] K. Rahner, "Anthropologie (theologische)," in: *Lexikon für Theologie und Kirche I* (2nd ed.; 1957), p. 622, speaks of a "*dei*" (Greek, meaning necessity), which, "from a historico-theological standpoint, is to be expected."

[26] G. Ebeling, "Die nicht-religiöse Interpretation biblischer Begriffe," in: *Zeitschrift für Theologie und Kirche* 52 (1955), pp. 296–360, shows how difficult and stratified the problems are. The discussion in Evangelical Protestant theology shows a great freedom and radicalism, which probably go together with the fact that the concepts of religion and church have here taken on a considerably less impervious and stabilized meaning than in Catholicism.

[27] *Ibid.*, p. 334. G. Ebeling much more profoundly develops D. Bonhoeffer's

On the whole, D. Bonhoeffer has no regrets, therefore, about the rise of a "world coming of age," of a world without religion. Along with K. Barth, he supports the conviction that there should never even be an attempt to make room once again for religion in the secularized world. The coming generation will be one completely without religion.[28] Yet here lies a new and great opportunity for the Christian message. For this message—in a world without religion—must also be without religion. Today and in the future, religion may be demanded as a prerequisite or way to faith just as unessentially as the Jewish circumcision was earlier. The world's lack of religion testifies to God's powerlessness in the world. And in this situation salvation is found, as became manifest in the crucifixion. "For I determined not to know anything among you, except Jesus Christ and him crucified" (1 Cor. 2:2).[29]

D. Bonhoeffer's summons for a "non-religious interpretation of biblical concepts" plays a central role in the Evangelical Protestant discussion about the problem of secularism. Religion is here classified with the "law." K. Barth has also seen in the Christian faith the fundamental antithesis to religion, and with good reason, if one regards religion as the attempt to have God and his work of redemption at one's own disposal and through the act of religion alone to force one's way to God. The "religious interpretation" of biblical concepts is then simply "legal interpretation." Understood in this way, "religious interpretation" in the end excludes what D. Bonhoeffer means by "non-religious interpretation."

This "non-religious interpretation" involves three things: first, a Christological interpretation, that is, in theological thought Jesus Christ is at stake: What does Christ really mean for us today?; second, a concrete interpretation, that is, intellectual sincerity must also be respected in theology, and the question strictly posed: What do we really believe?; third, an interpretation of the faith, that is,

---

concept of the paradoxical conformity between the Christian faith and the process of radical secularization. We cannot, however, go into this any further here.

[28] *Ibid.*, p. 333. The author says more cautiously: "In regard to the phenomenon of religion, we encounter something simply unknown."

[29] H. Fries, "Die Botschaft von Christus in einer Welt ohne Gott," in: *Verkündigung und Glaube*, ed. Th. Filthaut and J. A. Jungmann (Freiburg i. Br.: 1958), pp. 100–122, gives a critical explanation of D. Bonhoeffer's theses concerning the coming of age of the world, the concept of religion, the realization of salvation through the crucifixion alone, and so forth.

the theological thought must be adjusted to the message and must answer the question: How can Christ become the salvation also of those without religion?[30]

W. Hartmann sees in the "breakdown of profaneness and of the autocracy of the human capability to do everything" the only possibility for a new link with the autonomous man. The proper stewardship of the world as God's inheritance can hardly be the affair of an autonomous reason, because this reason consciously disengages itself from administering the world in the spirit of the creator and lawgiver. Any action in the world may not be separated from faith; solicitude for the world must not pass over to the autonomous reason alone. For when man rejects the gospel, he inevitably falls—in some way or other—"under the law." He further runs aground every time he tries by his own efforts to account for himself and the world. Human existence cannot be produced, but rather is acquired only from God. The modern profane man must therefore be allowed to guide his existence "under the law."

At the same time, however, W. Hartmann warns that any attempt to exploit the failure of secularism for religious purposes—in order to overcome its crisis—leads to an "obsolete religious outlook toward the world." Secularism cannot be rescinded; it must be surmounted by looking ahead. This looking-ahead also lies in the "non-religious interpretation" of the Christian content of faith.[31]

As with D. Bonhoeffer and W. Hartmann, so also for F. Gogarten the coming-of-age of mankind appears as the fruit of the Christian faith. The one under age is the man "under the law." Through belief in the gospel, man reaches majority: he is admitted to "sonship." Through faith he becomes a "co-heir of Christ" (Rom. 8:17), and in his alliance with Christ he bears a responsibility for the world. The Christian, who in sonship is set free for responsible action in the world, must by all means "hold back" his faith. Should faith itself attend to the doings of the world, it would wrong both itself and the world. Indeed, faith—and only faith—knows all about the world. But the believer must restrain this knowledge; it is not

[30] Cf. G. Ebeling, *op. cit.*, pp. 304–40. The works of D. Bonhoeffer which are especially important for our problem are: *Ethik*, ed. E. Bethge (3rd ed.; Munich: 1956) and *Widerstand und Ergebung*, ed. E. Bethge (7th ed.; Munich: 1956).

[31] Cf. W. Hartmann, "Säkularisierung," in: *Evangelisches Kirchenlexikon* III, pp. 768–73.

for him to desire to take the entirety of the world upon himself, because he would then fall under its law.[32]

Similarly, H. Schreiner affirms the genuine reality of the world, its self-subsistence, and its freedom from all external pressure and —what he especially stresses—from demoniac secularism, which leads necessarily to totalitarianism. Yet for him faith in no way remains "held back"; it is rather the only guarantee of a genuine world-formation. It must operate very concretely in the different domains. On this point H. Schreiner differs from F. Gogarten. This variance becomes even more evident when H. Schreiner to some extent offers concrete suggestions for the self-subsistence of all worldly realities found in the conscience bound up in God.[33]

Finally, H. Kraemer asserts that the initial excitement of the awakening has long since died down. Through the scientific and technical control of the powers of nature, modern autonomy has fallen into a "Babylonian pandemonium," the like of which history has rarely experienced. The coming-of-age of reason faces a multitude of modern idolatries. The progress of science has led not only to a heightened self-confidence, but also to a menacing spiritual dissipation and a sometimes insufferable loss of norms. The modern profane man has been outplayed by his own conquests and is no longer able to remain their master.

In the course of this evolution in modern profaneness, a number of areas have been snatched away from the church (education, social welfare, and so forth), so that the church has had to submit to a far-reaching privation of functions. But the work of the church has thereby become especially problematic in that a fundamental religious understanding of the world and life can "no longer find a place" in the fundamentally secularized orientation. And yet modern profaneness also has a positive meaning for the church: the relative autonomy of worldly spheres has become more clearly evident, and the church sees herself unavoidably compelled to rethink her own understanding of herself and the world.[34]

[32] Cf. F. Gogarten, *Verhängnis und Hoffnung der Neuzeit. Die Säkularisierung als theologisches Problem* (Stuttgart: 1953).

[33] Cf. H. Schreiner, *Die Säkularisierung als Grundproblem der deutschen Kultur* (publication of the Kirchlich-sozialen Bundes 73) (Berlin-Spandau: 1930). Some good surveys of this discussion in Evangelical Protestant theology are made by C. H. Ratschow, *op. cit.*, pp. 1288–96 and W. Hartmann, *op. cit.*, pp. 768–73.

[34] Cf. H. Kraemer, "Säkularismus," in: *Evangelisches Kirchenlexikon* III, pp. 773–76. Further literature: W. Hahn, "Säkularisation und Religionszerfall. Eine

III

A Theology of Earthly Realities

The task of theology is to abstract the truths of revelation from the sources, to thoughtfully enter into them, to order them into a complete picture, and to impart them to contemporary society. The truth theology has to proclaim is the one assigned to it; it is a truth which is to be found time and again and which should be expressed in an up-to-date manner. The way of theology proceeds from above, from God to the world and to man. Its method is a deductive one.

The following treatise, although it begins with reflections on the self-subsistence of the world, is only seemingly inductive. Even a "theology of earthly realities" is bound to the deductive method. But the theological answer should be given whence the question arises: it should seek the modern profane man where he exists. This speculative treatment will not, therefore, take up the problem of the self-subsistence of the world in order to keep the reflection strictly to its object, for this could be accomplished in other ways. This procedure is presented rather only as a help to make it clear to the reader—especially to one not versed in theology—that the theological consideration and statement do keep to the point.[35]

A. *The Self-subsistence of Earthly Realities*

What does this thesis concerning the independence of earthly realities mean? How is it to be explained?

1. *The concept of the thesis.* By the "worldly domain" we understand the different forms of human association and the material order as well as the activity connected with them: work, profession, society, science, culture, art, technology, and economy. These worldly domains all have a bona fide existence of their own. They have their own proper and valid existence, and thereby also their own proper

religions-psychologische Überlegung," in: *Kerygma und Dogma* 5 (1959), pp. 83–98, in which the author asks whether Western secularization implies a falling away from religion; F. Delikat, *Über den Begriff der Säkularisation* (Heidelberg: 1958), which contains an accurate research into the theological definition of the concept of secularization; M. Stallmann, "Was ist Säkularisierung?" in: *Sammlung gemeinverständlicher Vorträge und Schriften aus dem Gebiet der Theologie und Religionsgeschichte,* 227/228 (Tübingen: 1960), in which an introduction tracing the history of this concept is followed by a presentation of D. Bonhoeffer's and F. Gogarten's understanding of secularization.

[35] Cf. *Lexikon für Theologie und Kirche* I (2nd ed.; Freiburg: 1957), p. 623.

meaning and system of laws to which man in his knowledge and action must submit. Their proper existence must remain intact even when the philosopher or believer sees in them a transcendental relationship. Philosophy preserves an existence of its own as opposed to theology, as does culture as opposed to piety and mysticism, and economics as opposed to charity. There is not only God, but also the world. There is not only religion, but also economics, technology, art and science. And they all have an existence of their own. Religion cannot simply be everything; it cannot of itself dictate an order and posit norms for other fields. These areas must have "their own laws and their own, at least relative, autonomy in order really to subsist at all."[36]

He who believes that the world has come into existence through the Word cannot find it difficult to perceive that order, law-abidingness and meaningfulness prevail in the world as a whole and in all the component parts of the world. The more God puts the world, which is dependent upon him, on its own two feet, all the more he supports it in its own being; so the more divine his work appears. In the teaching of the natural law, the fact that earthly realms have their own set of laws is expressly recognized. Man must yield to the natural order, to the objective logic inherent in the individual worldly domains, and thereby uncover that truth and call forth that order which lies in the things themselves.

Since the beginning of modern times, science has devoted itself with growing interest to earthly realities as such. The result is that understanding of the world and of human life has been deepened and broadened to a remarkable degree. Man has become another person; he behaves differently toward the world and toward himself. His increased insight into the orders and laws of the world in great and small things vividly brings home to him the meaning of an existence that is both self-subsistent and endowed with its own laws. Science, in laying bare the truth of the world, has made a contribution which, however, should not be overestimated.

The insight that the world is temporally and spatially limited, and therefore measurable, also belongs to the perceptions of natural science. According to the ancients, the cosmos stood autonomous in itself. Beyond the cosmos, nothing further could be imagined. The cosmos itself was its own basis, law and meaning; the divine and

[36] F. v. Hügel, "Andacht zur Wirklichkeit," in: *Schriften in Auswahl,* selected, translated and introduced by M. Schlüter-Hermkes (Munich: 1952), p. 45.

the human were enclosed in it. The limited and measurable cosmos of modern natural science, however, cannot be understood as something absolute.[37]

More and more the conviction prevails that by measurability alone we cannot arrive at a decisive quality of the real. Even the smallest things refer to something beyond themselves: "Through themselves they point beyond themselves to the most profound depths." They point to man, in whom alone they become conscious and expressable.[38]

It goes without saying that theology neither could nor would want to shy away from the findings of modern science; rather, science can provide theology with some very fruitful impulses. The belief in the constancy of knowledge and of culture is theologically outdated. Even Thomas Aquinas thought that every good thing had esssentially been discovered by the dawn of the new era, about the time of St. Paul, and that all further discoveries could only be inferior ones. As God rested on the seventh day, so man also, after the birth of Christ, rested from all the work of civilization and restricted himself to the preservation of what had been achieved.

Thomas certainly knew that there would be new findings and cultural advances in the future course of history. But since the coming of Christ, they could not be good of themselves, but only insofar as they served religious purposes. In contrast to this view, Pius XII clearly stated: "Every human cognition, even when not of a religious character, has in itself its own value and sovereignty; it is, however, a participation in God's infinite knowledge. When it is used to elucidate God and questions concerning the divine, it thereby receives a new, higher value and consecration." [39]

2. *The meaning of the thesis.* We have already shown how the modern secularistic evolution has carried the self-subsistence of the world too far in an *autonomous* direction. Only the one-sidedly ra-

[37] Inasmuch as Greek thought had already explored "being," it was itself already on the way to surmounting the "absolute" cosmos. This thought is developed by W. Weymann-Weyhe in an unpublished manuscript from a radio broadcast in 1962: *Die Welt ist nicht immer die gleiche. Kosmos, Naturgesetz, Wahrheit und Theologie,* pp. 15–19. This contribution is stimulating in many other respects as well.

[38] *Ibid.,* pp. 25–38.

[39] Cf. A. Mitterer, "Die Weltherrschaft des Menschen also Naturrecht," in: *Naturordnung in Gesellschaft, Staat, Wirtschaft* (Innsbruck-Vienna-Munich: 1961), pp. 44–47.

tional had been acknowledged; any foundation of this self-subsistence in a transcendental relationship has been denied. The claim of a divine revelation has appeared as a heteronomous presumption. Since the Renaissance and Humanism, but above all since the Enlightenment of the seventeenth and eighteenth centuries, the consequences of this secularistic conception have been more rigorously thought out and steadily realized. Gradually the worldly arenas have shaken themselves loose from that guardianship of the church which was so matter-of-fact to the medieval man. The lords with their politics were the first to break away; then followed the common welfare and city life, scientific thought and morality, and finally the conscience of the people and their daily experience of pleasure and pain.

We have also shown how this development was a reaction—one necessarily expected, so to speak, from a historical-theological point of view—to the *integralistic* appropriation of the self-subsistence of the world. Here we should recall two forms of this appropriation, and what we have learned from their effects.

First, the world as world must not be plunged into the absoluteness of God. The fact that there is a higher being is no tacit permission to efface, as it were, a lower one. The absoluteness of God must be interpreted not in itself, in the abstract, but rather from the concrete history of salvation set in motion and sustained by God. The absoluteness of God must be interpreted in such a way that it brooks the "pluralism" of things. In the Catholic teaching of the *analogia entis* (analogy of being), the absoluteness of God is doctrinally expressed plainly enough, but its concrete understanding and realization in faith have often been *de facto* disregarded. This understanding and realization in faith were more orientated to Greek than to biblical thinking. Otherwise it would have been seen that God's creative love, in its giving and its being content to leave a being as it is, carries with it the possibility and also the guarantee for the world as it is in itself.

As to the second form of appropriation, the understanding of the world per se must never again be Monophysitically atomized in the church. The duality of orders, rightly understood, must remain untouched for the entire duration of salvation history. The concern of the church, and of those in the church who dedicate themselves to theology and kerygma, is focused on the integration of the world into the history of salvation. With such a viewpoint, it can easily happen that the "one thing necessary" in tow, as it were, becomes the only thing. In relation to this one thing, everything else becomes unimportant; to acknowledge that the other has its own reality even seems sacrilegious and sinfully secularistic. Those who know their history well and who interpret it have declared often enough how strongly and persistently this misunderstanding—call it divinism, hierocracy, or ecclesiological monism—has stamped concrete Christianity.

Just as autonomism has misconstrued the transcendental grounding of the world, so divinism has failed to appreciate that the world has a reality of its own. In order to do justice to historical truth, we should show, however, that theology has actually always been on the way to a denouement in which the world's deeper dimension and value are preserved.

In Christian antiquity (Justin, Clement of Alexandria), the *logos spermatikos* was everywhere operative and therefore could resolutely support the right of culture within the church. Toward the end of the fifth century, Pope Gelasius I made a sharp distinction between the spiritual and worldly realms of power, tracing both directly to Christ. This concept came to the fore time and again from the Middle Ages down to Leo XIII, who expressly made it his own. Beginning in the twelfth century (Suger, Abelard, Godfrey of St. Victor), theology began to reflect more keenly upon the self-subsistence of the earthly spheres. This was the time of the discovery of the world's reality as such. In the Thomistic concept of creation, the self-subsistence of creatures is definitively anchored in theology. Leo XIII concretized this view in numerous statements which recognized the "necessary autonomy" of the worldly orders and "an area of justifiable and legitimate freedoms." [40]

In *Quadragesimo anno,* Pius XI cites Leo's remark that the Church believes it would be wrong for her to interfere without just cause in earthly concerns. He rejects the authority of the Church to make assertions upon technical matters, since she has neither the means nor the competence for this. The competence of the Church confines itself to "what has a relation to the moral law." [41]

[40] Cf. A. Auer, *op. cit.,* pp. 270–76; also A. Auer, "Kirche und Welt," in: *Mysterium Kirche,* ed. F. Holböck, Th. Sartory (Salzburg: 1962), pp. 509–11.

[41] *Quadragesimo anno:* ". . . non iis quidem, quae artis sunt, sed in iis omnibus quae ad regulam morum referuntur." Herder edition (1931), p. 32.

Catholic social science sees here the unequivocal recognition that the various areas of civilization are self-subsistent and possess their own inherent system of laws. When the Pope says that economics has its own "principles," [42] he means exactly what we wish to express with the still relatively new ideas of self-subsistence (*Eigenständigkeit*) and "necessary" autonomy (*Eigengesetzlichkeit*): namely, that economics and all other fields have their own basis of being upon which they rest, and their own laws which flow from this basis of being and are therefore indispensable. O. v. Nell-Breuning sees in the phrase "*suis utuntur principiis*" ("things operate by their own principles") "a classical formulation of our own terms of self-subsistence and 'necessary' autonomy." [43]

In the evolving "theology of earthly realities," the earthly spheres —the human and the material—prevail as a proper theme in theology itself, thus no longer being relegated only to sociocultural philosophy and ethics. This "theology of earthly realities," in which the world as world finally is treated theologically, will have to consider more exactly the relationship of the emancipation of the worldly orders to their own self-subsistence, and, in doing so, must overcome many an integralistic prejudice.

B. The Relative Self-subsistence of Earthly Realities

As we already stated, the assertion that the earthly realities are self-subsistent and have laws which are proper to themselves does not express the full truth. This assertion must be integrated further so that the foundation of the worldly orders in a transcendental relationship of being can also be seen and recognized in reference not only to God the Creator but also to Christ the Head. These integrating statements about the world can be made only by theology, for their content has become accessible only through revelation. In the history of salvation, the transcendental determination of the world is thus presented in two great stages: in the mystery of creation and in the mystery of Christ. The latter develops

[42] *Ibid.*: ". . . oeconomica res et moralis disciplina in suo quaeque ambitu suis utuntur principiis."

[43] O. v. Nell-Breuning, *Die soziale Enzyklika* (3rd ed.; Cologne: 1950), p. 60. Cf. also his important treatment of the ethics of economics as "institutional ethics" in the article "Zur Wirtschaftordnung," in: *Wörterbuch der Politik IV*, ed. O. v. Nell-Breuning, H. Sacher (Freiburg i. Br.: 1949), pp. 274–80.

itself in the Church throughout history, and only with the second coming of Christ will come to a full revelation and realization.

The first level of the relative self-subsistence of earthly realities is their creatureliness, that is, their relationship to God the Creator

This statement must be set forth in its essential content.

a. The world *is created by God:* In an act of radical freedom and love, the world is placed in being out of nothing; by the same divine freedom and love it is continually preserved in existence. This creative action of God is accomplished through the Word, and for that reason certain *rationes seminales,* certain values and laws of order, are grounded in the world. Whatever possibilities and realities the world comprises come therefore from God.

This is the first decisive integration to which modern profaneness in its secularistic bent must yield. The world cannot be closed in on itself. The world need not necessarily exist; it does not therefore exist of itself, nor can it suffice of itself alone. The doctrine of creation draws the world into an immediate nearness to God and causes it to emerge as a direct and constantly actual expression of his creative love. The creator releases the world to a reality of its own, and so much so that the world appears to stand completely in itself; it is able to arouse the illusion of being fully autonomous.

b. Within the created universe the creator has set up an *ordering principle* comprising all things: *man.* Because it is ordered and meaningful, the world is present wholly in each of its components and is to be encountered in any—even the smallest—part. In man, however, the world is pre-eminently represented. The world is created for man and can find completion only through him. He is able to apprehend the world and thereby give things their names. He is entrusted by the creator with the task of fulfilling the world by his dominion in it. The world is the place of his existence, his "extended corporeality" (M. J. Scheeben). Since man is its center and head, this cosmos—in varying degrees—personally resounds with human corporeality into its uttermost ramifications apparently remote from man.

Sacred Scripture has not reflectively concerned itself with this anthropocentrism of the cosmos. K. Rahner notes that the anthropological truths of the Bible to a large extent employ categories drawn solely from an objective world, as well as ontology obtainable from these categories, "so that there is a danger of missing the theological individuality of man and seeing him, in a sheer objective approach, as a piece of the world." But the scriptural truths nevertheless have a clearly discernible "anthropological apex" insofar as they envision man as a spiritual, free person taken into partnership with God.[44] The fact that man is the image of God does not allow any evaluation of him as a stage in the development of the cosmos, as a being bound up in the same way as all the other beings, whereby he receives an even lower position than many others.[45]

J. B. Metz has recently shown that in Thomas Aquinas there is a speculative break-through from the ancient Greek cosmocentrism in which man is practically lost in the universe—or at any rate receives no special place in it—to the biblical-Christian anthropocentrism. The cosmos is now situated in the horizon of man, rather than man in the horizon of the cosmos. Man is no longer arranged as an arbitrary part in the universe. "The being of those things that exist is rather viewed and determined from this human subjectivity." In man, being, taken altogether, is very decidedly present. Subjectivity thus becomes "the primary place for the accessibility of being; thought is seen as making-present of being." In man, then, the universe is for the first time really present to itself.[46]

In this spirit of St. Thomas, J. Hommes speaks of a "human conditioning" or "personal meaning" of nature. Nature is fully immersed in the life of man; it is the "instrument of his existence," the "concrete part of his essence." Nature, with its personal conditioning, is given to man, but it demands at the same time man's own "independent spiritual-personal activity," which he can fruitfully unfold only in cooperation with other men in directing nature. "The human-personal conditioning of nature is something given to man in his existence, and therefore, as such, taken over by him as a determination of his very self. Man's ability to handle nature—

[44] K. Rahner, *op. cit.*, p. 620.

[45] K. Löwith, "Der Weltbegriff der neuzeitlichen Philosophie," in: *Sitzungsberichte der Heidelberger Akademie der Wissenschaften, Phil.-Hist. Klasse IV* (Heidelberg: 1960), p. 9.

[46] J. B. Metz, *Christliche Anthropozentrik. Über die Denkform des Thomas von Aquin* (Munich: 1962), pp. 41–95, esp. pp. 41–51. According to W. Weymann-Weyhe, *op. cit.*, pp. 34–39, modern physics (C. F. von Weizäcker, W. Heisenberg) is drawing nearer to this Thomistic conception, insofar as all being is taken into the thinking spirit and only here becomes itself.

as the tool of his existence—and his ability to handle the rational—as a possible way home—find themselves united in the human handling of the processes of nature." [47]

Christian anthropocentrism is obviously not only compatible with theocentrism but even grounded in it, for man has been placed by God the Creator in the center of the world. This Christian anthropocentrism is pregnant with meaning for an understanding of the world from the standpoint of salvation history. History is only possible to the extent that a person is involved. The only history is that of man.

Because the cosmos, as the "extended corporeality of man," is personally conditioned, human history must also become cosmic history. This means first of all that the destiny of the cosmos can be understood only as a consequence adherent to human-personal history. The history of man precedes the fate of the universe as a causative factor and guides it onward. And secondly, history, shaped as it is out of the freedom of man, becomes necessary for the destiny of the cosmos. In the beginning, the unity of man and cosmos was a unity of glory. Through the sin of man it became an association in disaster. In the Second Adam and in man whom he has liberated, this unity is brought back into salvation and raised up even beyond the glory of the beginning. At the end of history, this unity of man and cosmos will enter into the glory of completion.

The ordering of the world's being to mankind also includes the potentiality that the world could become entangled in possible ruin as a result of the fault of man. This potentiality has become a historical reality. *Sin,* to be sure, has its origin in the freedom of the human person. Because the human personality is essentially socially and cosmically determined, the guilt stemming from the person must necessarily affect the social and cosmic realms. In Romans 8:20f., Paul characterizes this consequence as *mataiotes* and *phthora,* as a true deterioration which became powerful in the world—and in things—after the curse of God and to which humanity is now subjugated as to a hard servitude.

One may interpret the "vanity" and "corruption" of Romans 8 as a partial loss of the transparency of creatures (an upsetting of values and laws of order), as the world's obstinacy toward man's will to form and rule, as its satanic misuse. In any event, time and again man comes to experience this corruption and is able to confirm this

[47] J. Hommes, *op. cit.,* p. 64. For the whole picture cf. pp. 60–64.

biblical truth from his own experience. The evangelist John describes the world as a sinister prodigy of power in which the evil spiritual potencies at work seduce man the pilgrim to a disordered use of the things of the world by the "lust of the flesh, and the lust of the eyes, and the pride of life" (1 John 2:15; cf. also John 12:31; 14:30; 16:11).

The Pauline and Johannine idea of the world as the epitome of evil does not cancel out the usual notion of the world—verified throughout the New Testament—as the embodiment of God's creation. The Pauline and Johannine idea intends rather to make more precise—to interpret—the latter truth within the framework of the history of salvation by bringing into account the mystery of sin with all its devastating consequences. The balanced interpretation of both aspects of the cosmos conception in the New Testament guards on the one hand against a naïve optimism which critically fails to appreciate the reality of evil and, on the other, against an unenlightened and basically unchristian pessimism which appears to exhaust all its energy of belief in the mystery of sin and has nothing left for the mysteries of creation and salvation.

c. Remaining to be established is the fact that from the very beginning, through God's creative will for the world, the world has been *finalized in Christ*. The incarnation of the eternal Word is the actual great goal of God's plan for the world. From the beginning, therefore, God not only implanted in his world all the "natural" forces and laws and values in such a way that they would expand themselves by virtue of an evolutional dynamism inherent in them and in the human spirit, but also embedded into his work of creation an altogether different dynamism, namely, the determination to salvation.

This statement includes the assertion that Christ would have become man even if there had been no sin. This so-called Scotistic viewpoint cannot be corroborated with absolute certitude; however, it is also not excluded by the New Testament. Were it to refer, as is sometimes said, to a merely possible or conceivable order, it would then surely be nothing more than a theological game. The question of whether Christ would have become incarnate even in the event there had been no sin is a question which the actual real order, the true plan of salvation, must help to resolve. The concrete fact of the development of salvation history, with its great stress on the concrete message of the New Testament, does not absolve us from the obligation of getting at the heart of the matter and exploring revelation for the "eternal" plan of salvation.

In any case, the plan of salvation culminates in the fact that the world created by God should be embraced in man and with man, its center, in Jesus Christ, and should be drawn into the inner life of God. The existence of the world and man has its foundation in Christ. We can never understand creation if we disregard him for whom it is determined, and this is revealed only in Jesus Christ.[48]

The second level of the relative self-subsistence of earthly realities is their relationship to Christ the Head

God plainly willed that his creation remain not just his "work," forever simply standing apart from him. He wanted to take his creation into his innermost being. "And this his good pleasure he purposed in him to be dispensed in the fullness of the times: to re-establish all things in Christ, both those in the heavens and those on the earth. In him, I say, in whom we also have been called by a special choice, having been predestined in the purpose of him who works all things according to the counsel of his will, to contribute to the praise of his glory—we who before hoped in Christ" (Eph. 1:9–12). What does St. Paul mean here?

a. The God-man is the head of mankind. Mankind is joined to this head as a body. The Fathers of the Church constantly emphasize this thought: Christ bears all men in himself; mankind as a whole is present in him. The human nature of Jesus Christ is, so to speak, a fulcrum which the eternal Word establishes in the world in order to draw all things to himself. Because his human nature stands in a real association with all human nature, Christ takes it into the solidarity of his person and thereby becomes the head of the human race. Now that mankind has become his body, he is able to elevate it to his communion with the Father, and also to let his own union with the Father overflow into this his body.

b. Henceforth man is the head and center of the cosmos. He is the living clasp by which the world of the spiritual and corporeal are fitted into one. In him the world encounters itself; in him it is present; in man it is seized into one. The world is primarily created for man so as to render possible to man his incarnate existence. As

[48] Cf. L. Scheffczyk, "Die Idee der Einheit von Schöpfung und Erlösung in ihrer theologischen Bedeutung," in: *Theol. Quartalschrift* 140 (1960), pp. 19–37.

the "extended corporeality of man," the world is personally conditioned. It must therefore follow that the God-man, in becoming the head of the human race, also becomes the *head of the whole material creature.*

The material nature is indissolubly united to man, even as his own body is united to him, though to a lesser degree and contiguity. If man himself in his full body-soul existence is taken into communion with Christ, the remainder of creation cannot be left out. In this way the God-man, through his union with human nature, becomes conjointly the hypostasis of the entire creation: he bears this creation in himself as in a root. Everything man comprises in himself enters into his incorporation into the eternal Word. The World made flesh becomes thus the new and actual place of the world.

c. But this is not to be understood to mean that a rigid and definitive state is produced, which would exclude any dynamism and further development. On the contrary, the eternal Word has united himself truly not with abstract essences, but rather with concrete men and things. Yet everything concrete stands in the stream of the historical. One can then say that the eternal Word has entered into full *solidarity with the total history* of man and his world. The God-man is not merely the encompassment into one of what is human and material, but also the encompassment of the development of man and things.

In himself, Christ sums up everything that is in history and carries it through into the last phase of the history of salvation. When this phase comes to an end, he will draw everything that is united to him into his return home into eternity. Among all men and things which are in the world and have their history in the world, there is nothing which could remain outside this union with Christ. There is not one thing that exists which does not have the vocation to be the "body of the Lord" and through him—in whatever form this may take—to participate in glory.

Jesus Christ bears the whole world and its history in his body. He is the one who gathers and summarizes into one, the universal mediator in whom the entire universe is "at home." In him the universe is where it belongs; in him it is brought to that place which was appointed to it ever since the beginning. The cosmos remains what it is, but it is inserted into the scope of its fulfilment. A definitive and irrevocable character marks this event which proceeds in

Jesus Christ, beginning with the incarnation and provisionally realized with the ascension of our Lord into heaven. There is no relapse from Christ, nor is there anything in the inner history of the world which can surpass him.

"Man does not pass beyond Christ; in him the end of things is attained. He alone is the ultimate, the eternal youth of the world. He is always the new: Christ, beyond whom there is simply nothing else, in whom the end of things is reached. With him, humanity has entered into the essential event; henceforth we can expect no progress—no matter how great it may be—which will be of the same importance as what we already possess in Christ."[49]

Through this vision of history, Christianity is radically removed from that theory of evolution for which Christ is at most only one stage, however important, of transition. History proceeds further, century upon century, until the Lord's second coming. But what will be effected by his second coming has in the God-man already been made present on earth and abides forever. For this reason, everything that the world is presses essentially toward Christ, because it can find its integration in him alone. No person or thing can eliminate from the world this existential inclination.

The relationship to Christ the head is the second level of the relativity in which every self-subsistence of the earthly realities is grounded.

In Jesus Christ the world is definitively embraced by God. This is a fact of salvation history. The explanation of this fact (also of the form in which it is presented above) certainly needs more careful theological clarification in many respects.[50] The term *anakephalaiosis* from Ephesians 1:10 means that Christ has made the powers subject, that he has restored the original unity, and through the recapitulation to one dominion has brought the world home again to God. But may this and similar passages be interpreted in such a way that one speaks of the world as the "body of the Lord," when, however, by "body of the Lord" the Church is usually signified? Or would it be more accurate to say: Christ is indeed united with the cosmos, but nevertheless the body of Christ must be distinguished from what is only related to him?

At any rate, there are theologians who think that the cosmos and

[49] J. Danielou, *Vom Geheimnis der Geschichte* (Stuttgart: 1955), pp. 97f. (Eng. tr.: *The Lord of History:* Chicago: 1958).

[50] Here is not the place to examine—even if it could be explained—what specific value is to be attached to the individual events of salvation: incarnation, death, resurrection, ascension.

animal life are "manifestly" no part of the Mystical Body or of the whole Christ.[51] One must be very careful not to exaggerate Christocentricism into a Christomonism. There is only one plan of salvation—Protestant Evangelical theology (K. Barth and D. Bonhoeffer) has also worked this out very impressively—and this one plan of salvation, without any doubt, culminates in Jesus Christ. But one may not on this account disengage the reality of creation from Christ.

K. Rahner clearly outlined the Catholic position in these words: "*We* encounter this unsurpassed high point of history (the partnership with God) within the whole framework of our history—in which, already knowing something about man (and certainly also about God), we discover man—when we encounter Christ and therefore understand that he is a man. Theological anthropology would necessarily be curtailed if it were pursued exclusively from the standpoint of its goal, Christology; for the last experience does not cancel out the earlier one."[52] What is said here concerning the Christian understanding of man also holds for the Christian understanding of the world.

We say that the world, as created by God, has its self-subsistence, but the Logos entering into the reality of the world has taken its self-subsistence upon himself. World remains world; it is only truly released to its own reality through Christ, but it remains thereby indissolubly united to him. This fact is plain to see throughout history in the Church and will be brought to fruition in the second coming of Christ. The relationship of the world to the Church and its relationship to its perfected form in glory are no new levels in the relativity of the inherent value of earthly realities; they are only the unfolding and realization of that relativity to Christ the Head.

The third level of the relative intrinsic value of earthly realities is their relationship to the Church

a. The Church is in *its essence* a sign that man and world have been embraced by God in Christ. Through the Church, Christ en-

[51] Cf. O. Karrer in a discussion regarding Teilhard de Chardin: *Christlicher Sonntag* 13 (1961). In his book *The Phenomenon of Man,* Teilhard calls the cosmos the "body of him who is and is coming"; in his hymn to matter, he calls it the "flesh of Christ." Cf. the recent, illuminating article by L. Scheffczyk, "Der *Sonnengesang* des hl. Franziskus von Assisi und die *Hymne on die Materie* des Teilhard de Chardin. Ein Vergleich zur Deutung der Struktur christlicher Schöpfungsfrömmigkeit," in: *Geist und Leben* 35 (1962), pp. 219–33.

[52] K. Rahner, *op. cit.,* pp. 626f.

throned at the right of the Father guides throughout history the work of *anakephalaiosis,* taking possession of the world and man in his corporeality. The Church is where the meaning of Christ for man and the world is preached, represented and made fruitful.

b. The most effective way in which this occurs is through the sacraments, especially the Eucharist. Here the union of all things in Christ is proclaimed and sacramentally realized. In the Eucharist, the cosmic-human association, founded in creation and exalted in the incarnation to brotherhood in Christ, progressively reaches reality. Its final form of realization is proclaimed until Christ comes again, but it also displays its hidden, powerful dynamism in the movement of history.

Mankind as a whole as well as its individual communities has within itself a natural ontological propensity toward the Eucharist. Thus he who in faith, hope and charity attends to the immanent dynamism and intentionality of the natural orders is from his very nature impelled, so to speak, to the mystery of the Eucharist.

A similar situation prevails in the material world, equally whether it directly constitutes the "body" of man or indirectly stands in his life and makes up his "world": in the Eucharist the bodily and worldly existence of man also comes to fulfilment. Just as the eternal Word at the incarnation united himself to a human body, so the *Kyrios* in the Eucharist unites himself to bread and wine. The eucharistic elements are exponents of the reality of the world in the same way that Jesus' human nature was in his time. In the Eucharist, the world is on the road to its fulfilment.

c. The *principles* for the concrete realization of the relationship of the Church and worldly orders were laid down by the Council of Chalcedon in 451. The Council, of course, spoke explicitly only of the relation between the two natures in Christ: his divine and human natures exist with one another not only without separation and division, but also without confusion and change, so that the distinction of the two natures is not abrogated by their union, but rather the individuality of each nature remains intact.[53]

This doctrinal statement, however, is valid not just for Christ as the head, but also for the Church as his body. The Church is truly the continuing presence of the God-man in history. If the Christological doctrine of the Council of Chalcedon is taken in an ecclesiological sense, it means that the Church and the world exist not only

[53] Denz. 148.

without separation and division, but also without confusion and change, so that the distinction of both orders is not abrogated by their union, but rather the individuality of each order remains intact. In other words, by the relationship of Church and world is meant the *principles of duality and integration.*

The principle of duality expresses nothing other than what we meant when we said that the world is self-subsistent and has its own proper worth and laws. When the "theology of earthly realities" provides for the liberation of the worldly orders to their own reality, it draws from the central mystery of Christology. Christ entrusts these worldly orders—which are also directed toward him—to their stewards and trustees directly, and not through the Church (the two-sword theory). The law of duality between the spiritual and temporal orders is valid for the entire duration of salvation history.

But the law of integration also prevails: the world is ordained to the Church, because here it is provided with salvation. The Church is where Christ effects the consummation of the world. Through the Church he takes the totality of the material and spiritual world, its being and its history, ever deeper into himself and fulfils it ever more forcefully with the power of salvation. Through the Church it remains evident that the inner-worldly realities can find no sufficiency in themselves, but rather, in order to be completed, must remain open to the kingdom of Christ.

The fourth level of the relative intrinsic value of earthly realities is finally their relationship to their perfected form

This perfected form is operative since the beginning as an entelechial dynamism. Its designation in creation was taken on by Christ, and proclaimed and realized in the Church through the Eucharist with increasing intensity. The Lord in his second coming will bring to fruition everything that he incorporated—or, to be more theologically cautious, ordered—to himself in the incarnation: thus the universal, evolving world of men and things which stretches out over all of history.

What we call "eternal life" will have the form of a community, and will "happen" in a corporeal manner in a transfigured cosmos. This is irrevocably pre-formed in the God-man, from the incarnation to the ascension. The human nature of Jesus has kept its individual being and is not tarnished in the light of glory. The dogma of

Chalcedon safeguards also the eschatological truths about man and world. The world will indeed perish. It will not evolve ever more sublimely into a historical infinity. It will not forever experience in an eternal cycle new deaths and new births. It will be annihilated, but it will not remain in annihilation. Its materiality, as a new bodiliness and new worldliness, will be converted into a state of perfect glory and will here find eternal existence.

The eternal life will be the city of God in which the elect dwell together in love and peace, in opulence and splendor. It will be the banquet community which unites all with God and with one another; the kingdom in which the enthroned Lord exercises his dominion; the everlasting marriage feast of the lamb with mankind in a transformed world. Duality yet integration, being its own yet belonging to Christ—these will all be consummated.

This is the basic outline of a theology of earthly realities: In the Word, world and man are placed in existence; in the incarnation of the Word, they are given a direction. In the "fullness of time" the Word made flesh incorporated everything created into himself, in order to free it from the servitude of evil by his death and resurrection and lead it into the inner life of God. In the Church this work of the God-man is made present throughout time until it is brought to revealed and perfected glory in the parousia and handed over to the Father. Then God will be "all in all."

The Christian and the World

Johannes B. Metz

Johannes B. Metz studied at the Universities of Innsbruck and Munich, earning doctoral degrees in philosophy (1952) and theology (1961). He is Professor of Fundamental Theology at the University of Münster. His most important published work is *Christliche Anthropozentrik*. He is coeditor of *Concilium*, an international theological series, and editor of new editions of *Geist in Welt* and *Horer des Wortes*, the principal philosophical works of Karl Rahner, S.J. He also contributes regularly to theological reviews.

The increasing secularization of today's world is a fact that confronts faith with a choice. Faith can either ignore the situation, take refuge in familiar habits of theology and piety, and thereby cease to appear as the real and necessary but merely as myth. Or it can recognize that Pentecost has come and that it is necessary to understand history and to accept responsibility for it.

There have been several attempts within recent years to give a Christian explanation of this increasing worldliness and to offer remedies for it. One approach seeks to push back the worldliness of today's world towards an immediacy to God through a "theology of terrestrial realities" similar to the medieval understanding of the world. Another approach attempts to teach the Christian an openness to the world that aims at catching up with today's worldly world and grounding it anew in the mystery of Christ. The first of these approaches seems anachronistic. Regarding the second, we wonder whether an emphasis upon Christian openness to a world seen as

Reprinted from *Theology Digest*, Vol. XIII, No. 2 (Summer, 1965), pp. 95–100, with the permission of the author.

the immediate material of Christian activity is always entirely serious in light of the complicated nature of contemporary worldliness and whether this view does not come dangerously close to an optimism tending to cause an uneasiness in one who takes this worldliness seriously. Be that as it may, here we want merely to draw attention to something which is common to these and all similar attempts: they presuppose as more or less self-evident that the worldliness of the world is, as such, something which fundamentally runs contrary to a Christian view of the world and which therefore has to be totally surmounted and subdued in a Christian manner.

History Assumed Into Logos

To us this "self-evident" presupposition seems highly questionable from the point of view of a theology of history. It does not seem to be entirely serious about the fact that the "spirit" of Christianity has been permanently infused into the "flesh of world history." Theology must not lightly reject the processes of the concrete history of the world, understanding the history of salvation almost in a monophysitic manner. Instead, we must see the process of world history as "assumed" into the Christian Logos. Theology must ask how this modern secularization of the world fits under the "law of Christ," how Christ is himself still in power as the Lord who governs history interiorly precisely as its transcendental guarantee.

It is true that the Christian understanding of history is always under the sign of the cross and that the secularization of the world is to a degree a permanent, immanent protest against God. Here we wish to consider this secularization rather in its positive aspect, i.e. as the historical appearance of the divine assumption of the universe.

World Testifies to Christ

Our task, then, is to inquire into the theological origin of this secularization. Our thesis is that this worldliness originated not in anything anti-Christian, but rather as a Christian event; and that therefore it bears testimony to the power of the "hour of Christ" as it is at work within history.

At first sight this thesis might appear strange, for it seems that the reality of salvation demands an historical dominion over history, and hence that Christianity be essentially a continual struggle against the secularization of the world.

For the time being we will leave this question, for which we hope to find at least an indirect answer by seeking a positive foundation for the thesis we have proposed. For this purpose, we simply concentrate on what has happened historically in Jesus Christ: God has assumed the world in eschatological definitiveness in his Son, Jesus Christ. Or, put in other words, God acted in historical activity upon the world in such a way that he irrevocably took it to himself in his Son.

The Christian God is a God of history. Our faith in him is the answer to a historically singular event and not the dramatically clothed objectification of a timeless, metaphysical self-consciousness of man. Nor is God a random fact within history, but rather a decisive moment for history itself. He dominates history interiorly not only as the decisive moment *in* history, but also as the constituting moment of history itself. It was founded through him and for him (Col. 1:17), and his reign *in* history, the Church, is the symbolic representation of this eschatological founding of history.

The "world" of which we speak is not a mere object, but always the world of existing men, this anthropocentric world which "becomes" through what happens to it in historical deeds and which consequently represents alternative possibilities of development. Such a concept is opposed to the Greek view of the world as a fixed framework of uniform recurrence. The definitive historical action of God upon the world establishes the world not only in its general historical character, but above all in its eschatological character: the new heaven and the new earth, the one kingdom of God and men. But this character the world has yet to achieve in its historical existence.

Christ Assumes the World

God has, in his Son, assumed the world in eschatological definitiveness. If we are to understand this, we must understand the meaning of "assumption" here. In Jesus Christ, man and his world have been definitely and irrevocably assumed in hypostatic union. What held for Christ's assumed nature holds also for the assumption of man and his world. What God took upon himself he does not do violence to. He does not do away with "the other" in its difference from him, but he takes it to himself precisely as something other than himself. He can and intends to assume it in that by which it is different from him, in its non-divinity, its humanity, and worldliness. And only because he can do this, did it please him to create a world at all and finally to assume it in his own eternal Word. The assumption by God is then more basic than the abandoning to the independence of the non-divine. This assumption, then, is a liberation of what is assumed for its own proper and essential existence, for the independence of the non-divine. God is not a competitor, but the guarantee of the world.

World's Potential Enhanced

In order to understand what happens in this assumption, we have to take friendship as our model. The more deeply one friend is accepted by another, the more does this other become himself, the more radically is he freed in his own possibilities. Similarly the assumption of the world into the trinitarian life of God does not contradict, but rather enhances the world's own possibilities. Finally, just as the liberated slave can more radically belong to a former master as a free friend, so this liberating assumption of the world makes possible the deepest form of belonging to God.

It is precisely when God takes to himself the non-divine that he rises above it as its transcendent Creator. Thus for Christianity, the understanding of the creatureliness of the world always stands against the background of the history of salvation through which assumption alone the world appears as entirely worldly and God as entirely divine. In light of these considerations, then, it should be clear that we do not follow a confused incarnational optimism that sees the world as immediately deified through the Incarnation of God and sees the history of salvation as the growing divinization of the world.

The "assumption" of the world in Jesus Christ must never be thought of as merely a single biological event in the life of Christ, but rather as the whole of his historical life. For God's descent into the "flesh of sin" is an assumption filled with suffering, and the liberating assumption of the world is perfected only upon the cross.

To be able to measure the significance of the world view which was opened in the Christ event, we have only to recall the Greek understanding of the world which preceded it. For the Greeks the world was always numinously bordered, always the twilight of the gods. In this view the world was not entirely worldly, because God was not entirely divine. The Greek god was not a transcendent creator, but a world-principle, a world-reason or law, an immanent regulator of the cosmos. Consequently, the apotheosis of nature and a piety based upon this view are not Christian, but genuinely pagan. The Christian God is transcendent; and precisely as God he does not appear within the horizons of the world, but lets the world be worldly. Consequently, wherever it has understood its origin, Christianity has had to appear not as a growing divinization of the world, but precisely as an increasing de-divinization and, in this sense, as a profanation of the world. Thus it was not by chance that the Christians were stigmatized by pagans caught in their Greek understanding of the world as the real and dangerous *atheoi* who delivered the world to godlessness. This ancient understanding of the world reasserted itself during the classical Middle Ages of Western Christian history.

Historical Process Christian

Thus, the process of increased secularization of the world which began in modern times results in its basic character from the Christological principle explained above. We are not saying that the historical process itself is free from the culpable confusion and deviation of an overbearing secularism, or that the modern secularization and understanding of the world at work in it is an adequate expression of the secularization set forth in the Christ-event. In fact, it is in light of these concrete dangers and confusions that the reserve and protest of the Church against the modern world's secular character must be assessed. We assert that, in its basic character, the process has a genuinely Christian impulse.

Thus, for instance, one can understand from a positive Christian point of view the separation of empire and priesthood which began in the late Middle Ages. Since Christianity now proclaims itself responsible for all the religious relations of men, the state is divested of its ancient numinosity and sacredness and is thus free to serve as the advocate of a secular world in true partnership with the Church.

Science Strives for Order

Similarly the striving on the part of the secular sciences for independence from a universal, theological order of sciences such as existed in the Middle Ages has come into existence ultimately not against, but through the spirit of Christianity. This independence was seen in its beginnings already by Thomas Aquinas, insofar as he saw the "philosopher" (Aristotle) as an authority with his own independent principles. By a dimly lighted path through the history of philosophy and theology this liberating process of philosophical reason has come to its recognition in Vatican I. In the history of modern philosophy, this path certainly has seen many aberrations and frequently has been misunderstood as a rationalistic emancipation of human reason. But precisely through this "secularization" of philosophy in which Christianity does not neglect philosophy in a fideistic way, but rather accepts it for what it is in itself, philosophical reasoning has in modern times attained a high and historically unique independence, especially in comparison with classical Greek philosophy which was never able to separate itself critically to the same degree from its theological origin. Thus the separation of the sciences of God and of the world in the last century is seen in its source, though not in all details, as a movement born of Christianity.

A third example of this liberation is the objectifying of nature which has taken place in modern times and by which the earth has become an object, the field of human experimentation. Thus nature can appear as it "is": not as God, but as created by God and everywhere mediated by the "work" of men. Admittedly the development of technology involves the danger that this very technology may turn against man himself and try to make him a means to its own purposes. Yet in order to orientate ourselves in such a faceless, objectified world we must recall that Christianity has made this situation possible and take our stance accordingly.

Such secularization, then, is not the expression of the powerlessness or the indifference of Christianity towards the world. It is not a secularization of the faith by the overwhelming power of a world hostile to the faith, but the secularization of the world by the historical power of this Christian faith which assumes the world and sets it free. Actually the misfortune is not the secularization of the world, but the manner in which we Christians have regarded it, mistaking or disowning our own offspring so that he early ran away and now views us with hostility. Does not much of the pride and false desire for autonomy of the world stem from the fact that we set that world on its own much too hesitantly, and indeed only with protest?

Secularization Asserts Itself

Today one may, indeed must, admit that the secularization of the world, a radically Christian event, often had to assert itself against a historical Christian miscomprehension of the world. For this reason, though not solely for this reason, this secularization has taken on really anti-Christian and secularistic features. This fact of opposition from Christianity itself renders the historical shape of the modern process of secularization ambiguous and unpredictable. But, be that as it may, in order to understand ourselves as believers in today's world, we must recognize that this process of secularization is grounded in the Christ-event.

Discovers Multiple Worldliness

In our considerations, therefore, we have discovered a three-fold worldliness: (1) that which has not yet been mediated through the historical encounter with Christianity and is in this sense an "innocent" worldliness—somewhat as in ancient paganism; (2) worldliness as it was set free by the efficacy of Christianity in history; and (3) the wordliness which misunderstands this process of liberation as an autonomous and secularistic process and which protests against its Christian origin and emancipates itself from it.

The Christian appears as the mediator of this liberation of the world. His is an active role, for this liberation does not take place through the world's merely falling away from God, but rather involves its coming to belong more closely to him. In what precisely, then, does this role consist? Basically, in an imitation in faith of the descent of God into the world, of Christ's liberating assumption of the world.

The Christian finds himself living a life which revolves in an eclipse about the two poles of his faith and the world, poles in a relationship which can no longer be clearly and obviously set and controlled by faith itself. He is aware that going along with the world does not always result in going along with God. Such action often gets stuck, as it were, in the pure worldliness of the world.

Between the vision of faith and life as he finds it, therefore, the Christian is aware of an ever-widening discrepancy. This difference cannot simply be disregarded and left unresolved, for in the long run it will be taken up and closed by the overpowering world of today and faith itself will become totally overshadowed from the side of the world. Nor, if we take the worldliness of the world with total Christian seriousness, can we resolve this difference by making an act of faith in the God-centeredness of actual worldly events. Rather, the believer ought to follow the pattern of Christ and "take up" the world, even though it continue to seem unrelated to faith.

Thus, for instance, the young man who has without any particular thought of God determined to be an engineer should by his faith encompass his plan of life so that the difference between the secular and religious phases, which cannot be eliminated, appears as initially posed and left to itself by faith. The worldliness of his existence as engineer ought to be seen as guaranteed by the freedom and discretion of his faith itself: "For it all belongs to you—Paul, Apollos, Cephas, the world, life, death, the present, the future—all of it belongs to you. But you belong to Christ, and Christ belongs to God" (1 Cor 3:22–23).

Faith Accepts the World

We must remember that the relationship of the Christian to the world in faith remains twofold. To us the worldliness of the world appears always as something unmastered, not penetrated by faith, and in this sense something truly pagan and profane. The world, it is true, is totally comprehended by Christianity, but not by us and in our historical situation of faith, but by God and in his original "yes" to the world. The assumption of the world in its very worldliness remains for us an eschatological event towards which we exist in hope. Our Christian attitude to the world is certainly not without embarrassment nor one of unquestioning optimism.

Still, the Christian faith and only the Christian faith is able to stand up to this uncovered worldliness and to accept it as such in calmness, without dodging it or throwing over it a cloak of ideology. It is not as though the Christian experiences worldliness only in a pure "as if" and only the unbeliever is able to experience it in its true "as such." The opposite is true. For the world has gained through the Christ-event its radical form of worldliness, and through the liberating assumption by God has in itself become so godless that man today can openly cope with it only with the strength of this event, without conjuring up new gods.

The unbelieving non-Christian will in the end always ideologically falsify this worldliness—either in the utopianism of a naïve faith in progress, of a paradise within the world, or in a tragic nihilism and resigned scepticism. But against these the Christian appears as the properly worldly man, for he alone can truly let the worldliness of the world "be" by the faithful reperformance of the liberating assumption of the world by God in Jesus Christ.

What Christianization Means

The worldly task of the Christian again and again has been formulated as "to Christianize the world." This phrase is subject to much misunderstanding. For the "Christianization" of the world should not mean to make of it something other than it was before, to cover it with something unworldly or super-worldly, to bring it up to a new dimension, or to "bring it home" from its worldliness into a numinous, glimmering divinity. Thus we must also understand correctly the phrases "Christian art," "Christian philosophy," "the Christian state," etc. The word "Christian" is, rightly understood, not an addition, an infiltration of something foreign, but rather an assertion of the world, art, etc., in its true and distinct nature.

Sketches World's Grandeur

To "Christianize" the world means to "secularize" it, to guarantee to it its own scarcely sketched, scarcely imagined heights and depths, which have previously lain buried in sin. It is precisely sin which has alienated the world from itself, for sin forces upon the world something other than its properly worldly being and is not liberty, but slavery. But grace is liberty and guarantees to things the depths of their being, calling and turning the world to its perfect worldliness. Grace perfects nature—this holds true also for the "consecration of the world" through grace. And the Church, as the historical, palpable sign and institution of this grace within the world, is therefore not the opponent, but the guarantee of the world. To be sure, this proper being of the world, its fully guaranteed worldliness, is not to be placed within history. It remains, as we have said, eschatologically the act of God in which will be accomplished for the world what happened by reason of its universal and historical "recapitulation" in Jesus Christ. What is originally and independently proper to the world, what its worldliness in a complete sense signifies according to content can be answered only eschatologically at the end of the whole of the as yet incomplete history of the world.

Christianity and the "New Man"

Karl Rahner, S.J.

Karl Rahner, S.J., internationally known theologian, is Professor of Christian Thought at the University of Munich. He is an editor of the *Lexicon für Theologie und Kirche* and the pastoral encyclopedia, *Sacramentum Mundi.* Included among the most recently translated of his several hundred books and articles are *Free Speech in the Church, Encounter with Silence, The Eternal Year, The Church and the Sacraments,* and volumes I, II, IV, and V of *Theological Investigations.*

Christianity is a religion with an eschatology; it looks into the future; it makes binding pronouncements about what is to come both by explaining what will come and by looking on these future events as the decisive guiding principles of action in the present. Indeed, Christianity declares that with the incarnation of the eternal Word of God in Jesus Christ, the last age has already begun, that the future has already been decided as to its final sense and content, and that now it only requires that which is already and remains to be revealed.

Christianity no longer knows any ultimately open salvation-history but declares that—since the coming of Jesus Christ who is today, yesterday and in all eternity—the end of the ages is really already present and that we live, therefore, in the last ages, in the fullness of time. One thing only remains for us and that is to await the coming of the Lord in glory, even though—reckoned in earthly measurements of time—this period of waiting may appear long to

Reprinted from *Theological Investigations,* Vol. V (Baltimore: Helicon Press, June 1966), pp. 135–56, with the permission of the publisher.

us and even though thousands upon thousands of years on this earth may pass through this one moment of the silence of the end of time before the real and ultimate end finally dawns. Christianity understands itself as the religion of the future, as the religion of the new and eternal man.

Christianity cannot be indifferent, therefore, in the face of an interpretation, planning and utopian ideal of the future which originates outside her and which tries to determine man's present attitude in view of his future. It cannot be doubted, however, that the spiritual situation of man today is essentially determined by the blueprint of the new man of the future. The man of today feels himself to a larger extent to be someone who must overcome himself in order to prepare himself for a new and quite different future. He feels himself to be someone whose present can be justified only as the condition of his future, though this future which justifies him is not conceived—eschatologically—as the gift of God dissolving temporal history but as something which man himself creates and conquers for himself. Hence, the question as to how these two conceptions of the future are related to one another is an unavoidable and, for the Christian, an absolutely decisive one.

Before tackling this question directly, we must make at least some attempt to give a clearer picture of modern, extra-Christian thought concerning the future, so that we may know with what we are really comparing the Christian eschatology. Naturally, the "picture of the new man" can be sketched here only in its most formal traits. Yet this picture of the new man cannot be simply presupposed as known, at least not from *those* points of view which must be our special concern here. We presuppose in this that this "new man" is already present today in his beginnings, in the sense that, to some extent at least, his further developments and final form can already be divined. Furthermore, in describing the new man, we are not concerned with laying down a binding, systematic view of the characteristics exposed.

The man of today, and even more so the man of tomorrow, is the man of a history unified the world over, the man of a global space for life and hence the man of a world in which everyone is dependent on absolutely everyone else. The "United Nations" organization is a small indication of this. And the boundary lines drawn by the various "curtains" today do not limit the meaning of what has just been said, for one's enemies are usually "closer" to oneself—

in the sense of being more decisive for one's own destiny—than one's friends.

Whereas in the past (prescinding from the only hypothetically and approximately ascertainable beginning of the human race) the history of individual peoples, and hence of individuals, was more or less clearly divided up by historical vacua; thus, for instance, what was happening at the time in the empire of the Incas was quite immaterial to the history of fourteenth-century Europe; today all the histories of different peoples are part and parcel of the one, real world-history. The "field" which determines the fate of the individual today is, not merely physically but also historically, the whole earth. The present and the history of individuals have become the present and the history of all, and vice versa.

The man of today and tomorrow is the man of technology, of automation and cybernetics. This means, in our present context, that man is no longer (or at least no longer to any large extent) the man who simply lives out his existence according to the given pattern of nature in an equally pre-existent environment, but someone who fashions his own environment. Man now inserts an external world made by himself in between himself (eking out and asserting his existence both physically and spiritually) and "nature" (i.e., the physically and biologically tangible environment which is the condition for man's own existence).

It is of course true that there has never been a man without any culture, a man—in other words—who was able to live like an animal in the sense that his struggle for existence (by procreation and upbringing of offspring, protection against the dangers of his environment, etc.) was related immediately to a purely pre-established reality, as in the case of the animal. But in the past, culture, understood as something external, has on the whole consisted merely in such slight modifications of man's natural environment as this environment itself permitted: it consisted merely in the *utilization* of animals and plants in a certain systematic way, without any deliberate transformation of nature in the inorganic and organic world in the light of freely chosen ends and under rational control.

Life today, which has been thus transformed, always and everywhere manifests the reason why such a transformed life in an environment determined by ourselves is possible: the modern rationality of Western man, his calculated planning, the disappearance of the feeling of awe which used to be inherent in the experience of the world itself, and the "profanation" of the world, turning it into the raw material of human activity, an idea which—starting with the Western world—has become the determining presupposition of any consideration of the raison d'être of the whole world and of humanity.

The man of today is not, however, merely the man of the rational, calculating creation of his own space of existence—the *homo faber*. Unlike the man of previous ages (especially since the start of the modern fashion of "turning in on the subject"), the man of today is not merely the man given to that sort of rational reflection on himself in which (at least at the first and important appearance) the object of reflection is not altered by the fact of reflection.

Rather, he is someone who applies his technical, planning power of transformation even to himself—someone who makes himself the object of his own manipulations. He no longer simply takes stock of himself, but changes himself; he contents himself neither with steering by his own history merely the alteration of his sphere of existence nor with the mere actualization of those possibilities which have always offered themselves to man in his commerce with his fellow men both in peace and in war. The subject is becoming its own most proper object; man is becoming his own creator.

It does not matter in the meantime that for many different reasons and in many different respects these possibilities of a planned self-alteration and adaptation are as yet relatively few. The important thing is that man has thought of the idea of such a transformation, that he already sees possibilities of realizing this idea and indeed has already begun to realize it. Against this background must be seen the Freudian depth-psychology, birth-control, human eugenics, the transformations of man, based on Pavlov's psychology, which override the free judgments and decisions of man in the Communistic world and which are practiced—in somewhat more careful doses—even in the West (one need only think here of the techniques of propaganda, advertising, etc.).

This man of the unified, planetary living-space which is to be extended even beyond the earth—the man who does not simply accept the world around him but creates it and who regards himself as merely the starting point and raw material for what he wants to make of himself in accordance with his own plans—has for these very reasons the impression of standing at a beginning, of being the beginning of the new man, conceived as a kind of superman who will show clearly for the first time what man really is. What comments are to be made on this ideology of the new man, if the situation and program just described are looked at from the point of view of the Christian faith?

I

Christianity has no predictions to make, no program and no clear-cut prescriptions for the future of man in this world; it knows from the very start that man does not have them either and that he (and hence also Christianity itself) must therefore go unprotected into the dark venture of his intramundane future. The eschatology of Christianity is no intramundane utopia; it sets no intramundane tasks and goals. As a consequence, the Christian is not given any concrete directions for his life in this world as such, which could relieve him of the anguish of planning the future and of the burden of his passage into the dark unknown. He has the moral law of nature and of the gospel. But he himself must convert these general principles into concrete imperatives which themselves are not merely applications of these principles to a static material of moral action with which he has to deal, but also represent decisions about some definite plan of action and about the choice of different possibilities—none of which can be clearly deduced from these general principles.

By the fact that man changes himself and his environment—and by the fact that, since paradoxically but truly this planning does not make all this any the less unpredictable but rather increases the uncertainty in equal proportion to the extent of the planning, these alterations themselves have in their turn the character of something unpredictable, of trial and a wandering into the uncertain—ever new and surprising tasks are imposed by very reason of the principles advocated by Christianity, tasks which earlier Christianity could not have dreamed of and which require a long, laborious process of acclimatization for the Christian and the Church before they can be mastered at all.

Yet it is not as if this passage into the unpredictable future were unimportant for Christianity itself and of no significance for Christianity both as a Church and as the Christian life of individuals and nations. Truly realized Christianity is always the achieved synthesis on each occasion of the message of the gospel and of the grace of Christ, on the one hand, and of the concrete situation in which the gospel is to be lived, on the other. This situation is always new and surprising. Consequently the intramundane and Christian task of the Christian is really and truly a *problem* whose solution must be looked for laboriously amid surprises, pains, fruitless and false steps, false detachment and restoring, timidly conservative reserve and false fascinations with novelties.

Thus the Christian too may stand frightened and fascinated before the future of intramundane tasks opening out before him. He too may feel himself called to action and to criticism, in brotherly union with all those others who salute this future and who know themselves called to bring it about. Since the mastering of the intramundane situation represents a task (insofar as this is possible for man) which is also really Christian—because eternal life must be effected in time—it is, sadly perhaps, possible to show that the Christians of this day and age occupy themselves far too little with the programming of man's future in this world, as if this did not present any problems or could safely be left to the non-Christians.

It is indeed true and a fact of decisive importance that the gospel does not offer or intend to offer any ready-made plan for the future and that the Church cannot give us any clear-cut and binding ideas about such programming. But this in no way means that *every* programming for the future—whatever it may be—can be reconciled with the Christian spirit and life and with the nature of man of which Christianity is the custodian.

Hence, it does not mean that even in their practical life Christians have no duty or obligation with regard to such practical programming. It is absolutely possible for Christians to have a task as Christian individuals which the Church as such does not have. And it may seem that Christians do not have a clear, courageous and infectious enough conception and love of this planning of the future and of these demands—which go beyond the abstract principles of the unchanging gospel—and that they merely seek to defend the spirit of the gospel by a *defensive criticism* of the dangers of plans for the future and of intramundane ideologies.

Nevertheless, it remains true to say that the Christian as such is not given any clear prescriptions by the gospel as to how the future is to look or will in fact look. He is a pilgrim on this earth, advancing into the uncertain and going out to venture in brotherly union with all those who plan the future of this world, and he may quite legitimately feel proud of being that creature who plans himself and of being the place (called "spirit" and "freedom") where the great world-machine not only runs its course in exalted clarity but also begins to steer itself.

II

Christianity draws man's attention to the fact that, while he is under the impression of standing on the threshold of a new and unheard-of future, this future too will constantly lead him back to himself as the finite creature he is. This future, planned by himself and to be built by himself, is inevitably finite for the Christian; he already recognizes, experiences and suffers it as something finite in advance. In other words, the future too is built out of materials with definite structures whose finite nature also sets internal limits to the possibilities of the future and renders them finite. Man does indeed over and over again express surprise at how he has underestimated his own possibilities, at how the world is greater than he had thought, at how new avenues open out to possibilities which he had up until now regarded as utopian.

Certainly it is dangerous in many respects to declare something to be impossible; for many times in the past such declarations have been the beginnings of successful efforts to make the impossible come true. Nevertheless, man is not and will never be the creator who creates omnipotently out of nothing—he is and will always be the creature who creates out of himself and out of the already existing realities of the world around him. And he and the reality surrounding him have structures and laws; these already existing realities, together with their determined structures, form the a priori law of what they can become.

These essential structures are not—this modern man has learned and this also differentiates him from the man of earlier ages, including the Christian Middle Ages—a static barrier which prevents any genuine process of becoming and change and being changed. These essential structures are most certainly endowed with an inner dynamism toward development. But precisely in this way they also form the law according to which this development takes place and the horizon within which the history of this development runs its course. And no matter how much this course may take us into the boundless, there are twists and turns in it which betray the finite and created nature of this course of becoming, the becoming to which it remains necessarily subject.

There are many such a priori, inevitable elements in the finite nature of man. There is his spatio-temporality: even if man should conquer a new part of the world for himself outside his earth (and if we stop to think, are we not still very far from this being true?), he will always face the immensity of the universe as someone who begins his short span of existence from the earth and not from anywhere else.

Then there is man's biological constitution together with all the limitations this entails: the different stages of life, his dependence on nourishment, the finite nature of his brain—the storehouse of his activities—which provide the basis for what he can really experience and by which alone in the final analysis all other (artificial) stores of usable content become really interesting for him, in the same way that someone finds interest only in *those* books of a library which he reads (and not in those which he can read) or at most in those which he could read *without* having to give up the reading of others. And finally there is the limited nature of his life which ends in death.

This brings us then to the most irrevocable and clearest limit of man: he dies, he has a beginning and an end, and this means that absolutely everything which lies within these "brackets" is under the relentless sign of the finite. We are able to prolong human life and in fact have already done so. But what a laughable alteration would it really be if we were all to become 120 or 180 years old? Who has ever claimed or prophesied that he could do more?

And who—even if he were to give but a little thought to such a utopian idea—could even merely hope or wish to live forever in the kind of human existence which is the only one given to us? The *inner* finiteness of human existence would turn the *external* endlessness of life into utter madness—into the existence of the eternally wandering Jew—and into damnation, since what is unique in a finite sense is impressive and sweet only if, and because, it is not always available; a time which I could really have to infinity whenever I liked, condemns the content of each moment to absolute indifference, since it is absolutely repeatable. And then: what significance does it have for *me—I* who will die—if I could help to make it possible that at some future date a man may be bred who will never die any more? None whatsoever! But we will have to come back to this point later on.

No, the message of Christianity about the finite and created nature of man remains true even today. And the more it might be possible to achieve what today lies still in a utopian future, the less could this achievement blind us to the finiteness of the achieved or deaden the pain of this finiteness. This is all the more true since it is an unproved supposition that the possibility and the pace of new developments experienced by us today could never be followed by a certain phase of stagnation, or that the time of pre-planned and self-directed development—once started—must unceasingly flow on in ever greater acceleration to ever new shores.

It is just as possible that the development may, as it were, stagnate again (although this time on the higher level reached by then) just as it did in many earlier centuries as far as the progress of technology and the external style of living were concerned. And since society is always and inevitably composed of individuals (it being quite indifferent for this whether one adopts an individualist or Communist view of the exact relationship between the individual and society), the finiteness we have spoken of determines not only the existence of the individual as such but permeates right through the life of society.

Since society cannot pass on culture by biological heredity, it must to a great extent always begin again at the beginning. No matter how cunningly exact and comprehensive our planning may possibly be, it will never be adequate but will always produce surprises and failures, for a finite consciousness inevitably contains more objectively unreflected elements than elements which have been fully reflected upon. This is so even simply because the act of reflection cannot itself be reflected and yet a great deal about its content depends on it and on its characteristics.

Indeed, it may be that there is an absolutely finite optimum of what can be planned. All planning must work with unplanned factors; the proportion between the unplanned factors, which are of practical importance for the result of the plan, and the planned factors and their certainty for the planned result is variable; it can easily happen that the more complicated plan which is calculated to avoid more mistakes works out worse in practice than the simple plan which works with less explicit factors. To put it more simply still: even the culture and civilization of society, which is seemingly growing into infinity, will always remain conditioned by the individual—in other words, by the finiteness of his consciousness, by the limited number of individuals and the finite nature of the life of individuals. And so this culture and civilization remain finite.

It can happen, of course, that this finiteness does not appear—at least not explicitly—in all its existential radicality in the consciousness of the individual and in the commonly expressed opinion of a group or of an age, etc. Perhaps the movement is experienced enthusiastically as a movement into infinity even on account of its very presence alone, for the simple reason that one has overlooked the fact that a movement—even though its limitation is not clearly experienced—never attains anything beyond what is finite, and because one has not adverted to the fact that an infinite potency does not by any means promise an infinite act.

In any case, this intoxicating experience of infinity will always end up in cruel disillusionment—at the latest in death. And the pretension to infinity found in man—which according to the teaching of Christianity stems from the infinite promise of grace—will always weigh up again what has been, and what can be, achieved in this world and will always find it to be of too little weight.

III

Christianity knows an individual and existential notion of time which those who dream of a future paradise on this earth do not possess, and the lack of any such notion shows the latter conception to be insufficient. Let us take a closer look at this. It is said—and no doubt rightly—that the future has already begun. It is said, both in the West and in the East, that we are moving toward a glorious age: man will conquer outer space, there will be enough food for everyone, there will no longer be any underdeveloped and undernourished countries, everybody will have what is required to fulfill his needs, class distinction will be abolished.

The Christian must not indeed act as if all these plans for the future are proved wrong simply by his declaring skeptically that paradise is not to be found in this world. Anyone who simply counters such ardent dreams of the future with sober skepticism is—presumably—not experiencing hunger, is not at present in danger of cancer and hence is not particularly interested in finding the means by which medicine may at last conquer this disease. Yet the Christian is right in the long run when he points out that this happy future has not yet arrived, that he himself will not be alive to experience it and that he cannot agree that the question of *his* existence is solved by saying that it will be solved for others in the future.

The fight for a better future does consciously or unconsciously live on an evaluation of man, and even of the individual, which attributes an absolute value to man as a spiritual person. And this is quite right. For why should someone living today sacrifice himself for someone in the future if the future individual is just as insignificant as the present-day individual is thought to be, and if the present-day individual could be sacrificed precisely because he is insignificant?

The Communist who today sacrifices himself in true freedom and quite unselfishly for those who will come after him, affirms by this very fact that he as a person and those future persons have an absolute value, whether he admits this explicitly to himself or not. Anyone who affirms someone else to be of absolute value does the same for himself. He does not consider himself to be necessary in his biological existence, but he does acknowledge himself to be necessary in the dimension in which he takes the decision of self-sacrificing affirmation, namely, as a free, personal spirit.

Any conception which regards the future as something which does not simply come about by itself but must be conquered by sacrifice, acknowledges implicitly what Christianity affirms explicitly: the future of the human, spiritual person in no way only lies in *that* future which will be present at some later date but is the eternity which is brought about as the result of the spiritual act of the person.

Christianity is quite right in saying that there is a personal, existential time which is the coming-to-be of the unconditioned finality of the free decision and of existence—and which works in time by overcoming merely continuous time. All ideologies concerned with the future which declare that the future that is yet to come in a *temporal way* is something absolutely inevitable and not something to be merely overcome in the same way as the bare present must be overcome, borrow this notion of the absolute nature of the future from that future which is really absolute, namely, the future of the free person.

This future of the free person will not come later on but is present in the spiritual person and his free act; it realizes itself in the sphere where life—open to the bounded in its linear temporal nature—is brought to an end by biological processes. If every existing thing were completely subject to that time, whose every moment is indifferent since it passes away into an equally indifferent later moment in time which in turn unmasks its own insignificance by disappearing once more in the next moment, then we would have no reason for preferring a future to the present which is no longer the future of the one who has this preference. The present is necessarily the only true and valid reality for someone who is simply passing away, if indeed he ever becomes at all conscious of himself and of his transitoriness. Only if there is a future of the personal individual spirit is there any real sense in fighting for a better future in this world for those who will come after us.

It is clear from these few cursory remarks that Christianity has a notion of time in its teaching about the individual and freely achieved finality of the person, which goes beyond the notion of time employed by any ideology and utopian view which—concerned only with this world and its future—thinks of time purely as a sort of line passing into what is yet to come. The Christian notion of time goes much further, for it provides whatever is genuine and morally justified in these ideologies about the future with the only foundation which will really hold water, and opens up a supramundane and suprahistorical "future" for man which is above the eternal flux of time, namely, eternal life which finds its temporal expression and proof in time and which is the only future that has really already begun even now, in every present moment of the free decision of believing love.

IV

Christianity has already surpassed all ideologies about the future and all utopias in a completely different way still—by its teaching on the incarnation of the eternal Word of God and the universal salvation already ushered in by this event. It is first of all very striking how pale and shallow everything becomes when those who believe in an intramundane future (conceived as a beatifying paradise and as the triumph of successful man thus bringing nature to its own proper completion) are asked to explain what this future they are striving for will really look like.

We will be able to circumnavigate the moon and will perhaps

be able to land on Mars; Russia will have surpassed America's meat production; no one will suffer want any more; there will be enough time and money to give everyone the best education possible and to offer him all the cultural goods he desires, etc.; everyone will have everything he needs. And so the catalogue goes. But one gets the impression that all this is not very much different from what is already possible and in part already normal even today—in other words, that the "new man" will look hopelessly like the old one.

In contrast to this (not in the sense of mere contradiction but of a message regarding a completely new and different dimension of human existence), Christianity proclaims that man can have a direct encounter with the Infinite and the Absolute—with the One who from the outset surpasses everything finite and who is not constituted piecemeal by finite moments of progression. Christianity proclaims that man's business is with God himself; it tells us that this unspeakable mystery we call God does not merely remain the ever-distant horizon of our experiences of the transcendent as well as of the finite, but that the Infinity as such can also descend into the heart of man which is "finite" in such a way that it can nevertheless be given the grace of this unspeakable Infinity.

Christianity proclaims that we will come face to face with the Infinity of absolute Reality, with the inaccessible Light and the Incomprehensible who is infinitely beatifying life. It proclaims that this personal Infinity has already begun to assume the finiteness of the spiritual, personal world of man into his eternal life by the fact that Jesus Christ, the eternal Word of God, has already made this finite quest for the infinity of God (i.e., human nature) his own and has replied to it with the answer of the eternal Word.

Christianity teaches that God has already broken up the world and has already opened up an exit for it which leads into his own Infinity, even while the world still pursues its course along the interiorly crooked paths of its finite history—even while it is still subject to change by the fact that it can only replace *one* finite thing with another finite thing which, even though it may be better than what has gone before, will always remain both a promise and a disappointment and nothing more for that spirit who recognizes and suffers his finiteness. In the actual world, creation no longer means merely the bringing-into-existence of something out of an infinite foundation and the perpetual keeping of this originated reality distant from its incommunicable source, but means rather the production of the finite as something on which the Infinite lavishes himself in the form of Love.

This history of the infinite endowment of the creature with God's reality is indeed primarily the history of the personal spirit and certainly takes place primarily as the existential history of faith across the temporal progress of the history of the material cosmos. Yet this fulfilment of the finite by the infinity of God does nevertheless refer to the whole of created reality. Christianity knows no history of the spirit and of existence which could be conceived simply as overcoming and repulsing the material, and for which the history of the cosmos would at most offer the external stage on which the drama of the personal spirit and his divine endowment would enact itself in such a way that, when the play is over, the players would leave the stage and would leave it dead and empty and abandoned to itself.

After all, the history in which God himself takes part by entering personally into it is the history of God's becoming *flesh* and not only the coming of a merely ideological spirit. Christianity professes belief in the resurrection of the body and means by this that in the last analysis there is only *one* history and *one* end of *everything*, and that everything reaches its end only once it has taken possession of God himself. Christianity, indeed, only conceives and knows a matter which is different from spirit and out of which the spirit cannot simply develop as the very product proper to that matter, as is taught by dialectical materialism. Yet Christianity knows only a matter which is created and exists from the very start *by* the Spirit who is called God and *for* the spirit called man, in order to make spiritual, personal life possible and to act as a basis for such a life.

The spirit is not a stranger in a spirit-less world which follows its own paths quite unconcerned about this spirit, but rather this material world is the corporeal presence of the spirit, the extended being of man, and has therefore ultimately the same end and destiny as man. Even in eternity—when the spirit will be fully achieved—the material world will be the expression of this achieved spirit and hence will participate in the final state of this spirit in—as we say—a "glorified" manner. Hence we profess that the end will be a new earth and a new heaven.

We cannot say very much about this achieved, final state of

the bodily, mundane spirit: and this precisely because every intramundane achievement could only be an achievement constituted of finite elements, and so not at all an absolute achievement. Precisely because God's message has given us the boldness to believe in an infinite achievement, the only way we can in principle describe this consummation in its material content is to say that God himself will be this consummation. And since God, the Infinite, is the mystery which can be named and called upon only by a *via negationis* and by pointing silently beyond anything which can be put into words, we can speak of this consummation only negatively in images and likenesses and in speechless reference to absolute Transcendence.

Our consummation, therefore, is not fitted to become the subject of party tirades, of glowing imagery, of plastic descriptions or utopian conceptions. And when the man of today reads the old descriptions of this consummation which were less burdened with the images of an apparently intramundane utopia but employed an apocalyptic rather than a properly eschatological imagery, he will feel less at ease in all this than the man of previous ages. He will "demythologize" in a manner both justifiable and necessary if he is to be truly orthodox. This does not mean, however, that he has thereby in any real sense moved further away from an understanding of the reality itself. On the contrary, he knows that the truly infinite nature of his consummation is something unspeakable embracing all the dimensions of his being (but each of them in its own way) and that it—precisely as achievement by God and in God himself—is something unattainable by man himself, something given to him as a gratuitous gift of pure grace.

By the fact that this coming of God himself is the true and the only infinite future of man, Christianity has always already infinitely surpassed all intramundane ideologies and utopias about the future. The infinity of this future which is already beginning embraces all intramundane futures; it does not exclude them, nor does it make them unlawful (as long as they are mindful of their limitations as created forms). Again, it is not as if the man who believes in the coming of God's future can no longer acknowledge himself to be called to cooperate in working for these intramundane futures; and his supramundane, eschatological outlook does not necessarily have to dampen his inner urge for such cooperation.

Even if we leave it an open question whether God does not in fact realize certain things (which he wishes to be achieved in the world) through the *guilt* of men and not through the actions of those who love him, it must still be said in principle that the Christian is absolutely justified and qualified—and indeed to a certain extent obliged—to take an active part in working for the progress of the human race and thus of the world, by developing his own immanent powers and those of the world. For the consummation to be brought about by God does not, in the last analysis, expect a dead but a living humanity which has gone to its very limits and so is burst open by salvation from above by developing its own powers. For man's finiteness and the essential tragedy and fruitlessness of all human history, inherent in all finite development, become manifest more relentlessly in this way than it would in a purely static world.

V

However much the Christian—the man of a divine future—is a citizen of the world to come and not merely the child and supporter of the present world, and however great the development of this world into the unlimited may be thought to be, the Christian must nevertheless live at present in this world which is always a world of a future already begun: a new world full of earthly goals, tasks and dangers. It would be a complete misunderstanding of everything that has been said so far, if one were to think that a Christian may withdraw into some dead corner of world-history, as it were, or that he is someone belonging historically or socially to that class of people to be found in every history and development, i.e., the people of yesterday who are no longer really attuned to the times—the adherents to what is over and done with—the conservatives who weep for the good old days.

It cannot be denied, of course, that the good Christian of Christianity often gives this impression. It is true that Christianity has not been given any guarantee by God that it will be unable to sleep through the present. Christianity can be old-fashioned, it can forget that the old truths and the values of yesterday can be defended only if and when one conquers a new future. And it has actually to a great extent fallen into this error, so that today's Christianity often gives rise to the painful impression that it is running mopishly and in a disgusted, critical mood behind the carriage in which the human race drives into a new future.

One gets the impression that God's immense revolution in his history, in which he lets the world burn up in his own infinite fire, rests on the shoulders of people who really put their trust in what has proved itself in the past, although this is ultimately also only of this world and hence brittle, ambiguous and transitory, just as what is still to come in this world. Why are Christians so often to be found only on the conservative side? They really would not be forced to subscribe to other people's plans for the future if these are unchristian and inhuman. But then they ought also to have their own list of imperatives for the next couple of centuries and not just for eternity—and not merely general principles which they declare to be valid yesterday, tomorrow and always.

All these facts do not need to be covered up but can be admitted without any qualms. They do not alter the *principle*, however, that the Christian can truly achieve his own proper Christian being completely and fully only if he lives evidently and unconditionally in the present and in the future, and not merely in the past. This does not mean that someone who is going to build a new future in this world has already lived and proved his Christianity by this fact alone. But it is part of the convictions of a full Christian life that Christian faith and morality are in fact and of necessity exercised by using the concrete raw materials of human existence and not in some other, extra-worldly sphere.

It belongs to these convictions that these raw materials of Christian self-realization consist in the whole reality of the world created by God. This, however, makes the task of the Christian one which he does not freely choose himself but which is pre-arranged for him—in short, the concrete existence, the historical hour, into which he is placed. He may and indeed ought to be able to master this task in a different way from the non-Christian. Yet he must fulfil this task and no other. Wherever and whenever one does not want to face up to one's own peculiar situation in one's own particular age but tries instead to take refuge in a world of yesterday—a dreamed-up world, a dead corner of history, a social set-up which was alive and powerful yesterday—one not only falls down on one's earthly task but in such a case Christianity itself suffers both from the artificiality of this existence and the false pretences of the fictitious.

The fact that being a Christian imposes a task within the world does not mean, of course, that "official" Christianity, i.e., the Church herself, must therefore take it into her own hands to develop and advocate a concrete program for an intramundane future derived solely from principles which Christianity alone must advocate. It is impossible to stress that intramundane cultural affairs are relatively autonomous in their own sphere (to stress, indeed, that the Church today must inevitably live in a pluralistic society and cannot under any consideration lay claim to any immediate and direct ruling power in "mundane" matters) *and* at the same time to bemoan the fact that the Church has nothing very clear and stirring to say about the future now dawning and about the way it should be shaped.

But Christians themselves must surrender themselves to the future and regard it as their most proper task, even though this may expose them to uncertainty and risks. Christian lay people, in particular, are not merely organs for carrying out the instructions given by the official hierarchy of the Church, but must themselves try to discover God's unique will for them and for their times.

This again does not mean, however, that the official Church in the most strict sense, i.e., the Church in her own inner life, does not have any tasks arising precisely out of this situation. On the contrary, the Church has many such tasks. She ought to think a lot more about how she can arrange her life and message so as to avoid creating *more* difficulties than are necessary for the man of today and tomorrow—for the men of tomorrow who already live today. The Church is still far from having accomplished this task, and this not only because this task is ever new and must always be solved anew. The Church has also a lot of ground to make up with respect to what she has failed to do in the last one-and-a-half centuries. For during the modern age which is now coming to an end, her thinking and feeling, and her familiarity with the situation, have not kept pace sufficiently with modern developments; during this period she has become more of a conservative power defending herself than was right.

By the fact that she is in arrears with her accomplishment of old tasks, the Church has naturally become overburdened in the fulfilment of her present ones. There are many new tasks for her in Church life and worship, in the reform of the liturgy, in the adaptation of the way of life of the Religious Orders, in the courage to express the old truth in a new way in theology, in the reform of Canon Law. She ought to be reflecting on the problems posed for her by our modern pluralistic world and society, such as the problems arising out of the debate with other religions (or rather, out of the loving attempt to understand them), problems arising in connection with the formation of a type of Christian who can survive and endure the unavoidable and permanent secularization of the world of today, or in connection with the activation of a public influence suited to the society of today and tomorrow.

She should be making her presence felt in this sense through organs which meet the demands of the present and the future, by stirring up courage for planning such as is taking place today (in contrast to previous ages) in all the other dimensions of human existence. She should be presenting the demands of Christian morality in such a way as to make it apparent that they are not incomprehensible imperatives imposed from outside but rather the expression of what is objectively right. She should be establishing a relationship between the clergy and the laity which corresponds to the present condition of lay people and which, while conserving the permanent structure of the Church, does not confuse it with an old-fashioned patriarchism and does not buttress it with taboos about authority which can be safely "demythologized" even within the Church.

If, at the end of these reflections, we now take another look at the brief and formal portrait of the ideology of the future discussed at the beginning, it may be in place here to point out the following: the Christian is completely capable of regarding the planetary unification of world-history under a positively Christian aspect—indeed, from an aspect necessarily demanded by Christianity. In other words, if the universality of the Church is to be or become something real, and is not to be merely something belonging to the basic definition of Christianity, then this can be achieved by Christianity in the concrete only in, together with, and by the creation of this globally unified history.

The Christian will not be surprised to learn, therefore, that this fusion of the history of every nation into one had its real starting point in the very birth of Christianity and in the place where Christianity first took roots in the world and in history, namely in the Western world. If this world of the future is a world of rational planning, a demythologized world, a world secularized by the creature in order that it may serve as the raw material for man's activity, then this whole modern attitude—no matter what particular elements in it we may be able and ought to criticize—is basically a Christian one.

For in the Christian outlook—and only in this outlook—man has become the subject which Western man has discovered himself to be; only in Christianity and by its teaching about the radically created nature of the world as something confided to man to serve as the raw material of *his* activity and as something which is not more important and powerful than man but is meant to serve and is created *for* man, could there spring up that attitude to the cosmos which demythologizes it and which legitimizes the will to control the world. In a metaphysical and theological (Christian) sense, man has always been for Christianity someone who has control over himself and over his own final destiny.

If we consider the doctrine of freedom and of absolute responsibility for self—and the doctrine stating that the particular fate (and eternity) of each individual person is the result of his own free acts—then it becomes clear that the possibility gradually dawning on man today, namely the possibility of making himself the object of his planning and formation, is merely the echo and particular application of that deeper self-responsibility which Christianity has always acknowledged man to possess and which it has always steadfastly refused to relieve him of, since it has always regarded it as his own—sometimes painful—burden.

In the last analysis, therefore, the spirit of the approaching future is not at all as unchristian as the pessimists and the timid often think. Christianity has always been the religion of an infinite future. When Christianity tells us that the future which it professes has always already surpassed all the ideologies concerning the intramundane future of the new man—and when, *even though* in a critical spirit, it examines and tones them down, demythologizing them also, so to speak—then it does this out of a truly Christian, eschatological spirit and not out of a spirit of static conservatism. In this way, Christianity makes man morally responsible to God in his justified desire for an intramundane future—to be created by man himself in unlimited development—and opens this desire to the infinite life of God. This is the life of which it will always remain true (and of which it always becomes true anew) that it has been promised to us as our most proper future by grace.

Religion, Scholarship, and the Resituation of Man

Walter J. Ong, S.J.

Walter J. Ong, S.J., Professor of English at St. Louis University, is a scholar in the fields of Renaissance literature and contemporary civilization. Twice the recipient of a Guggenheim Fellowship, he has also been a Fellow at the Center for Advanced Studies at Wesleyan University and a Fellow of the School of Letters at Indiana University. Among his many published works are *In the Human Grain, The Barbarian Within,* and *American Catholic Crossroads.*

In today's technological society, what does religion expect of scholarship, in particular, of humanistic scholarship? The grounds of the question and of any acceptable answer are not what they would have been a few generations ago. The operations and range of humanistic scholarship have shifted, and the relationship of religion to human society has changed.

The vagaries of the concept of the humanities through the course of history are interesting and informative. Cicero, Aulus Gellius, and others use *humanitas* in the sense of liberal education, mental cultivation fitting a man, good breeding, elegance of manners or language, refinement—more or less synonymously with *doctrina, litterae, eruditio.* The concept was opposed to what belonged to mere brute animals, the infrahuman, and, by extension, to what was servile. By the fifteenth century the English cognate "humanity" is used somewhat in the sense of secular as opposed to sacred, as when William Caxton's edition of the *Golden Legend* speaks of a person as having "floured in double science . . . that is to say dyunyte and humanyte." The Renaissance, manuscript-oriented as the Middle Ages had been and further influenced by the invention of printing, tended to associate *humanitas* with reading and writing, giving particular play to the concept *litterae humaniores.* But this association of the humanities with letters helped dissociate the concept from philosophy. The subjects beyond grammar and rhetoric which were grouped under the generic name of "philosophy" were taught in the Middle Ages and much of the Renaissance by lecture and disputation without the use of written exercises. Under these conditions humane letters came to mean the study of grammar and of a rhetoric which was in practice, if not in theory, controlled far more by written expression than ancient rhetoric had been.[1] Since the study of literature as a formal discipline ended generally with rhetoric, to which poetry was more or less assimilated, the humanities were rather generally restricted to elementary and secondary schools until rather recent times, despite the plans of the great early humanists.

Today we vacillate in our use of the term; by the humanities we sometimes understand the study of literature and sometimes all the subjects covered by the term liberal education, that is, the broad or general fund of consciously cultivated knowledge which forms the core of our educational tradition and with which all educated members of society must be given at least some elemental familiarity. In a brilliant study, Alphonse de Waelhens describes the problem of humanism in phenomenological terms as that of "man facing his future and his past in his present situation," [2] and explains that this problem is quite centrally one of expression, although, since all works of culture are modes of expression, humanism extends itself far beyond the arts of communication. The problem of facing the future and the past in the present, Professor de Waelhens points out, appears less acute at some periods than at others, but in our own time, with our high degree of self-consciousness, it is acute in the extreme. Here, although I cannot undertake to repeat Professor de Waelhens's brilliant and circumstantial analysis, I shall understand humanism in something of his sweeping sense, since this is certainly in accord with current usage as well as with his telling

[1] See Walter J. Ong, "Latin and the Social Fabric," *The Barbarian Within* (New York: Macmillan, 1962), pp. 206–19.

[2] "Le problème de l'humanisme, dont on nous parle tant aujourd'hui, s'est posé à toutes les époques, car il n'est autre que celui de l'homme confrontant son avenir et son héritage dans sa situation présente" (Alphonse de Waelhens, *Existence et Signification* [Louvain: Editions E. Nauwelaerts, 1958], p. 143).

insights. Here, then, except when the context indicates otherwise, the terms humanism, humanities, and humanistic refer in this large sense to disciplines or activities centered in some manner around language and literature but including also the study of philosophy, history, religion in its historical and theoretical aspects, sociology, anthropology, mathematics, the fine arts, and related subjects.

When we take the term humanities in its large sense, we tend, somewhat hesitatingly, to oppose it to the physical sciences, or at least to technological subjects however intellectually demanding such subjects may be. But we are not quite sure of our ground here, and our hesitancy hints at the existence of a problem, which is perhaps the great secular problem of our age: What is the relationship of man to things, particularly now that he is so much in control of them? Antiquity tended to oppose *humanitas* to the brutal. The ancient *humanitas* implied primarily a contrast between man and animal and, by extension, between an upper social class and a brutalized, servile social class. Today our concept of humanistic suggests more overtly a contrariety between man and a world of inanimate things (where work is not necessarily physically brutal at all). Our tendency to contrast the humanistic with the overspecialized reinforces this suggestion, for, in a society where details are becoming more and more the business of computers, specialization strongly suggests some sort of mechanization of intellectual function.

The changed relations between man and the physical world around him impart a nuance not only to the concept of the humanities but also to the way in which religion affects man's life. The central shift of religious interest here is that which has changed the relation between man and natural or cosmic religion. This shift, which began to be manifest at the time of the Enlightenment and has become spectacularly evident in our technological age, has affected those who profess a supernatural, revealed religion as well as those who profess a natural religion or no religion at all.

Man has never been entirely immersed in nature, for he has from the beginning adulterated it with his own fabrications. Nevertheless, in earlier times man had closely aligned his religiosity with the mysteries of nature around him, exploiting for religious purposes the sun and moon, waters, vegetation, and the whole panoply of natural objects which Mircea Eliade has discussed in his *Patterns in Comparative Religion* and which he, Jung, Daniélou, Beirnaert, and others have shown to have a kind of objective symbolic content accounting for and warranting their world-wide acceptance in quite diverse human cultures.[3] Religious attention to nature may be more or less pantheistic, but it is not necessarily so, and natural symbolism is built into the monotheistic religions and even into those religions (Judaism and Christianity) which, in the terms of Eliade and others, inculcate a respect for history and time, rather than a flight from their terrors. Nevertheless, although the waters of baptism or the bread for the Eucharist and other such symbols have a permanent place in Christian life, this place is assured primarily by the fact of their connection with historical events of some two millennia ago when they were instituted, and with the symbolic sense which then reigned not only in Israel but through the world generally. If the symbolism in Christian rites were unsupported today by association with the realities of man's past, if this symbolism were launched for the first time in our abstract twentieth-century glare, it would hardly be convincing.

When pretechnological man addressed himself to nature and in or through it to God, he was addressing himself to something in which he felt himself deeply involved, from which he could not stand off in objective contemplation. Hans Urs von Balthasar distinguishes in man a threefold relation to truth: a relationship to the "coordinated being that meets him, usually and misleadingly called object of knowledge" (the relationship which engenders abstract science), a relation to the cosmos "based on his own bodily being and the immanence of the human spirit in the world," and "a relation of assent to the absolute and to the 'light' and the 'word' that flow into him from there because of his 'openness.'"[4]

Earlier religion, like much early philosophy of practical cast, such as Stoicism, drew heavily on the second of these relations, that based on man's bodily being and spiritual immanence. Confronting the universe in terms of his continuity with it and immanence in it, supported by traditionalist institutions which he had little ability or

[3] Mircea Eliade, *Patterns in Comparative Religion,* translated from *Traité d'Histoire des Religions* by Rosemary Sheed (New York: Sheed and Ward, 1958); Jean Daniélou, "The Problem of Symbolism," *Thought,* 1950, *25:* 423–40; Louis Beirnaert, "La Dimension Mystique de Sacramentalisme Chrétien," *Eranos Jarhbuch,* 1950, *18:* 225–86; Jung's voluminous work is well known.

[4] Hans Urs von Balthasar, *Science, Religion and Christianity,* translated from *Die Gottesfrage des heutigen Menschen* by Hilda Graef (Westminster, Md.: The Newman Press, 1958), p. 29.

desire to explain abstractly, early man felt strangely at home in the cosmos, even when it was doing him the utmost violence. By the same token, he had little occasion to encounter himself as distinct and alienated from his surroundings, alone. It was I-and-my-context or man-and-context which preoccupied the mind—a form of thought which Dorothy Lee finds persisting today in the concept of the self among "primitives" such as the Wintu.[5] In this pretechnological culture the concept of man is poetically rich because it has so broad a support, suggesting as it does so much else with which man is in contact. It was through this same world with which he felt himself continuous that early man's religiosity expressed itself.

From this world of nature man has pulled further and further away. He no longer feels much at home in it—although the relations with it, hinted at by known evolutionary processes and structures, are now opening the possibility of renewed acquaintance. Man's present changed relation to the cosmos has come about as the result of a long series of shifts, the basic sequence of which Auguste Comte tried to catch in his three-stage pattern of social development: the magic stage, the philosophical stage, and the scientific stage. Whatever the ultimate validity of this proposed description, we are now living in a different world from that of earlier man, one in which two principal termini of development can be conveniently located for our present purposes. These are mechanization and man's encounter with himself.

The mechanization effected by technology has a long history, running back to such distant sources as the quantification of thought in the Middle Ages.[6] It stands as one terminus of a great effort at abstraction, which has enabled man to hold things at a distance from himself, to extricate himself from his context and to deal with it as something in which he is purportedly for the moment not involved.

What I mean by man's encounter with himself is in a way a correlative of mechanization. For mechanization is an operation which affects not only man's efficiency but his very sense of his place in

[5] See Dorothy Lee, "Notes on the Conception of the Self among the Wintu," *Explorations* (University of Toronto), 1954, No. 3, pp. 49–58; a revision of an article which appeared earlier in *The Journal of Abnormal and Social Psychology*, 1950, *14:* 538–43.

[6] See Walter J. Ong, *Ramus, Method, and the Decay of Dialogue* (Cambridge: Harvard University Press, 1958), pp. 53–91, 306–18; cf. R. Hooykaas, *Humanisme, Science et Réforme* (Leiden: E. J. Brill, 1958), and John U. Nef, *Cultural Foundations of Industrial Civilization* (Cambridge: Cambridge University Press, 1958).

the universe and even his self-possession. To gain control over the material world, we have had to move away from it, in the sense that we have had to operate on it more and more indirectly. The old agricultural activities, for example, rich with folklore which emphasized man's continuity with nature, have been in great part replaced by activities still agricultural in aim but carried on in distant factories, in botanical laboratories, and in cost accountants' books. As man's presence becomes more and more effective and his responsibility for the world more and more actual, his individual operations become more and more remote from the end result. Gadgetry intervenes between us and the universe at the very time when the universe appears within our grasp. The plight of the spaceman becomes symbolic. How will he ever be genuinely present to outer space, when he is so thoroughly insulated from it in his pressurized suit? And how will he be present to other men, and other men to him? The problem of survival in physical, personal isolation is one of the major problems of the space projects, which are in so many ways the most typical endeavors of our age. Man needs a sense of community to keep his own self-possession. Deprived of this sense, he is more than isolated or lonely; he is alienated or estranged from himself.[7] Technology works against the communal sense on several fronts at once, both openly and insidiously. It is not surprising that the themes of isolation and alienation have become a commonplace of literature and the arts today.

And yet this is no adequate view of technological society. Technological society has indeed created certain special conditions favoring isolation or alienation, but it has not invented these states, which have been long known to man, although they have been brought about by diverse causes in diverse cultures. We must not forget Lear

[7] The term alienation and its cognates perhaps warrant a special note. From the ordinary dictionary sources, we learn the following: The English term "alienist" was first used largely as a legal term for a physician skilled in handling mental diseases; but the association of alienation with mental aberration goes back to ancient Latin. We find *alienatio* in Celsus and Pliny in the sense of an aberration of mind, a loss of reason, delirium. The term originally meant the transfer of property from one to another (*alius*), but then it came to signify also a casting off or aversion, in the sense of a withdrawal of warm, friendly feeling from another person (cf. the English "alienation of affection"). It is remarkable that out of this concept grew that of mental illness, loss of sanity, which is obviously conceived of by the early Latin-speaking world as an "othering," a separation from oneself (cf. the English "I am beside myself"). The key perceptions of contemporary existentialism thus seem to have obvious roots in the Latin past.

and Hamlet and the bitter human experience which made these *isolés* plausible to their own ages, as well as to ours. As a matter of fact, moreover, mechanized, technological society has placed the conditions for the encounter of man on a basis more intimate than ever before. Society has not, of course, created this encounter, and it can even be perverted so as to prevent it. Only love can create a genuine encounter between man and man. But there can be no doubt that technology has made possible an enlargement of the range of love.

Technology has made possible the total exploration of the earth's surface. It has brought the separate human colonies scattered across this surface, unknown to one another for certainly hundreds of thousands of years, into contact with one another, and it maintains this contact daily and hourly. The resulting sense of the solidarity of the human race is new, and it has immediate religious relevance. A Christian in the West today can live with a sense of involvement with his non-Christian brothers in Asia such as could hardly be acquired by medieval Christians, hampered as they were by the quasi-militarist concept of Christendom which was rooted in a lack of contact. Society has become more and more self-conscious about its responsibility for its individual members. Our development of communication, our study of personality structure, of intergroup relations, of depth psychology, of sociology, of the fuller significance of literary and art forms—all have made person-to-person relations accessible to explication as never before. To explicate relations between man and man is of course not to create them. For this, love is necessary. But I see no indication that love is less active today than it has been in the past, provided that we view the past as it was in actuality and not in some romantic transformation.

The preoccupation with isolation and alienation in our literature is itself an encouraging sign, for to know one's disease is to increase the possibility of a cure. The present trend toward isolation and estrangement, with its special roots in technological society, has paradoxically called attention to man himself and his own human problems more explicitly than was ever the case before.

This does not, however, restore man to his context in nature. His estrangement continues insofar as his relation with nature is concerned. And this presents a special problem in man's encounter with his fellow men. His encounter with them is now relatively stark, naked, direct, rather than cushioned in the living forces of nature, real or imaginary. If man today feels that next year's corn crop may be threatened, he does not organize the community for a rain dance which, however meteorologically ineffective, at least in the past established a bond between man and man based on their common dependence upon natural forces. The farmer concerned about his crop nowadays consults an agricultural expert to find what sort of hybrid seed corn is available, produced especially to fit the rain patterns of his particular area. He and the agricultural expert are not linked to nature as to something on which both depend to the extent that obtained in the past. The two are managers of nature, meeting not in nature but above it, looking down on it.

Under these conditions, human encounter takes on a new importance because of its starkness. Outside nature, men are all alone—but they are all alone together. They are more obviously than ever one another's context. One can describe the situation in the terms which Ludwig Binswanger has made current in phenomenological and existential psychology, the *Umwelt,* the *Mitwelt,* and the *Eigenwelt,* which represent three modalities of man's world.[8]

By the *Umwelt,* Binswanger refers to the world of objects about man, the natural world, the world which man shares with other animals, in short, approximately what we mean by environment. The *Mitwelt,* on the other hand, belongs to man alone: it is the world of interrelationships with human beings. This world differs drastically from the environmental world, for action within it is personally reciprocal. It is the world of personal relationships, of encounter between man and man. Here one individual does not influence another in the way in which environment influences us, for in encounter one man influences another insofar as he himself is influenced by the other. For me to become acquainted with you does something not only to me but also to you—one can only hope that it is not too disastrous. The *Umwelt* by contrast is inert: environment is not expecting us in the way another person is. Binswanger's third world, the *Eigenwelt,* one's "self-world," is the one in which one encounters, faces up to, lives with oneself. It, too, is a world known only to man.

These three worlds, or "three modes of world," are interrelated,

[8] See Rollo May, "Contributions of Existential Psychotherapy," in Rollo May, Ernest Angel, and Henri F. Ellenberger (eds.), *Existence: A New Dimension in Psychiatry and Psychology* (New York: Basic Books, 1958), pp. 61–65; see also Ludwig Binswanger's contributions in this same volume.

and the disruption of one necessarily disrupts the others. Within the past few centuries, and more intensively within the past few generations, as the *Umwelt* has become more subject to him, man has consequently had to turn his attention in some ways more to the *Mitwelt* and to the *Eigenwelt*, to make special adjustments.

As he looks out on the world today, man's chief problem is thus himself. We do not genuinely worry any longer about technological advance—perhaps we never did, for advance thrives not on worry but on enthusiasm. Although one or another technological problem may enter deeply into the concern of one or another individual whose work is technological, collectively we are not troubled about technological development. Given time, it will come, somewhere or other. We even state in advance and in public how many years it will take to be able to shoot a dog or a man or a space ship into orbit. But we *are* concerned about ourselves. From the university professor's lectures to the Sunday supplements, we find the same theme harped on: Can man survive his own responsibility? Accidents still happen, and they always will in individual lives. But more and more, when things go wrong, it is likely to be not nature but man who is accountable. He has failed in properly running through the countdown.

This situation of man has profound religious implications. Heretofore the religious matrix was I-and-my-universe (including other men) open to God. Now, with the physical world more and more at our command, the religious matrix is becoming more and more I-alone or we-alone open to God. In the perspectives suggested here, one can see some reason for the puzzling fact that, as technology has become more and more dominant, personalist philosophies, philosophies of "presence," of encounter, and of dialogue come more and more to the fore. It is not merely that the depersonalization enforced by technology generates a personalist approach to existence by way of compensation, although this is a partial explanation. At least equally cogent is the fact that man's control of things has made objects or anything treated as an object less fascinating in many philosophical circles than formerly. One turns from objectivity to intersubjectivity, not simply because one is overwhelmed and surfeited with objects but because one finds the more central problems really are the intersubjective ones.

In the shift from a world in which man finds himself embedded in nature to one in which he finds himself more and more externally managing nature lies the core of the problem concerning the relation of religion and the humanities today, if by the humanities we mean those disciplines which are of special concern to man as man and to his place in the scheme of things. For this place itself is undergoing a profound change. One still comes across explanations of the state of humanistic studies and of religion which querulously imply that the secularization of life and the increased prestige of technology are due to some kind of *trahison des clercs*. This is a provincial explanation which fails to get to the bottom of the problem, for what has been at work is not a greater and greater willingness of humanistic scholars or religious men, first Western and now Eastern, to compromise with the mechanics in the pits, but a major development having to do with man's gradual discovery of himself in the universe, a discovery connected with much larger movements, such as the growing together of isolated cultures, the development of mass languages, of exploration, of communications, and the extrusion of the mechanistic, technological armor which was the price man had to pay for freeing himself more fully from a contingent environment.

The occurrences of the past few centuries which are relevant to the present discussion can be summed up as follows. After a very slow start and an initial diffusion in tiny pockets across the surface of the globe, man has gained more and more mastery over the physical world. The knowledge and techniques developed by one or another group of people have been communicated to others as the scattered human colonies grew in size and finally established permanent contact with one another. The concomitant processes of populating the earth to an efficient density, gaining control over natural processes, and improving communication are by no means complete, and doubtless never will be, but the general pattern of consolidation and subjugation is unmistakable. At the present time man tends to find himself less embedded in nature, in the sense that he is less able to turn to it for psychological refuge, for nature is less his mother now than heretofore and is rather something over which he has assumed responsibility. As man looks out on the globe today, he more than ever finds that he is face to face with himself. This is the age of man's encounter with man. Such a fact cannot fail to affect the meaning of humanism. And it cannot fail to affect man's encounter with God.

Under the present circumstances, when man is plunged into a stark encounter with himself because of his new dominance over physical forces, there is one answer which immediately suggests itself to the religiously committed person when we ask what religion can expect from the humanities. One may simply respond that religion expects more and more attention to man as a religious being. But this answer is trite and unilluminating. Religiously committed institutions and persons presumably know of the need to be aware of man's religious activities, and, for religiously uncommitted or partially committed scholars and institutions, detailed suggestions concerning possible lines of thought and action which throughout the curriculum would call more attention to man as a religious being have already been spelled out in a number of volumes—for example in *Liberal Learning and Religion* or in *Religious Perspectives in College Teaching.*[9]

I shall pass over what these and similar books have treated and consider the question on a more fundamental level. Under the present circumstances, what religion would most welcome from humanistic scholarship, I believe, is the resituation of man within the natural universe, from which his quite unavoidable development of technology has removed him. When I answer the question this way I am of course speaking from the viewpoint congenial to the Judaeo-Christian tradition—at least, to the extent that I am supposing that man's situation within the material universe is a matter of positive religious interest, that his viatorial status is not something of itself evil, and that, while it is the business of religion to keep man from making too much of purely material things, it is not on the other hand the business of religion to insulate man from time, history, and materiality, but rather to orient him within the temporal and material universe in which he comes into being. Other religious traditions may regard the situation differently and consider time and matter as evils or illusions from which it is necessary to free man. Certain religious traditions which espouse such views have much to contribute to the Judaeo-Christian understanding of the universe, and I believe that a Christian such as myself has much to learn from them. Yet in the cosmos as we know it now, especially since the discovery of evolution, it appears that this negative or fearful or hostile attitude toward time and matter is no longer a viable one, although individual insights associated with it may prove to be of great, and even unique, worth.

[9] Amos N. Wilder (ed.), *Liberal Learning and Religion* (New York: Harper and Brothers, 1951); Hoxie N. Fairchild and others, *Religious Perspectives in College Teaching* (New York: The Ronald Press, 1952).

The resituation of man within the physical universe is called for because, in trying to express and handle man's present problems, we have overspecialized of late in helping him to know himself as an interior consciousness, and neglected relating him to the cosmos in its sweeping evolutionary structures. Never has man been more articulate about his own interior. He is to some extent prepared by literary and artistic productions and by humanistic studies for the new situation in which he finds himself, that of encountering himself as man has never quite encountered man before. Poetry, fiction, and drama—not only in Rilke, Kafka, Bernanos, Marcel, or Sartre but also in protoexistentialists such as Henry James or Conrad—have presented us with a literature of alienation and encounter; and phenomenonological and personalist philosophies have developed many of the tools for analyzing the person-to-person relationship or its absence. Specifically religious thinkers such as Martin Buber, Eugen Rosenstock-Huessy, Hans Urs von Balthasar, and others have gone into the religious implications and the dynamics of the dealings between man and man in dimensions far beyond those ordinarily considered in a treatment of "social" life. In the United States the interaction of self and other, including the "generalized other," has preoccupied George Herbert Mead and his followers, and John Dewey and his school have seen communication as paramount in mental life. Since Wittgenstein, linguistic and logical analysis has taken a definite social turn opening into interpersonal relations. Psychology, anthropology, and semantics are all deeply concerned with intersubjectivity and the problems of personal identity.

Yet this kind of thinking, which provides such fine and real insights into the isolation of each individual human soul and the encounter between self and self, is not enough. Man does encounter himself in the universe today more starkly than ever before, so that he needs this kind of thinking; but he still encounters more than man. He still finds "things," the *Umwelt,* his physical environment. Indeed, although he is less intimate with nature, he is nevertheless related to it in greater detail than ever before. Especially since Darwin, one of the major intellectual enterprises of man has been that of pinpointing his connections with the physical universe in which he has put in his appearance. As the evolutionary universe has opened itself to us in the past few generations, the pinpointing has run back now, at least in sketchy fashion, over billions of years of past history. Man no longer has to rely on guesses to know fairly well where he came in.

This knowledge of man's physical place in the cosmos, in space and time, has, however, been assimilated hardly at all to his knowledge of his own interior. The *Angst* of the existentialist hero or anti-hero appears to have nothing whatsoever to do with what paleontology tells us of man's past. Space novels, even those of C. S. Lewis, are of little help. The more we situate man in space, the less we situate him in his own interior, and vice versa. When the phenomenologists probe his interior, they lose sight of the stars. Man seemingly cannot be relocated in nature any longer.

The difficulty lodges in part in the fact that man's connection with the cosmos today is established abstractly and intellectually, whereas earlier it was established emotionally and infra-intellectually. The primitive felt his world as the reality around him. With the rest of things he was in no physical contact and virtually no intellectual contact. Today we are intellectually in contact with the most distant places and times. We calculate the precise period and location at which civilizations emerged. Thus oneness with nature in terms of a felt internal experience means less and less, whereas continuity with nature as a documented fact means more and more.

What is needed in this situation is to unite the interior and exterior, to restore man to his home in the cosmos. It is obvious that in this mortal life man will not find his permanent home here. And yet the material universe is in some sense his home: his material body is a part of his person, and in Christian teaching it becomes again a living part of each individual in the resurrection. In the Preface in the Mass for the Dead (echoing 2 Corinthians 5:1) we read:

> Thus for Your faithful, O Lord, life is changed, not taken away, and when the house of this earthly stay has crumbled, an eternal dwelling is made ready for us on high.
>
> *Tuis enim fidelibus, Domine, vita mutatur, non tollitur, et dissoluta terrestris huius incolatus domo, aeterna in coelis habitatio comparatur.*

Even in this context of death and decay, the body is spoken of as a house or home (*domus*), with an ease which today is enviable. Advocates of both religion and the humanities commonly decry the materialism of contemporary man. But we must not forget that the remedy for materialism—making too much of merely material things—is not to be sought in getting away from material things, for this is quite impossible. Even the most high-flown varieties of Platonism will not help us here. Materialism is not cured by flight from this world but by establishing our bearings within it, by impregnating it with intelligence and love.

Because of their concern with the human center of the cosmos in one way or another, the humanities seem particularly qualified to help man resituate himself in the universe by relating his interior and exterior points of reference. Are there any salient developments in contemporary scholarship which particularly indicate that within this scholarship such a resituation may be under way? Those that exist, I believe, may be conveniently grouped under two headings: the growing tendency of historically oriented studies to focus in the present, and the growing tendency of a great many disciplines to group themselves around anthropology.

For some time humanistic scholarship has been historical and evolutionary in outlook and method. This point is obvious and commonplace. But within the historical outlook there is a growing tendency to give explicit attention to the present, bringing knowledge of the past to rest there. This tendency is evident, for example, in the sensitive area occupied by linguistic studies. Here, while it is true that research on ancient languages continues to make progress, a whole new area of interest in contemporary usage (from English to Hopi and beyond) has come into being. In the teaching of English literature, the center of activity has moved, in the United States at least, from Old and Middle English, past the Elizabethans and Jacobeans, into the contemporary period. Work on contemporary literature can easily be superficial; but even after the necessary culling, the bulk of truly serious work on contemporary writers is overwhelming and without a real counterpart in earlier ages.

At its best, the trend to an interest in the present is not at the expense of an interest in the past. On the contrary, the latter has grown. We are faced with a paradox: as modern scholarship penetrates farther and farther into past ages and cultures—for the farther we get from the beginning of things the more our common store of knowledge about the beginnings accumulates—our interest in the present proportionately grows. Of course, an active and detailed knowledge of both past and present is not held in one and the same mind or minds; but it is possessed by society as a whole, and it is accessible to those who wish it.

Often enough, therefore, serious literary scholarship brings a circumstantial and detailed knowledge of the past to bear on the interpretation of the present—as it is indeed forced to do in interpreting the works of a T. S. Eliot or a James Joyce. The conscious exploitation of the past for the illumination of the present which we find in creative writers such as Joyce and Eliot is itself significant. But the trend to a present-focused historicism is not due merely to the existence of such writers or artists. Rather, their work and that of scholarship itself follows a common trend, observable also in other fields. In sociology, for example, the study of primitive cultures has enriched, and profited from, elaborate studies of the societies in which the sociologists earn their livings. In political science, the study of contemporary institutions has become a major undertaking. In history itself, a deeper and deeper penetration of the past continues; but the historical documentation of the present (as, for example, with the Roosevelt, Truman, and Eisenhower collections) proceeds along an even wider front. And this is true of many other disciplines.

This present-focused historicism undoubtedly manifests a growing interest in bringing our contacts with all reality to bear more immediately on man's present and future situation and thus to help him situate himself in the universe as a whole.

In *The Myth of the Eternal Return*, Mircea Eliade has shown how the concept of a Golden Age to which one dreams of returning represents a certain flight from time and the responsibilities of life in time. The present state of scholarship is such that a nostalgia for a Golden Age, which haunted even the learned in antiquity, no longer troubles us. Most nostalgic attitudes toward the humanities (certainly in learned circles) must be at least partly concealed to persist at all. The special kind of scholarly antiquarianism which marked the Renaissance and lingered on through subsequent centuries has now fairly disappeared. What antiquarianism we have appears not so much in scholarship as in Frontier Days' celebrations and other commercially stimulated folk activities, which scholars find it hard to take seriously, except (and this is highly significant) as manifestations of contemporary culture.[10] Yeats's "Byzantium" makes good poetry, but it does not tempt paleontologists or tease city planners out of the twentieth century.

[10] For an excellent study of such celebrations as contemporary culture, see W. Lloyd Warner, *The Living and the Dead: A Study of the Symbolic Life of Americans* (Yankee City Series, Vol. 5; New Haven: Yale University Press, 1959).

Closely allied with the present-focused historicism of scholarship is its tendency to orient itself around an anthropological center. The older focus of attention on nature (in all the many senses of that word) in our day has yielded to a new focus on man and to a detailed study of man's relation to his environment quite unknown in earlier days. This anthropological shift has thus registered within the humanities themselves the changed status of man in the cosmos, his relative independence of nature and his growing success in subjugating nature to his own interests. Earlier philosophies talked of the dominance of the microcosm within the macrocosm, but this dominance was realized in a quite limited way.

The cultivation of anthropology as a field of inquiry had to wait until mankind had built up a certain population density around the earth, and then, by expanding travel and communication, had become conscious of itself as a whole and of the diversity and unity of the social structure. Anthropology is thus the product of the present stage of human self-consciousness. By now, anthropology has become a point on which a great many scholarly and scientific operations (perhaps in a sense all of them) more and more converge. This alliance with anthropology was noteworthy in philosophy from the nineteenth century on,[11] not only in those Continental currents which were to move into contemporary phenomenology and existentialism but also in Anglo-Saxon linguistic and logical analysis, in which an interest in the sociology of knowledge and the role of communication has been especially manifest since Wittgenstein. The alliance with anthropology was doubtless to be expected in paleontology, archaeology, history, and psychology, but the anthropologizing which linguistics and semantics now entail—for example in work of the sort done by Bronislaw Malinowski and Benjamin Whorf—was hardly foreseen a few generations ago. Sociologists such as Johan Huizinga and Eugen Rosenstock-Huessy have entered into sociology and anthropology through the door of philology or even textual criticism—"grammar," in the large, classical sense of that term. Depth psychology, linguistics, and the weight of the sociological element in today's thinking have generally drawn literary criticism into the anthropological orbit. Northrop Frye's *The Anatomy of*

[11] See Balthasar, *op. cit.*, pp. 28–61. The anthropologizing of philosophy can be observed also in neoscholastic circles with the appearance of books such as George P. Klubertanz's textbook, *The Philosophy of Human Nature* (New York: Appleton-Century-Crofts, 1953), which represents a focus of attention unknown in medieval scholasticism.

Criticism is a good case in point: it is virtually impossible to decide whether this work is a literary or an anthropological study, for it is both, and very likely, in some sense, inevitably both. And even fields not commonly associated with the humanities, such as architecture, are quite explicitly caught up into anthropology, with the present developments in the sociology of city planning.

The present-focused historicism and the anthropological drift which mark scholarship in the humanities at this hour, even at their very center, where the humanities are concerned with human expression, language, and literature, represent trends which are religiously promising today. It is not easy to gauge trends so pervasive as these. Yet they appear to indicate that, as our scholarly knowledge of ourselves and the world around us grows, it is becoming more feasible to join a knowledge of intimate interior states to a knowledge of the exterior structure of the universe in time and space. A historicism focused on the present does something to the human consciousness that is different from what the more antiquarian variety does. Relating events from history and prehistory (which are always relatively external in their reported form) to man's sense of the here-and-now, it relates the exterior structure of the universe to a state of mind. For the present, in which alone man enjoys the interior sense of the *presence* of another (there is no *presence* in the *past*), is more directly personal and immediately interior than the past-as-past can ever be. The greater focus on the present in historical treatment thus represents not merely a shift from one "point" in time to another "point" (time really has no "points") but an altered state of mind affecting the exterior-interior relationship. The situation can be seen in *Finnegans Wake*, where past external events are transformed in a newly realized interior consciousness. Joyce's work is not, of course, precisely the same as that of a professional historian. Yet, more than the work of a professional historian ordinarily can be, it is directly representative of the contemporary historical state of mind. Ezra Pound's *Cantos*, shouting their author's defiance of the artificial order achieved by the selectivity of history and favoring more personal recollections, are representative in another but related way.

What we have styled the anthropological drift has similarly pulled the interior and exterior into a more explicit relationship with one another. Anthropology roots man in external environment, in time and space, descriptively and scientifically. Yet in doing so it in turn invites the relating of this external environment to man—which is to say, to an interiority, for it is in his possession of an inviolable interior, a personal conscious center, that man differs from other phenomena in the universe. When anthropological studies become involved with man's interior (as they are more and more), they develop their present keen interest in communication, which relates them not only to linguistic and literary studies, to psychology, sociology and philosophy, but also to something more directly religious —love itself. Informed work in communications today proceeds with an awareness of the human consciousness as a realm in which the interior and exterior meet, where interpenetration takes place between person and person. Fully informed studies of communication show an intimate awareness that communication and human knowledge, which is inevitably communication, cannot exist at all except in a context of love. At this point, scholarly interest abuts on what is specifically and centrally religious.

I do not mean to suggest that anthropology has fully succeeded in linking man's interior with the external world, but only that it gives promise of some more unitary vision. In the remarkable efforts of the late Pierre Teilhard de Chardin, we certainly encounter some kind of major anthropological and religious breakthrough. It would seem that the fascination which *The Phenomenon of Man* has for alert thinkers through the entire world today lies in the fact that it seeks to formulate, perhaps for the first time fully and consciously, the work which lies ahead of synthesizing our awareness of the person with our knowledge of the evolutionary universe. Father Teilhard was an anthropologist (more specifically, a paleontologist), who had, moreover, besides a Catholic priest's concern with the spiritual, a keen interest in depth psychology and in his own strain of phenomenology. He was not much taken with "humanism" as an ideal. I recall talking with him on one particular afternoon in the garden of the Jesuit house in Paris where we were living in 1951 and feeling him bridle a little, in his gentle and smiling way, at the term *humanisme*. "Ça, c'est fini," he protested with emphasis. To him, humanism signaled a harking back, an attempt to catch the world vision of fifteenth- and sixteenth-century man, possibly an educational system in which training (in literature at least) is an attempt to integrate today's knowledge around such a pole. Nothing, he thought, could be so futile. And I agree. If humanism can mean only this, we must have done with the term. We must indeed know the past intimately to know ourselves; but any synthesis must be a creation of our own time.

Religion, centered on God, is a unifying force; and from humanistic scholarship it demands as far as possible an integral view of man. Man's personal salvation, we can assume, is the business of religion itself. But religious man needs a knowledge of the whole background, as far as this can be ascertained, against which his personal salvation is being worked out. In the Judaeo-Christian tradition, the entire universe, no matter how far extended in space or time and no matter how deeply hidden in some of its aspects within man's consciousness, is seen as God's universe, despite its imperfections and despite sin. Alfred North Whitehead once noted that the scientific mind, which is traceable back to medieval Europe, has its roots in the Hebraeo-Christian tradition even more than in the Greek, because by believing in one God who created all things without exception and who was infinitely intelligent and wise, medieval Christians approached the universe with a conviction far beyond that of the pagan Greeks that everything in it ultimately admitted of explanation, no matter how difficult it might be to find what the explanation was.[12] Scholarship needs this kind of conviction to serve religion today—and very likely even to survive. Its maximum service to religion, as to itself, will be realized by continued dedicated work, specialized and generalizing, carried on under the persuasion that there is a unity to be found in the relations, however complex and however changing, between the human interior and the universe in which man has appeared.

[12] Alfred North Whitehead, *Science and the Modern World* (Cambridge: Cambridge University Press, 1926), p. 17.

Consecratio Mundi

M. Dominique Chenu, O.P.

M. Dominique Chenu, O.P., editor of *Revue des sciences philosophiques et théologiques* for fifteen years, is Professor of Religious History at the Sorbonne in Paris. He received his theological training at the Angelicum in Rome and was a *peritus* at Vatican II. Among his many written works are *The Theology of the Twentieth Century, Toward Understanding St. Thomas,* and *The Theology of Work.*

Consecratio mundi—not too long ago this phrase seemed quite commonplace in the current vocabulary and, if one may use the expression, more "pietistic" than formally meaningful. Today, however, it takes on a definite meaning in technical richness and in ecclesial significance: a fortunate result of the Church's renewed awareness of herself as the Christian community involved in the world. This, in turn, is a reaction against the break between the Church and civil society which has occurred for a great number of reasons.

Consequently, the phrase draws its original power from the fact that it refers to the role of the laity in the building-up of the Church, its role in the "presence" of the Church within the world. As testimony in its favor, it will be sufficient to cite one notable text which, without having full magisterial solemnity, is nevertheless supported by it by the highest authority. During the Second World Congress of the Lay Apostolate (held in Rome, October 5–13, 1957), Pope

Reprinted from *The Christian and the World* by M. Dominique Chenu, O.P., translated by G. O. Alcser (New York: P. J. Kenedy & Sons, 1965), pp. 161–77, with permission of the author.

Pius XII proclaimed the work of the faithful layman to its full extent:

> Aside from the small number of priests, the relations between the Church and the world require the intervention of lay apostles. The *consecratio mundi* is essentially the work of the laymen themselves, of men who are intimately a part of economic and social life and who participate in the government and in legislative assemblies.[1]

In its wording, in its doctrine and context, no statement confirms this better than what the then Cardinal Montini wrote several years later in his pastoral letter of 1962 to the Church of Milan:

> . . . This is why she [the Church] will call upon the laity, her good and faithful lay Catholics, to form a link between her supernatural domain, wholly devoted to religion, and the temporal domain of society in which they live. By a sort of delegation, she will confide to their docile and skilled collaboration the difficult and very beautiful task of the *consecratio mundi,* that is [note carefully the words used], to permeate the vast realm of the profane world with Christian principles and powerful natural and supernatural virtues.[2]

Yet within the large body of writing which uses this expression to define the object and the end of the lay apostolate, one cannot fail to observe a certain wavering usage; its meaning is sometimes expanded, sometimes restricted, sometimes taken as rigorously conceptual, sometimes surrendered to oratorical exhortation.[3] In view of this instability of usage, it is not inopportune to analyze both the precise conceptual content of the phrase and the supple connotations which, in its periphery of ideas, bring out the delicate interplay of complementary truths.

For it is one of the laws of language—and theological language must observe these laws—that words and spoken sounds are not rigid, inflexible units, but call for an aura of radiations and fringes around an essential semantic nucleus; although they are quite indeterminate, these fringes are extremely useful for an understanding

[1] AAS 49 (1957), p. 427; NCWC translation: Washington, D.C., par. 19.

[2] *Osservatore Romano,* March 23, 1962.

[3] This is the case in the many commentaries which Pius XII's statement aroused. For example, see *Wort und Wahrheit* (October-November-December, 1958) on the nature and the requirements of a *consecratio mundi;* also, the articles of G. Lazzati, professor at the University of Milan: "La *consecratio mundi* essenzialmente opera dei laici," in: *Studium* (December, 1959); "L'apostolato dei laici oggi" in a special issue on the Catholic laity, *Orientamenti pastorali* (March, 1961), published under the auspices of Milan's Center of Pastoral Orientation.

of the realities which they signify. To put it into a formula: words have a precise, specific meaning about a content determined by a "formal object" and an order of specific causes; they also have a generic meaning, corresponding to the signified reality's zone of influence, according to its connections with adjoining realities. As the logician would say, the specific meaning is limited in extension to the same degree that it is determined in comprehension, while the general meaning is proportionately more extended as it remains indeterminate in comprehension.

For example, the word "society" can be taken in the very general sense of any grouping, however little it may be organized; but it can also be taken in the precise sense of a definite group established by a contract, subject to an authority, having an administrative body and a government, for the purpose of defending interests, and so on —that by which it is distinguished from a different group, called a community, whose constitutive characteristics are different.

Both meanings of the word are legitimate and even necessary for a fruitful understanding. It would be a mistake to discard the use of a general sense on the pretext of strictness of expression and technical precision; but it would also be a mistake to disregard the findings of an analysis which has defined the semantic nucleus and has established the "formal" concept of a reality.

All this applies also to *consecratio mundi* as it is accepted in today's terminology. From a theological, spiritual and apostolic viewpoint, this is a favorable time to weigh the full force of the expression; it is particularly fitting to determine its precise, formal meaning, with full allowance for the truth and the effectiveness of its general meaning. It is this estimate which we shall attempt to establish here.

The Scope of This Analysis of Meaning

There is no question of yielding to scholastic subtlety to devise an abstract definition to be used among specialists. As the authorities quoted testify, the phrase itself expresses well the actual role of the faithful in the profane world, the land of God's kingdom, the scene of the incarnation of divine life among men. What is the real influence of man's activity in the world, carried on by a man who looks on the world in the light of his faith and is committed to its upbuilding through the resources of grace?

Here we find ourselves at a crossroads: on the one hand (through the growth of civilization as evidenced by a rapid evolution of the structures of mankind), the world is becoming vividly aware of the earthly values which it bears; meanwhile, on the other hand, the Christian community is searching for the impact of its faith on these profane values—values which are more and more emancipated from the close religious tutelage of the previous era. The desacralization of nature and of society seems to be a natural result of a scientific and technological civilization. Consequently, we are not going to define the role of the Christian layman through an abstract deduction from theoretical principles, but rather by an examination of the human material which he will have to take into account, first for his own benefit, then for the earthly well-being of his brothers, and finally for the concomitant upbuilding of God's kingdom.

In recalling the copious investigations conducted from every angle, both pastorally and doctrinally oriented, we are sure that one of the chapters in the theology of the relationship between nature and grace is being written today in the full life of the Church, in her apostolic activity and in her Christocentric teaching. The phrase *consecratio mundi,* however, certainly does not try to express the whole of this experience and this truth, but only one of its essential themes.

The coming of Vatican Council II has given a public, or, we might say, an institutional utterance to this problem. One of the chief topics on its agenda has been just that—to determine the relation of the laity within a Church which has come to understand that she is not a levitical, "clerical" society, but a community of believers structured through an apostolic hierarchy.[4]

"Consecratio"

What is the precise meaning of *consecratio?* We are seeking to fix the meaning of a specific concept and, as we just pointed out, its comprehension as well; this will give us the occasion to indicate the limit of its extension to other connected, though marginal, realities.

Consecration is a process by which man, whether commissioned by an institution or not, withdraws something from common usage or draws a person away from his primary availability in order to set him apart for the divinity with the purpose of giving full homage to God's mastery over his creature. Thus, it is the abstraction of a

[4] Cf. the monumental schema of Vatican Council II, as well as *De Ecclesia,* promulgated at the end of the third session. (Translator's note.)

reality from its own end, from that finality which is defined by the laws of its nature—the laws of its physical nature, its psychological make-up, its social involvement, or the free disposition of self, if we are speaking of a person endowed with freedom. It is an alienation in the best (or the worst) sense of the word, a transferral to him who is the highest sovereign, to the source of all being and to the end of all perfection.

After it has been set apart, the sacred object is untouchable, in an almost physical sense of the word; so much so, that a person will handle it only with approved gestures, with "rites" which manifest this seclusion. A sacred place must no longer be used for the ordinary needs of life, under pain of sacrilegious violation; no one enters it without surrounding himself, both exteriorly and interiorly, with the isolation of the gods. A sacred action—from the ancient anointing and coronation of kings (and even the protocol of today's heads of state) to the common, everyday burial of the dead—breaks, in its gestures and in its outcome, with the habitual conduct of social life, with its services as well as with its vulgarisms.

At least within the bounds of his consecration, a consecrated person must be separated in thought and feeling, in body and dress from the occupations, work, interests and behavior of other men. Social and religious historians attest to all of this, even in the most meaningful of corrupt practices (such as superstitious taboos), and in still more concrete terms than theologians in their classic definitions.

Evidently, this sacralization can have different levels, both in intensity and practical application; in fact, its limits are quite variable according to the times, the milieu and social customs. In short, consecration has its own depth; we can evaluate its original character if we compare it to a lesser action, which is a simple *blessing*. In a blessing, the object is certainly referred to the divinity, to whom it is offered or who takes it under his protection; but this object keeps its natural function, its earthly usage, its utilitarian ends. Blessed bread is respected, but also eaten.

The sacred appears in all its individuality if we compare it to the *holy*. The two concepts are certainly subject to constant confusion, and even to some justifiable synonymous usage. But the fact is that, formally, and without pushing the abstraction of this analysis too far, *holiness* has characteristics which differ from those of *sacredness*. God is "holy," the Holy par excellence; yet he is not specifically sacred. Holiness is the pre-eminent dignity within the very innermost self of the being, which is acquired by participation in divine life. Despite this close union with him who transcends, holiness does not relinquish its original state. During its beginning, its "initiation," and in its growth, it may require certain sacral means of operation and separation; yet these are merely the earthly conditions of a "grace" which, in contrast, seizes the being in the fullness of its real nature—in its profane nature, we might say. In becoming sacred, the profane ceases to be profane; in becoming holy, it remains profane.

A Profane World

The profane confronts the sacred. A profane reality—object, act, person, group—is that which preserves in its existence, within its workings and in its ends, the basic stability of its nature. But if this reality is a being which is conscious of its activity and its purpose, then this consciousness of its activity and purpose is at once both the primary value and the rule of its perfection. Wheat gathered in the harvest, processed and marketed in the economic order for the nourishment of men, clearly remains a profane reality, even though those who harvested and processed it worked for the glory of God, toward their personal holiness, and in the service of their brothers.

When the agricultural engineer leaves for an underdeveloped country in order to organize the rich productiveness of its land for a better world according to modern techniques, through his charity he performs a work which is sanctifying to a high degree, both in personal grace and within the Christian community; yet his involvement in Catholic Action does not make him leave his profane calling, his "laicity," any more than it suspends him from economic laws in buying and selling. The same holds true for a nation which is clearly permeated by Christian values in its institutions and its legislation; it still remains a political society, autonomous in its field.

Persons and things, therefore, can be involved in the over-all movement toward a supernatural end and be fully affected by Christian virtues; their dedication to supernatural ends and Christian virtues does not diminish the objective content of their nature, nor does it dispense from its laws. To be a gift of God, wheat must nonetheless still be cultivated. Likewise, the nation which attains its common good, both naturally and supernaturally, does not become a theocratic society. *Gratia non tollit naturam, sed perficit.* Grace does not "sacralize" nature; in making it partake of divine life, it restores it to itself, so to speak.

The examples are not hastily chosen to illustrate an abstract thesis; they represent the characteristic activity of a new civilization. In such a civilization, through his scientific discovery of the forces of nature and through his technological control over his powers, man no longer feels so struck by the mystery of nature's powers, which formerly forced him to appeal to the awesome might of the divinity. Now that he is acquainted with them, as he uncovers their underlying causes and even lays hold of them in order to build a universe in which his spirit becomes flesh, man desacralizes nature by making a kingdom out of it for himself in an exalting act of sovereignty. Such is the new condition of man in a civilization of work, in which man molds nature into human form.

The individual and collective repercussions of such a revolutionary mode of thinking are somewhat disturbing to man's religious sensibility. Yet in itself this sacralization is natural; and if in the twentieth century it takes on a cosmic dimension, this is due to an over-all application to mankind as it becomes aware of its earthly destiny. This progressive awareness can be observed by anthropologists and ethnologists in earlier civilizations, all things being equal, as well as in the stages of Western Christian civilization itself.

Furthermore, and in order to thwart a certian panicky imagination in the face of what is called the atheism of an industrial civilization, let us firmly understand that to desacralize the world, to purge it of its gods and demons, lies within the deepest law of Christianity: "in making it an object of creation external to God, he released it for men and made experimental science and technology possible" (J. Lacroix). We can question whether the Hindu, Buddhist, and even Islamic religions will resist the spread of a scientific and industrial mentality; but Christianity can give its straightforward consent, since it is the Word of God addressed to men, and not an outgrowth of a referral (*re-ligio*) of nature to God.

Faith is of a different order than "religion"; and if it can become psychologically, morally, cultually firm only through certain religious acts, at least by giving religion its proper place, it keeps itself untainted by a heaviness harmful to its gratuitous character. "True science," as Paul VI said, "has demystified, desacralized the phenomena of nature; it has contributed to purifying the faith of its slag, of certain superstitions, and of a certain dread or insecurity complex." [5]

A "Missionary" Church

Here we come to the profound reason for the new relationship between the Church and the world which is beginning in this day—a reason at once institutional and evangelical, the strategic and doctrinal focal point of all the problems which have gripped the Christian consciousness and which find expression at the highest level in Vatican Council II. *Ecclesia ad intra, Ecclesia ad extra:* beneath this balanced formula lies an incisive program,[6] oriented not toward two juxtaposed problems but toward a single issue—what must the Church be, in herself, to bear witness to the Word of God in the world, in the new world of the twentieth century? This is no longer merely the question of the relationship between science and faith, as at Vatican I, nor only the question of harmony between Church and State. It is an even more radical issue—the relationship between civilization (the building of this world) and evangelization.

As a result of progress which is ambiguous but good in itself, the foremost characteristic of this new world is the direct acceptance of responsibility for the common needs of mankind by diverse economic and political communities. Such is the happy result of socialization, as John XXIII understood it. Henceforth, the essential components of all human society—physical subsistence, economic organization, organs of culture, care for the sick and the aged, reconstruction after natural disasters, and, beyond all this, a striving toward social justice, toward a peace in brotherly solidarity among men which reaches beyond race and continent—all those things which, until today, have been more or less directly inspired and directed by the Church in the West for more than a thousand years, have become the common good of all mankind itself, the object of its highest hopes. Likewise, man becomes conscious of the laws of *his* nature insofar as he discovers and uses the laws of *all* nature. The world *exists*. Yet this does not make it less liable to "contempt."

[5] Interview with Cardinal Leger regarding the Council, quoted in the French newspaper *Le Monde* (July 18, 1963).

[6] Note that at the end of the first session of the Council, Cardinal Suenens defined in these very words the theme around which the material to be debated must center, although this was not brought out clearly in the preparatory schemata.

The autonomy of the world from the Church does not imply an absolute independence; however, it does go beyond the realm of mere empirical concessions and practical opportunism. The good ordering of terrestrial reality, the common good of human groups on all levels (family, corporation, nation, humanity itself), possesses value as an end, a secondary one and beneath the final end, but an *end* and not just a means. Within this integrated ordering of human values, the transition from sacred to profane is not the collapse feared by Augustine's theology, for whom the profane was merely a world to be made holy.

The historic arrival of this autonomy shows that if in the course of history the Church has eminently filled high social functions (aid to the poor, care for the sick, collective security, popular education, peace), she did so through a *substitution* for the ineffectiveness of human groups which were inadequately organized. Today, in a universe which is consciously building itself, we leave behind us a "Christendom," that is, a Church endowed with specifically earthly powers merged with her real powers received from Christ and used temporally to spread the gospel. The sacralization of institutions and ways of life was the means for collective and personal sanctification; on occasion it even substituted for evangelization.

The Church of the twentieth century no longer has to take upon herself the ordering of civilization or the building of nations; rather, she must spread evangelical leaven among these civilizations, within the structures of mankind. It is not the business of the Church to nourish mankind, to oversee economic projects, to provide measures of security, to undertake agrarian reforms, to establish a level of culture in underdeveloped countries. But she must collectively pledge her faith, her hope, and her charity, her "political charity" (Pius XI) to serve the upbuilding of a fraternal humanity. Her task is not to construct a "Christian world" at her own expense and on her own initiative, but to Christianize the world exactly as it is being built. In a way, the Church must go out of herself; she must be *missionary.*

For this very same reason, the involvement of the laity in the building of God's kingdom is in no way whatever a subsidiary function, a complementary role in the service of the clergy, the ones entitled to the task; theirs is a constitutive role within the realm of true evangelical responsibility, where obedience in doctrine and discipline does not dilute the quality or the truthfulness of the engagement. The involvement in *profane* organization is precisely what makes the function of the laity within the ecclesial body essential to the spread of the gospel. Neither theocratic imperialism, nor premature sacralization, nor clerical mandate replaces the universal rule of the grace of Christ.

The Cosmic Dimension of the Incarnation

But then, how is this universal rule of God to become effective over all human reality? How else, if not through a "setting apart" for God, as in the natural religions?

The incarnation of Christ is developed and fulfilled in an incorporation in which all reality, including every human value, enters into his body, and in which all creation will be "consummated." "For the universe itself (and not merely mankind) is to be freed from the shackles of mortality and enter upon the liberty and splendor of the children of God" (Rom. 8:17–23). For the Logos incarnate, the redeemer, fulfilled the work of the Logos creator: the identity of the Person does not allow the work of redemption to be severed from the work of creation; this identity gives cosmic scope to the incarnation, in which all creation finds its unity. The Church, Christ's body, cannot be considered as a pure and simple "case apart" within creation any more than the hypostatic union, just as creation cannot be considered alone, as achieved and complete in itself from the viewpoint of theology, without recourse to the incarnation.[7]

In a manner of speaking, there is nothing "profane" about a Christian any more ("All is in us, we are in Christ"); the distinction between the profane and the sacred has dissolved. But by eliminating this distinction, we no longer show sufficiently the individual depth of every created being which comes from the Word creator under the sanctifying assumption of the flesh by the Word incarnate and redeemer. Thus in Christ, the personal identity of the Word, creator and incarnate, does not decrease the autonomy of his human activity under the ruling Word. Monophysitism is not merely the heresy of some bad teachers; it is the bent of an "idealism" which thinks of the profane only as material for the holy.

[7] Here we refer, sometimes even word for word, to P. B. Dupuy's analysis of the recent works of K. Rahner, A. Grillmeier and F. Malmberg on the mystery of the incarnation in connection with creation. *Revue des Sciences Philosophiques et Theologiques* (1963), pp. 106–10.

In using the broad sense of the word *consecration* too freely, we once again risk falling unwittingly into theocratic and clerical usages (the word can never be transferred to mean sacralization itself). Even a certain devotion to Christ the King is not free from such an unfortunate time-lag, a devotion nearer to the regulations and requirements of the Old Covenant than to the gospel. The same would hold for a type of spirituality centered on Christ the High Priest, if the sacral categories should overemphasize it; whereas the epistle to the Hebrews uses these categories only to bring to mind a Priesthood whose reality transcends all rites and in the end gives them their true meaning.

The Timeliness of a Vocabulary

In brief, the problem at hand is one of using cultual categories to express the Christian mystery and to make it relevant.

First of all, such a usage is clearly essential, from the very fact that worship is needed in which faith in the mystery finds outward expression, adapted to the human condition and to the specifically "religious" requirements of an encounter with the God of faith. Consequently, if union with God in Christ is basically a movement of the *theologal* life which enlivens man's whole existence, then it remains that faith, hope and charity are also nourished within worship in which the *moral* virtue of "religion," in regulating the relationship with the divinity, rules once again in full power.[8]

What is more, an external and tangible worship is within the very logic of the incarnation, whose mystery continues in fact and is expressed in the sacraments; from baptism, or incorporation in Christ, to the Eucharist, the earthly fulfilment of the mystery, these take the form of "consecrations." It is here that we must recognize a properly Christian meaning, within the word itself, which to a great degree exceeds the restricted sense which we would be tempted to reserve for it were we to forget the true nature of the sacraments. Actually, these sacraments have meaning only in relation to a reality—*res sacramenti*—which is that of life itself in Christ, gathering the universe unto the glory of the Father and restoring all the values of primordial creation.

Finally, the cultual vocabulary has been spiritualized, deritualized, according to the explicit current of thought in the New

[8] Cf. St. Thomas, *In Boethium de Trinitate,* q. 3, a. 2: "Whether faith ought to be distinguished from religion."

Covenant ("worship in the spirit" in St. John; the epistle to the Hebrews). The use of the word *consecration* has spread beyond the various forms of "separation," of "setting apart," which the sacramental order itself recognizes. Henceforth, it is the normal thing to use cultual categories for presenting sanctifying and sanctified realities, in thought as well as in speech. This is what justifies, to a certain degree, the use of the word *consecration* to designate an aspect of the sanctification of the profane through the grace of Christ.

The expression *consecratio mundi* is likewise valid and beneficial. But to use it well, and in a valid way, is possible only after an immediate and necessary adjustment, by placing it correctly within an entire framework whose good balance, both in doctrine and in practice, ensures the most refined truth. Indeed, the great size of each room within this structure of the economy of the incarnation very readily involves an overemphasis, a gain which conceals other essential elements for a greater or lesser interval of time. Through much hard work, we have been able to recognize this in the consequences of Counter-Reformation theology.

Moreover, for several centuries, beginning with a Christendom in which the sociological sacralization of the civil order and of human values served as an earthly support for the expression of the Christian mystery, we have belittled both in doctrine and in practice the specific truthfulness of natural realities and secondary causes, the object of "profane" sciences. The building of the world, and, for example, each man's professional work, were no more than the occasion, the intentional matter, for the sanctification of the Christian in the world, the dull locale of a provisional existence. Whence the simply negative role of the faithful layman, busy with his own toil.

Today, through a new awareness recorded in Vatican Council II, the Church rediscovers her relationship to the world *as such,* within nature and within history. At the same time, she returns to the lay Christian his place in the very constitution of the Church, not by a masked clericalization, nor by his chance involvement in Christian institutions, but by his very being, by partaking in the mystery through the virtues of faith, hope and charity: theologal life, beyond all cultual "religion." All his works, in knowledge and in action, are sanctified; they become "holy" in Christ the consummator, without necessarily being sacralized or clerically institutionalized. The universe is permeated, invaded by grace, without being set apart from its natural destiny. Consecration of the world means the sanctification of men.

True, all reality is taken up within this sanctifying grace, which is individual and collective (within the Church); all reality is swept on by the supreme end, recapitulation in Christ, far beyond what it has by nature and its temporal destiny. True. But this eschatological finality does not reduce secondary causes to mere means, the makeshift scaffolding of a heavenly dwelling. Profane activities, and especially science, economics and politics, lose none of their own vigor beneath the imperative of the final end which will fulfil them. The order of created things remains under the control of their own ends within that order, according to the creative plan, although they are subordinated ends. Hope does not become alien to the world.

Let us say, then, that *formally* speaking the expressions "construction of the world" and "consecration of the world" have contrary implications.[9] By definition, the Christian layman involved in the world does not consider himself or his works as "set apart." Of course, as a son of God, he is certainly not "of the world"; but the lofty spirituality of the *exile,* of *contempt for the world,* of man the *pilgrim,* is true only within the core of the whole Christian mystery—the mystery of a recapitulation of all truth and all goodness by Christ, in whom creation once again finds its unity.

Therefore, if the theme of *consecratio mundi* carries a beneficial truth, if it is worth being put forth and discussed in its generic sense within current teaching, it would not seem timely to attribute to it the value of a doctrinal definition built up from the exact meaning of the word *consecration.* For then, in the present juncture of doctrinal and pastoral theology, there would be a serious danger of rendering ambiguous both the eventual positive definition of the layman and the exact determination of the relationship between the Church and the world. When it comes to language, truth demands timeliness.

[9] Contrary implications which have become manifest in the wording of texts at Vatican II; one of these texts described *consecratio mundi* as the task proper to the layman, and another (the famous Schema 17) spoke of "the presence of the Church in the world," a world desacralized according to the legitimate profane autonomy of the causes and standards of its construction.

God, the Universe, and the Secular City

Patrick A. Heelan, S.J.

Patrick A. Heelan, S.J., teaches the Philosophy of Science at Fordham University in New York. He studied physics in Dublin, St. Louis, and Princeton, and philosophy in Louvain. He holds doctorates both in physics and in philosophy. He is author of *Quantum Mechanics and Objectivity,* which treats of the epistemology of modern physics. He has written and lectured on the cultural aspects of natural science, on the foundations of physics, and on the phenomenological aspects of scientific investigation.

Not long ago, physicists at Princeton and at the Bell Laboratories reported that a certain kind of radiation from outer space in all probability represented the dying rays of the original cosmic fireball from which the heavens and the earth evolved over a period of approximately ten thousand million years. It was mentioned in the weekly science column of *The New York Times,*[1] but the secular judges who pronounce what is really significant for our society—artistic, literary, or political—ignored it.

I am not, I trust, so naïve or so ill-natured as to complain that the public failed to be sufficiently interested or enthusiastic. But I took the occasion to ask myself a question which I have often puzzled over: How is it that science—or cosmology, to give it its old name—lost its place as the unifying theme of human culture so that today, even a glimpse of the distant birth of our own universe seems to be

[1] *The New York Times,* December 20, 1965, p. 1, col. 5. Reported more fully in *Science,* Vol. CLI (1966), pp. 1416–18. A popular account can be found in P. J. E. Peebles and D. T. Wilkinson, "The Primeval Fireball," *Scientific American,* Vol. CCXVI (1967), 28–37. The authors are two of the original researchers.

merely a matter of peripheral interest to religion, philosophy, and the humane arts? Before attempting to trace some of those historical relationships between science and other, particularly religious, aspects of human culture, allow me to enlarge a little on the significance of what was recently observed at both Princeton and the Bell Laboratories.

Evidence seems to show that at the birth of our universe approximately ten thousand million years ago, there was a fireball, like that of a hydrogen bomb, that filled all the existing space. By "birth" I do not mean an absolute beginning like the moment of creation, but the beginning of the cosmic cycle in which we are living; it would be hard to exclude the possibility that cosmic matter has passed through many cosmic cycles, each ultimately terminating in catastrophic collapse. The cosmic fireball, bathed in an intense radiation glow, like the inside of a furnace, was the protogalaxy. Although the protogalaxy filled all the existing space, the volume of that space was paradoxically small because there was no space (not even empty space) outside the protogalaxy. As the cosmic fireball expanded, it formed more space within it, and finally, where the matter was cool enough, a portion of it condensed into a galaxy. The radiation heat trapped inside the cosmic fireball, however, remained. It became more attenuated as the universe grew because the galaxies within the fireball were flying apart with speeds approaching that of light. This attenuated background radiation is what has been recorded by the physicists.

One of the original galaxies was the Milky Way in which our sun was formed. Around this galaxy, about five thousand million years ago, the earth began to spin in regular orbit. After many more stages of cosmic history, some of the matter of that protogalaxy apparently coalesced to form man. This small grain of matter contained something that was not in the original fireball—consciousness. Hence, this grain of embodied material consciousness, man, had eyes and mind to reach out and embrace the entire cosmos from which it had come. Looking deep into that cosmos, man can examine the beginnings of cosmic history; the rays that arrive on earth from distant corners of the cosmos have traveled for millions, sometimes thousands of millions, of years, and they carry coded information about those early and distant epochs of cosmic history. The significance of the recent discovery is that, in a very real sense, man has been able to catch a glimpse of our universal birth in a fiery chaos; the span of time from the beginning to the present has been bridged by this ability.

I am aware, however, that for many contemporary people the scientific cosmic origins are too abstract, too abstruse, too impersonal to be of much relevance. And perhaps these esoteric matters should be of small concern, compared with the agonizing problems of human purpose and divine calling.

There is in Western culture, however, an alienation of the humane arts and religion from the technological and scientific aspects of our times. This is the topic I want to discuss. One aspect of the present "death of God" crisis has its roots in this alienation. Modern man's view of himself, of nature, and of God differs from past views largely because of the transformations brought about by the scientific revolution.

Science has always been proud of its objectivity, that special impersonal quality of scientific truth that raises it above the whims, fashions, and tastes of an epoch and guarantees certainty of success, whether he who uses it be a Christian or a communist, a genius or a fool. The common man, though he is often felt to be blinded by passion, foolish by nature, and inconstant in the search for truth, supposedly overcomes his failings and hereby attains scientific objectivity and, with it, the vision of scientific truth—bright, clear, eternal, and unfailing. The desire for a form of knowledge that possesses this kind of objectivity has always motivated the work of scientific thinkers. Parmenides was the first to separate the Way of Reason, which led to the bright, unfailing vision of Truth, from the Way of Opinion, which terminated at the illusory pictures that flood our sensation. Pythagoras discovered that mathematics was the key to the harmony of music and guessed that it was also the key to the harmony of nature. Plato completed the consecration of mathematics to nature by making mathematics the form by which the Demiurge-Creator put order into the original chaos. From these early beginnings in Greece came the science of the Renaissance and, eventually, modern physics, chemistry, engineering, and the cosmology of the cosmic fireball.

Modern science is characterized by its use of mathematical and formal symbolic forms. Although these forms fascinate the layman, they also repel him because they represent a world of pure cerebral order without human passions or failings, without prayer, repentance, love, or humour. Purely objective knowledge, it has been argued by generations of philosophers, is not merely human knowledge, but a sharing in the divine. To compute eclipses, to calculate the seasons from the stars, to make calendars of the feasts, to preserve and hand down the mathematical formulas which govern the cosmic machine—these have been priestly functions from time immemorial.

The Renaissance rediscovery of mathematics as the key to the science of nature was accompanied by a new attitude toward God and religion. In many respects this attitude was antagonistic to the mysterious speaking God, the Lord of History, whom Israel and Christians worshiped. The new notion of God was that of the Geometer-God or the Mathematician-God. He lived in the immensity of space, filling it with light, the basic substance of all things. Out of the criss-crossed rays of light, form came into being. Form was essentially geometrical. Although the universal eye of God and the mathematician interpreted reality in terms of Euclidean forms, individual men—each constrained to see reality from one point in space—saw reality as a set of two-dimensional profiles sketched according to the laws of perspective.

There is a story told of Brunelleschi, architect of the Duomo of Florence, claiming that he painted on a wooden tablet a picture of the piazza in front of the cathedral that was correct to the most minute detail from the perspective of a point one meter inside the cathedral door.[2] Then he drilled a small pinhole in the tablet at the point where the perpendicular from the center of perspective met the face of the tablet. He filled the area of open sky on the painting with a burnished sheet of silver. In front of the painting he placed a mirror. The eye, when placed at the pinhole at the back of the tablet, was located exactly at the center of perspective of the painting; it saw in the mirror the piazza reconstructed by the reflected rays, with the burnished silver sky reflecting the actual clouds above and adding movement to the otherwise static representation.

In this illustration we see an example of what the Renaissance and post-Renaissance scientist was trying to do and thought he had achieved. He hoped to construct an objective model of the world, a model of the world *as God sees it,* occupying an immensity of

[2] Recounted in *Vita di Filippo di Ser Brunnellesco* by Antonio Manetti (1623–91), excerpts from which are translated and published in Elizabeth G. Holt, ed., *A Documentary History of Art,* Vol. I (Princeton: Princeton University Press, 1947).

three-dimensional Euclidian space. God himself, who filled the immensity of space, saw this reality with an omnipresent eye. The human subject, however, occupied what was in fact little more than a point in this immense space. In art, and sometimes in architecture, when the presence of a human subject was acknowledged, he tended to become no more than an abstract point of perspective, the eye in a pinhole gazing out at what God's all-seeing eye saw in every detail without perspective.

This scientific world-view, the view of Galileo and Kepler, of Descartes and Newton, harmonized well with the tendencies that transformed Europe in the fifteenth, sixteenth, and seventeenth centuries. At the end of the fourteenth century, Europe was an aggregation of feudal domains. From the cosmological point of view of its inhabitants, each domain constituted a qualitatively different little universe, bounded by a piece of familiar flat earth below and the vaulted skies above. Beyond this domain, thought the inhabitants, lay a region of chaos inhabited by mythical beasts, ogres, and the banished gods of antiquity. Within this chaotic region, however, were pools of organized space, such as Rome and the pilgrimage places of medieval Christendom—Compostella, Vézélay, and St. Patrick's Purgatory. But these pools of space did not flow into one another to constitute one greater space in which all peoples shared. Local domains had local cosmologies (although it must be admitted that a cosmology for medieval people was not intended to represent the structure of the explorable and visible world), and, on the whole, medieval cosmology was a complex set of symbols through which the unseen realities were comprehended in their hierarchical order.

The new space of the Renaissance artist-scientist was, in the first place, a naturalistic representation, not a symbolic one. It was, moreover, the first attempt to depict an open connected space without horizons. A horizon was understood as the limit of an individual man's view, whereas space itself, as seen by God's own universal eye had no horizon. Renaissance space, therefore, was an open field ready to be explored, mapped, and conquered. Out into this field went the Renaissance and post-Renaissance man, to America, to China, and to the South Seas. He crossed every horizon fearlessly because he knew that in God's world-view there were no horizons; horizons were merely a matter of perspective and a product of man's limited vision.

With the geometrizing of space, went the geometrizing of time.

Time as a dimension of human life gave way to time as a dimension of God's life—a time whose created measure and substitute was the mechanical clock. To follow a mechanical clock, then, was to imitate the order, discipline, and regularity of the divine life.[3] The discipline of bourgeois life, of the counting-house, of the factory, and of the army, which, on their face value, were merely secular instruments of efficiency and convenience, came to be endowed with a religious significance in what has been termed the "Puritan ethic." Robinson Crusoe insisted on living the regular life of a petty clerk even on a desert island. And how well do the heroes of Dickens and Thackeray conform to this ethic! The notion of God presupposed in this view was not the traditional Christian one, but a distorted notion that arose out of the scientific and artistic activities—for they went together—of post-Renaissance man.

I remember a visit I once paid to the study and bedchamber of Jansenius, author of the *Augustinus,* in one of the towers of the old city walls of Louvain. His bed was a shallow alcove whose ceiling was not more than three feet above the thin mattress. On that wooden ceiling above the bed was a faded painting of a triangle representing the Trinity and, inside the triangle, the never-sleeping Eye of God, the symbol of the Lord during the eighteenth and nineteenth centuries. The Eye of God is even represented on the dollar bill of the United States of America. The new scientific modes of thought penetrated deeply into eighteenth- and nineteenth-century bourgeois culture and moulded its notion of God, of nature, and of the self. The historical dialectic which transformed these notions followed somewhat the lines suggested below.

Historically, the notion of God was the first to suffer depreciation. In the classical scientific world-view, God was represented as an omnipresent eye and mind who guaranteed the objectivity and rationality of scientific discoveries. He was a metaphysical and metascientific condition whose existence was required to sustain the hopes evoked by the scientific enterprise.[4] When these hopes were turned into concrete fruits, God became logically and psychologically superfluous. The "God-hypothesis" was no longer needed to motivate the scientist or to guarantee the validity of the scientific

[3] Cf. Lewis Mumford, *Technics and Civilization* (New York: Harcourt, Brace & World, Inc., 1963), pp. 14, 197.

[4] Cf. for example, Descartes' justification of science in his *Discourse on Method* (1637) and in his *Meditations* (1641).

method. Scientific investigation had become an institutional occupation in its own right, and it was carried on by its own momentum and by a variety of human and material interests vested in its concrete achievements. God was neither part of the object of the natural sciences, nor an explanatory principle, nor a scientific cause. We know that God is not an empirical datum; his characteristic works—miracles—cannot be scientific data because they are, by definition, exceptions to scientific laws. Thus, the development of science in the eighteenth and nineteenth centuries led easily and naturally to the view expressed by Laplace to Napoleon: "We have no need of this hypothesis!"

It was, however, only the Geometer-God, the God whose all-seeing eye sustained the objectivity of the scientific picture, which was rendered superfluous. On the other hand, the Christian God, the Lord of History, whose actions are recounted in the New Testament and Old Testament; who defended the poor, the oppressed, and widows; and who allowed himself to be moved by prayer and repentance, was only dimly heard, if at all, in scientific academies and in bourgeois homes of the nineteenth century. The Christian God probably continued to reveal himself to the poor, the oppressed, widows, and the men of good will even in Europe; but, from reading the history of Europe of that period, I get the impression that God himself was possibly just another of the religious dissidents who left Europe for the American frontier!

Philosophy, in search of a metaphysical absolute, turned against the scientist's notion of God; for a God outside the process of nature, it substituted a God immanent in nature. God became a *natura naturans,* the immanent source of movement, development, and emerging rationality in nature. God and nature became identified at the deepest level, and this pantheistic trend constituted the central theme of the nineteenth-century romantic revolt against industrial society and utilitarianism.

The end product of the historical dialectic on the post-Renaissance notion of God, then, was to dissolve the reality of the Newtonian God. In some sense, today's "death of God" crisis is a retarded effect of the crisis through which science passed in the last century, a crisis that involved not the Christian God, but the God of the scientist and of bourgeois society.

The same historical dialectic was at work to destroy the classical scientific notion of nature. This time, the instrument of the science-nature dialectic, which followed and accompanied the cultural changes wrought by the scientific revolution, was science itself. First, the development of non-Euclidean geometry raised the problem about the objectivity of spatial relations. The question was raised: Is Euclidean geometry really the modality under which God's all-seeing eye views nature? Or is Euclidean geometry just a convenient human construction that man has mistaken for objective reality? These were questions that dawned slowly on the scientific community and cast doubt on the validity of the entire scientific enterprise as defined in Newtonian terms. Kant had already said before the turn of the nineteenth century: "When Galileo caused balls . . . to roll down an inclined plane . . . a light broke upon all students of nature. They learned that reason has insight only into that which it produces after a plan of its own. . . [Reason] must not [stand before Nature] in the character of a pupil who listens to everything that the teacher chooses to say, but of an appointed judge who compels the witness to answer questions which he has himself formulated." [5] Throughout the nineteenth century and especially in the early twentieth century, the scientist was clearly doing more than merely drawing aside the curtains and observing the reality displayed before him in objective space-time. He began to realize that the scientific eye was blind without a special kind of light, a light different from that which illumines the senses—an *intellectual* light. This light was provided by a scientific theory under whose guidance the scientist explored nature. The theory was, however, the scientist's own creation. Unlike the Newtonian scientist, who thought he was looking at nature illuminated by God's own light, the modern scientist began to realize that he himself was both eye and light to the nature he explored. The success of the exploration, however, was not guaranteed by a priori principles, as Kant seemed to think, but by sufficient experimental evidence. The old question, however, took on a new sense of urgency: Has nature the forms that the scientist finds necessary for successful scientific prediction, or are these mere convenient fictions? The answer no longer appeared so easy. Clearly, however, the scientist would never have discovered the scientific forms if he had merely looked out on nature from the perspective of Brunelleschi's pinhole.

The success of Einstein's theory of relativity in the first half of this

[5] I. Kant, *Critique of Pure Reason,* (2nd ed., 1787), trans. by N. Kemp Smith (London: The Macmillan Company, 1963), B xii-xiii, p. 20.

century underlined the same elements: the radical uncertainty of any scientific theory, on the one hand, and the abstract quality of fundamental theories, on the other hand. Relativity theory defies imagination and is intuitively implausible. It tells us, for example, that things shrink when they move, and it denies the existence of an absolute universal time. One implausible consequence of this is that when Astronaut Shirra came down after orbiting the earth for fourteen days, he was actually younger by a fraction of a second than he would have been had he remained on terra firma all the time. Surely, however, the criterion of success or acceptance of a scientific theory is neither intuitive plausibility, nor beauty, nor simplicity, nor clarity, nor mystic symbolism, all of which have been taken in the past as signs of the divine intelligence at work; the only criterion is practical utility in human experiment and experience.

If the search for scientific objectivity originally meant the search to see things not as man sees them, but as God sees them, then this notion received another blow with the development of the quantum theory. The elementary atomic system is a very peculiar entity, and it certainly cannot be imagined to exist like a table or a chair in an objective Euclidean space. As an atomic system moves, it follows no path, and the precise location of its apparitions are erratic and unpredictable; it makes its appearance in the space of perception momentarily and then disappears. Moreover, and this is the feature which has caused the Newtonian view of science to collapse definitively, the quantum theory apparently requires for its physical interpretation an analysis of the relations which exist between a thing and the scientific observer. "At this point we realise the simple fact," wrote Heisenberg, "that natural science is not Nature itself, but a part of the relation between Man and Nature and therefore is dependent on Man." [6] Whatever the idealistic overtones of Heisenberg's statement, gone is the belief that science attains things as they exist in objective space-time under the all-seeing eye of God. This belief was an illusion traceable to the historical association of Galilean science with Renaissance art; from this association science derived the view that its function was to construct a geometrical model of nature.

Finally, the reversal of the notion of self within the Newtonian

[6] W. Heisenberg, "The Development of the Interpretation of the Quantum Theory," *Niels Bohr and the Development of Physics,* W. Pauli, ed. (London: Pergamon Press, 1955), p. 28.

scientific view must be examined. As we have said, the self, which as a scientific observer warrants scientific knowledge, was God's universal eye and mind, present in the immensity of space. When the scientific irrelevance of God had been generally recognized, some human substitute was needed to give objective meaning to a scientific theory. The fact that a scientific theory seems to have a meaning and validity independent of its discoverer refutes the immediate idea that the mind most capable of giving authentic warrant to a scientific theory is the mind of its proposer. The history of science is full of cases in which subsequent investigators have had to correct the mistakes and misinterpretations of the original author. Furthermore, the nature of scientific objectivity is often explained without any reference to a particular human author, stressing the timeless character of truth in science that accounts for its universal character.

In this respect, a scientific theory is different from other creative works of man. A great work of art or of poetry reveals the inner soul of its creator. Michelangelo's *Moses* is a stone expression uttered by the artist. But when we turn, say, to the Mechanical Law of Falling Bodies, we cannot discover anything significant about the author. Certainly we receive no clue that it was the work of the great Florentine whose bones rest in Santa Croce. Nor could we deduce from the Law of Falling Bodies that its author was an old man, scarred by many theological battles fought and lost, and devoted to a daughter who was a religious sister with whom he opened his soul and loved to picnic in the garden of her convent at Arcetri. Because of this anonymity of scientific discoveries, the humanist says that the scientist must render himself anonymous if he is to be successful. He must hide his face, empty himself of individuality, deny the historical dimension of existence. He must become one who merely seeks to conform to some abstract pattern of man-in-general.

To discover what the scientific self is, let us consider the following question: Who is capable of giving a warranted objective meaning to the following scientific statement, "The Universe began with an exploding cosmic fireball, the remnants of which are visible in the sky today"?

Whoever the true subjects might include, they certainly could not include men who did not and could not exist. There was no human observer at the beginning to witness the cosmic fireball, nor could there have been. There were no observation posts outside the fireball since there was, paradoxically, no space outside it; and inside it a human observer could not survive long enough to register a sensation. Nor can we appeal to a disembodied human mind immune to nuclear radiation; having no senses, such a mind would have no windows to the material world; it would see neither light, nor heat, nor movement; it would be a paralyzed mind. Must we conclude that every man who has existed is a true scientific subject? In order to understand what a nuclear fireball is, one must know what black-body radiation is, what electric charges and magnetic moments are, what strong and weak forces are, etc. But all of these involve relations between complicated instruments that are the product of a highly developed technological culture. Not even the mind of Aristotle, for example, would have been able to grasp the concept of electric charge, or magnetic field, or elementary particle without the use of high voltage electricity, isotopes, computers, and cyclotrons. Even if Aristotle were, indeed, the wisest man of his generation in Athens, without the instruments of the modern physical laboratory, he would have been incapable of giving meaning to the terms of nuclear physics.

The true scientific self, which contemporary science needs to warrant its objectivity, is not then any learned man of any epoch or even all learned men of all epochs, but none other than the contemporary scientific community itself. This was the thesis first put forward by M. Polanyi in *Science, Faith and Society* (1946) and elaborated in *Personal Knowledge* (1948). It is false to think of the scientist as acting merely in the capacity of an abstract universal mind, artificially withdrawn from the processes of human history. The self which warrants science is the contemporary scientific community, totalizing as it does the cultural and scientific history of the West up to our own time. Teilhard de Chardin wrote that evolution was not a hypothesis, but the condition of the possibility of all hypotheses. Scientific hypotheses and theories mark the course of human history like the dynasties of kings. Some fail, but often their seed is incorporated into a subsequent theoretical dynasty. Each theory, however, has its beginning in some epoch and only thereafter does it define a meaningful horizon for man's existence in the world.

This fact reveals a new and generally overlooked dimension of science—its historical dimension. The idea that science is transhistorical is an illusion created by the fact that the explicit formulation of a theory does not mention any particular man or epoch. The formulation is, to be sure, transhistorical; but formulations need men to give them meaning, and the meaning of a scientific theory is revealed only to a community living at or subsequent to a certain historical epoch. A scientific theory illustrates one of the ways a man of this epoch could explore reality if he so wished, and it expresses a perspective that a historical community has of the world. When we say, "The universe began with an exploding cosmic fireball," we utter words that only contemporary man can comprehend, words that have relevance only within the contemporary scientific community. Thus, the scientist, no less than the artist, the poet, or the statesman, initiates new stages of cultural history.

The picture which a scientist gets of the world is not an absolute, timeless picture, not a God's Eye view of nature, but one penetrated by his temporal role as representative of an historical scientific community. This, I believe, is a most significant conclusion. Although it does not yet represent the public attitude of our culture toward the role of the scientist, it represents the attitude that an increasing number of scientists take of themselves. Still, a more or less public attitude of hostility exists between the philosopher-humanist and the scientist-engineer.

The philosopher-humanist is irritated by lyrical accounts of the frontiers of scientific research; he is unsympathetic toward scientific enterprise and regards it as a rival that both draws men away from the "good life" and presupposes an interpretation of man at variance with that life. Science, he has learned from Nietzsche, is the expression of man's desire for power over nature and over other men. The philosopher-humanist sees no way in which science can serve the values he esteems—communion, love, sentiment, and human understanding. Science examines nature in an artificial environment and is cold to the struggles, loves, fears, and accomplishments of man; indeed, it could not be otherwise with an approach that systematically reduces everything to the mute, anaemic tokens of numbers, symbols, and equations? This attitude is true of much philosophy, especially existentialism and phenomenology, which conceives of its purpose as a dialectical polemic against scientism, against an overweening belief, characteristic of nineteenth-century positivism, in the value and power of science.

Oppressed by similar fears and alienated from the actual world of scientists, an artist may feel that the only freedom he has left lies in the ability to create a world of fantasy—a kind of anti-nature in opposition to the nature that has been seduced by science.

Much of modern abstract art, I think, is permeated by this fear and rejection of machine civilization and attempts to assert desperately the uniqueness and value of the individual person. Abstract artists seem to say: "Though you reduce my external life to a mere function and subordinate my skills to a technically superior machine, yet I am more than a function and a machine. I am free and a creator of worlds."

Undoubtedly, the fears expressed by the artist and by the intellectual are well founded. One has only to recall the functionalism of Nazi Germany, of Russia under Stalin, of any milieu in the West, where spiritual values have failed and materialism rules man and his organizations. George Orwell's *1984* is not without foundation.

But to prevent the horrifying possibilities of a *1984*, it is imperative to humanize the scientist and the engineer. The humanizing of the scientist and the engineer, however, is not a simple cultural matter, nor, paradoxically, is it primarily something to do with the scientific milieu. To be humanized means to be accepted by and admitted into the humane culture of an epoch. This implies a twofold willingness—a willingness on the part of the scientist to put aside dogmatic scientism and positivism and to embrace a fuller culture; and, more importantly, a willingness on the part of the humane culture to accept scientific activity as a valid human activity, to realize that science is a humanism, a dialogue between man and nature, as creative of new horizons as the work of the artist. The home of imagination today, Elizabeth Sewell has shrewdly pointed out, is scientific technology, not the arts.[7]

We may wonder whether or not the obstacle to the humanizing of science today is not, in part at least, the undiscerning, uncomprehending attitude that characterizes much of our humanistic culture. Science expresses itself in recondite symbols which speak only to the initiated. Among the noninitiated, distorted models of science gain currency, and frightening horrific images of the barrenness of a scientific culture pass into circulation. The scientist, by virtue of his profession, is obliged to play a specific role, that of being a modern primitive and barbarian. "The scientist today," wrote Ortega y Gasset, "is a learned ignoramus, which is a very serious matter as it implies that he is a person that is ignorant,

[7] Elizabeth Sewell, "Science and Literature," *Commonweal,* May 13, 1966, pp. 218–21.

not in the fashion of the ignorant man, but with all the petulance of one who is learned." [8] Whoever has lived in close contact with communities of research scientists realizes how absurd the statement is on its face value. If for "scientific" we substitute "doctor," "classicist," "critic," the statement is equally true and equally false. Its significance, however, does not lie in its truth or falsity, but in the attitude of malevolence that it manifests toward scientific culture. Certain brands of humanistic culture in the West are more deliberately opposed to science, I think, than they are to religion and to Christianity. Teilhard de Chardin was aware of this, and in the various scientific and religious conferences he organized towards the end of his life, he found the philosophers generally unhelpful and incapable of understanding the terms of the problem.[9]

Here, I believe, lie the deeper roots of our religious problems today. Humanists still see themselves as confronting and rejecting a Newtonian God, which the scientists have long abandoned and which was never, in fact, the Christian God. On the other hand, the scientists, isolated from an integral humanist tradition largely because of the exclusiveness of that tradition itself, have failed to find a fully humane meaning for their occupation that includes the relevance of social and transcendental values to their personal and professional lives. Although many scientists *have* found a fully humane meaning for their lives, they have generally done so in a predominantly technological environment where they are not expected to play the role of "learned ignoramus" in a social morality-play composed for them by philosophers, dramatists, and poets.

What relevance does the Christian God have for modern scientific culture and its incarnation, the megapolis? Harvey Cox's answer in *The Secular City* has produced much discussion.[10] He says that the Christian God speaks in the depths of modern man, calling him to commit his energies to the development of urban society. This God reveals himself to man as the first universal cause of movement in history, a movement that is directed toward the goal of a technological urban civilization. Cox's statements are pro-

[8] Ortega y Gasset, *Revolt of the Masses* (New York: Norton, 1932). The passage is cited in Philipp Frank, *Philosophy of Science* (Englewood Cliffs, N.J.: Prentice-Hall, 1957), p. xvi.

[9] Claude Cuénot points this out in his biography *Teilhard de Chardin: A Biographical Study* (Baltimore: Helicon Press, 1965), pp. 347–61.

[10] Harvey Cox, *The Secular City* (New York: The Macmillan Company, 1965).

phetic and acclaim modern man's desire for personal redemption, not by withdrawing from the secular city to a pastoral hermitage, but by working.

The function of a prophet, however, is to prophesy, to announce God's message. He does not have to prove it, or articulate its logic, or satisfy the pedantic critics who ask how we recognize that man's yearning for salvation by work is a revelation of the Christian God? What guarantee, other than the prophet's word, have we that the secular city can become a manifestation of the People of God? Although we, too, hope and believe, our minds boggle at the attempt to articulate the difficulties, and Mr. Cox does not really help us.

The answer of Teilhard de Chardin is no less prophetic. He also believes that the secular city is the divine milieu in which the People of God is taking shape today. Teilhard, however, tries to rationalize his prophetic and mystical insight. He developed the outlines of a dialectical logic that provided a progression the mind could follow by its own powers from familiar things to unfamiliar ones. Throughout the progression, prophetic gusts are somewhat tempered by a dialectical logic.

The form of Teilhard's argument reveals quite clearly the role he believes the Christian God and Christ himself play in the secular city. It also describes the sense in which he believes the Christian God is relevant to our contemporary scientific society. Unlike the scientific Newtonian God, who was the guarantor of scientific objectivity, the Christian God for Teilhard is always the Lord of History. Teilhard approaches God with a two-legged stride; I thus call his logic "dialectical." One leg represents scientific evolutionary synthesis; the other represents the fact of the Church in the world.

He called the first leg of his argument, a "hyper-physics," that is, a science of the evolutionary movement in the heart of matter. This argument is developed in the *Phenomenon of Man* and again in *Man's Place in Nature*.[11] Matter, he held, was endowed with a twofold energy—energy to move and energy to combine. The former he called tangential energy, the latter radial energy, or psyche, or consciousness. Evolutionary development is the expansion of

[11] Pierre Teilhard de Chardin, S.J., *The Phenomenon of Man* (New York: Harper and Row, 1959), and *Man's Place in Nature* (New York: Harper and Row, 1966).

this radial energy under the Law of Complexity–Consciousness or Centro-complexity. Cosmic matter then generally follows a unique irreversible trajectory through space and time with stages marked out by the appearance of successive levels of synthesis—life, animal consciousness, rational consciousness, local cultural communities. In the course of time and with the thickening of the human envelope over the limited surface of the globe, the process led to a common universal culture or psychic atmosphere, which he called the Noosphere. The Noosphere itself, he surmised, was intrinsically unstable; wars, competing ideologies, greed, race conflicts, all tended to disrupt it. To achieve a stable and definite state, a love-center capable of drawing all men to itself was needed. Teilhard called this personal love-center, a postulate of his pure dialectical reason, *Omega*. The common act of love would unite men, not in the way in which fanaticism or mere ideology does, but in the way love unites man and wife; it would unite people, although still preserving and heightening their personal differences.

The other leg of Teilhard's argument is found in *Le Christique* and in *The Future of Man*.[12] It consists of an examination of the Church in the world. Out of Christian revelation comes the identification of Omega with the incarnate Christ, who, as Paul says, came to "deliver creation from its slavery to corruption into freedom of the glory of the sons of God for which cause all creation groans in pain until now." [13] From this identification of Christ with Omega, it follows that the trajectory of geological, biological, and human history was, from the beginning, a supernatural one. Furthermore, the disorder, physical and moral, of the substratum of individual human beings in ceaseless activity is the existential or experiential reality of original sin.[14]

We can see now that the ultimate destiny of matter in the *parousia*, or resurrection of the body, is a point continuous with human history and that its moment should come when certain con-

[12] Pierre Teilhard de Chardin, *The Future of Man* (London: Collins, 1964). As far as the author knows, *Le Christique* has not yet been translated, but a summary of it with ample quotations will be found in Cuénot's biography referred to above, pp. 370–77. Two excellent studies of Heilhard de Chardin's thought are Christopher Mooney, *Teilhard de Chardin and the Mystery of Christ* (New York: Harper and Row, 1966) and Pierre Smulders, *The Design of Teilhard de Chardin* (Glen Rock, N.J.: Paulist Press, 1967).

[13] Rom. 8: 20–22.

[14] Cf. Smulders, Appendix iii.

ditions are fulfilled on earth—when, that is, the planetary Noospheric community makes its common act of love of the incarnate Christ, the love-center or Omega of Teilhard's "hyper-physics."[15]

The condition for the formation of the Noosphere is a world-wide network of industry, transport, and communications. The instruments which unite men into the kind of community in which the Noosphere is formed are the instruments of technology and science that help construct the secular city. Science and technology also provide the symbols through which man unites himself to God and to Christ in the modern world. These are symbols representing, not as abstract intellectual knowledge of God, but a conscious experience of sharing in God's creative activity or purpose in the universe at the beckoning of Christ.

Teilhard would have appreciated the dramatic moment when astronomers recognized that they were observing remnants of the original fireball. He would have especially applauded it, seeing in it, as in every scientific achievement, so much energy and love brought to focus that otherwise would have been dispersed in random and unrelated strivings. Scientific research for Teilhard was the model of a liberating discipline; it cannot be commanded by force or achieved by machine-like organization. It needs not mechanical discipline, but control that flows from love and dedication. Achievement under these circumstances brings the scientist a great experience of human liberation. Teilhard took this experience as the symbol of the parousia.

The contemplation of the parousia recalls the world's primordial beginnings, the exploding fireball whose echoes are still reverberating throughout the universe. It seems that every generation has interpreted the good of man in cosmological terms; similarly, man has expressed his image of God through cosmological symbols. Through what symbols will the man of the fireball universe express the goals of human existence? How will he unite himself to his divine Lord through the symbols of an exploding cosmic fire? It is still too soon to answer these questions without attempting prophecy. The new symbols, however, are unlike the old Newtonian ones; they are neither formal, nor geometric, nor static. They are pregnant with novelty—not with the novelty of a new theorem derived from old axioms; nor with the novelty which is merely the actualization of an old potency; but with free, creative novelty, the product of nature's

[15] Cf. Smulders, Chap. vi.

play rather than of her work. Surely through symbols like these, man cannot fail to realize that he himself is a spark of transforming cosmic fire, and he will choose a destiny in accordance with this image.

How, then, will he approach his God? Perhaps, like Christians of every age, he will approach him in a trinitarian fashion. As God the Father, he is the creator of energy. As Christ, the Son of God, he is a citizen of the secular city playing creatively with man. As God the Holy Spirit, he is the spirit of love which draws all men to the divine love-center of the universe. "The Incarnation," wrote Teilhard in *The Future of Man,* "is a renewal and restoration of all the forces and powers of the universe. Christ is the instrument, the center, the end of all animate and material creation; by Him all things are created, sanctified and made alive." [16] We need a theology which takes account of both the fireball universe and the secular city. To what extent the contributions of Harvey Cox and Teilhard de Chardin will be accepted by Christians of our age still remains to be seen.

[16] Teilhard de Chardin, *The Future of Man,* p. 304.

What Is Wrong with God?

Theodore M. Steeman, O.F.M.

Theodore M. Steeman, O.F.M., is a member of the Dutch province of the Order of Friars Minor. He studied at Leyden and Harvard Universities, where his special concentration was in the sociology of Christian religion. He has published articles in *Social Compass* and *Concilium* and has written an important position paper on the sociology of atheism for the Vatican Secretariat for Unbelievers. He is presently on the theology faculty of Boston College.

Come to think of it, Nietzsche's famous phrase: God is dead, has a peculiar ring to it. It is not an unqualified statement of atheism, a simple denial of the existence of God; it is rather the announcement that someone who was alive at some time has died. God existed, he exists no more. A straight atheism would have tried to prove that God is not, does not exist, cannot exist. Not so Nietzsche: for him God has died. The one who is acclaimed by a long tradition as the Immortal, has disappeared from the scene, his time is over. God is dead.

It would be too easy an answer if we decided that, in any case, Nietzsche is dead. We can perhaps qualify Nietzsche's statement and say that in view of the faith of ever so many theists, God is not really dead yet. But, somehow, we have to agree that something is wrong with God. It would be accurate to say, resuming Nietzsche's imagery, that if God is not really dead, he is at any rate sick. If he has not disappeared yet, it is at least clear that his appearance is not quite what it should be. And it seems timely to ask: what

Reprinted from *New Blackfriars,* No. 554 (July, 1966), pp. 508–24, with the permission of the author.

is the matter with God? Or, again more closely to Nietzsche's language: what has become of God?

I think we can dispense with arguing the actuality of the problem. Ever since the Bishop of Woolwich wrote his *Honest to God*, it has been clear that God has become a problem generally, also within the fold of the Christian churches. Bonhoeffer's program of a life in a world come of age "as if God did not exist" also finds a rather amazing following. And it has been reported from the United States that a whole school of young theologians is emerging who try to develop a christianity without God. The notable thing about these authors is that here too, as in Nietzsche, connection is sought between the new problem of God and *modern* man. If not all these writers go all the way to a straight affirmation of God's death, the problem seems to be very much linked to specific characteristics of man of our times. If the God of our fathers hasn't died, he is at any rate not quite fit for an age of space flights, technological civilization, world unification, pragmatic politics—for modern man.

The historical dimension which is brought in in this way is indeed so prominent that it seems hardly possible any more to discuss atheism, or any other religious problem, apart from an explicit reference to the type of man who is asking the question. This is in itself the most peculiar feature of the present quest for clarity in matters religious. Modern atheism, too, is not so much a denial of God's existence in itself, it is much more a statement of modern man's inability to believe that there is a God or to believe in God. That is why we can speak with some significance of God's death. The historical connotation implied in the concept of death points to the kind of life God once had: in the faith or in the conviction of man. God is dead because man is not able any more to believe in God in the same way as former generations did.

We have to go even farther. If, for historical analysis, the growth of atheism can be explained by modern man's inability to believe, modern religious thinkers appear to be very much aware of this inability and are trying to build a kind of conceptualization that would be acceptable to modern man. This means that we are turning the tables, so to speak. There has been a time when the atheist turned away from the Church or was ousted from the Church; now the Church herself is—or at least some of her theologians are—struggling with the problem how to formulate a faith that would fit the mind of the modern unbeliever or atheist. It would seem that man's willingness and capacity to believe have become the norm of faith. This is, as I hope is evident, far too rash a statement to be taken seriously, but it should help to make clear that the present situation is an intricate one indeed.

It is perhaps advisable that, before entering upon a discussion of modern atheism, we remind ourselves of some of the basic features of the problem as such. The problem "whether God exists or not" is obviously a fake one, or at any rate, it does not seem to be the proper way of asking the question. For one thing, in order to ask the question meaningfully we would have to explain first what these concepts stand for, what we mean by "God" and by "exists." But, furthermore, we would have to explain what the thrust of the problem is, why we think the question is worth asking. What if, after our long exposition of the arguments for the existence of God, someone told us: So what? What difference does it make? What I am trying to say here is that as far as I can see most of the proofs for the existence of God and most arguments about this age-old problem really miss the point when it comes to deciding the question. St Thomas is obviously not really asking whether God exists, but how God's existence can be proven, and so are most of his followers. And it is beyond doubt that St Thomas and Kant are not talking about the same kind of thing, even if they both presumably talk about God. Thus we should say that there is a whole set of problems that should be treated before we can arrive at the stage of rationally arguing God's existence. This is not to say that the question whether such a God exists in the sense that he has being of himself and in himself objectively, independently of our belief that he exists, is meaningless. But the matter is not really decided on the level of rational and philosophical reasoning. The latter functions far more as a process of taking account of one's position in life, of being aware, and reflexively aware, of what really carries one on. It also helps to control one's attitude, to be consistent, to bring order, to rise above the level of passing moods, and to bring life to a focus, and we should be very careful not to devaluate the functions of reason in human life—but part of being rational is being rational about one's own rationality. And it is good to be aware of the fact that when talking about God we are talking about much more, we are talking about ourselves too.

This essay should be not a personal statement of faith, or unfaith, or doubt, but an attempt at analysis of the modern problem of God. We should try to explain why modern man has so much more trouble to believe in God and how it is possible that atheism has become a quite respectable attitude in modern society. Thus we are faced not with a properly theological or philosophical question, but with a cultural-historical one. And we have to use sociological and psychological rather than theological concepts and modes of expression. We are dealing with man and his unbelief, not with God and his rights in this world or the sin of unbelief.

The Roots of Belief

Now, why should man believe in God? What in his life would induce him to accept the existence of something or someone beyond the reality of his life and this world, which or who would have an influence on his life and on his way of life, bind him morally, be his ultimate concern? Why should not he just accept the reality of human life as it comes, try to enjoy it, and accept the fact that it is a transitory thing? Why should man try to reach beyond himself, and seek a reality more stable than his own, and center his life around a reality other than this own? Why, in fact, should he look away from the joys and pleasures of his life and from the fulfilment he can find on this earth, and sacrifice them to a kind of life and happiness and fulfilment that he can never be sure will come? Why should not man be content with what life has to offer?

These, and similar, questions sound very reasonable and perhaps we should take them more seriously than we usually do. But that is not the point here. The strange thing is that we have to accept as sheer evidence that in fact, in a long long history, man has always developed some sort of belief in a world other than his own and found life in this world lacking in wholeness and meaning. Atheism, as a culturally defined and respectable stance, is a newcomer on the scene of history with an as yet rather short past. This is, of course, no argument against atheism. Electricity too is a new phenomenon (the technical use of it, that is) so is atomic power, and democracy as a widely accepted system of government, and science as a means of improving man's life situation, and the worldwide network of communications, and international traffic. Atheism too could turn out to be a cultural achievement of modern man. It has been described in such terms, as the final victory of man over his anxiety and as a sign of his coming of age. Nietzsche's solemn declaration that God is dead is the proclamation of man's triumph.

But this should not prevent us from trying to understand why, then, man has always believed that he should seek refuge in the reality of the superhuman and why he should not do so any more.

Human life is really an open-ended question, a question which does not contain its answer. And this question is not asked academically, by the people in the universities and schools, but it is a question to which the answer must be given by every man. There are many many attempts to define human existence, to define man; some of these definitions are optimistic, some rather gloomy, some funny, some serious, some very deep, some mysterious, some flippant. But somewhere along the line all these descriptions have to acknowledge the basic fact that man knows about himself. They are all self-definitions. They are all attempts to say what we are. And, therefore, they are all saying in one way or another that man is a problem to himself. This is a basic feature about us which we cannot avoid, and which makes us, whether we want it or not, more than just living creatures. We should note this well. This is not a condition we can choose. Life, human life, comes to us as a self-conscious life, a life that knows about itself. We could add this one to the list of definitions of man: man is the animal that asks questions about himself.

Life as Task

There is more to this: the life man knows about is not of his own making. It comes in a certain way—it comes as a finite thing, a life that has to end in death, a life that is insecure *vis-à-vis* the powers of nature, a life that is threatened even from within. It is a life that imposes itself on man as a task but does not bring with it the kind of satisfaction and fulfilment man would ask from it. In a way, we could say, life does not keep its promises, it is stacked with frustrations. We can also say that we are too big for the smallness of the life we have received. Our hopes are always more than can come true, our demands on life larger than life is willing to give. There is little help in being more realistic about it all—facing life as it comes makes it look like an odd enterprise, and absurd undertaking, or it makes us live at a subhuman level, denying the very fact that we are human. There is a strange kind of discrepancy between what we know our lives are and what we are inclined to think they should be.

Nevertheless, life is a task, it imposes itself upon us. Life cannot be lived if it is not accepted, if man does not take it upon himself to live it. To live it in face of the frustrations that beset it, to make it human, means to live it actively, to make something of it. Human life as it comes is an invitation, a challenge. It demands a sort of devotion, an active commitment, an acceptance of the task of living. What it will be depends on this willingness to make it work. Thus it requires the courage to be, the courage to live—in the face of death, of nothingness, of failure, of suffering.

These are quite common insights, nowadays, as is the insight that on the basis of this kind of analysis of the human condition we can account for the phenomenon of religion, of a religious faith, of belief in some god. What, in fact, is more natural, more understandable, than that out of his hope for the fullness of life and in the face of death man should develop a belief in a life beyond death? That out of his experience of life's goodness man should believe in a goodness that can conquer the evils that beset human life? That in his search for meaning man, not finding the full meaning of life in life itself, would call upon a source of meaning that transcends his own life, his own being, the smallness of his own existence?

We should be careful, though, not to make these connections too easily. The religious phenomenon, as found in history, is more complex and the human reality on which it rests is not so simple either. Notably one should be aware that religion is not only built on a human need for security, God being some kind of refuge, but also on the need for a motive to live, God being the ultimate concern, and it is by making this distinction that we can perhaps throw more light on this rather new thing in religious history: atheism.

The Problem of Life and the Problem of Living

When we go back to what we said before about the human condition, there are really *two* main problems, not just one. The first is the fact that life is beset with frustrations and that we should like life to be more in accordance with our own needs. The second is that whether we want it or not, we are called to live this life. We could say, perhaps, that there is a problem of the meaning of life and a problem of the meaning of living. The two problems are really quite distinct. It was Camus, I believe, who said that the basic problem for man was the question of suicide, i.e. why to live at all. That would illustrate the problem of living. It has also been suggested that the basic problem is whether man is alone in the universe. And this would perhaps illustrate the problem of life.

The two questions are not unrelated. Any good textbook on psychoanalytic theory will have some remarks about the need for relative security as a condition for an adult active life, but will at the same time define adulthood in terms of the ability to cope with the anxiety problem and to live an active and constructive life. That is, the anxiety problem, or the problem of wholeness, or—to take up our own terms—the problem of life, should be solved or dealt with before the problem of activity, creativity, living can be tackled, but the latter belongs to man's maturity, his coming of age. This is a remarkable theory because the suggestion is that maturity is not reached when one has come to terms with the problems of life, but rather when one has acquired the ability to live without being hampered by the problems of life or the anxiety problem. One has passed a stage and enters upon active life. The problems of life are left behind in order to take up the problem of living.

We can perhaps bring this view into a larger scheme of reference. What we are thinking of here is a distinction more or less in line with the one Bergson made between open and closed religion, open and closed morality. One of the striking things of life, especially in an evolutionary perspective, is that it never really submits to being fully closed. At the moment that a form of life is fully integrated in itself the form is broken open or cast aside. Evolution, growth is not possible except when the form is torn apart. This is a law, I would say, of human life too. A life that is too well integrated becomes sterile. It is the people who are still struggling who make the real contributions to the wisdom of the race, to its technical achievements. We should go even further. The fact of evolution and growth itself is apparently as much a law of life as its attempts at integrated forms, but these two are, if not completely at odds, at least in constant tension with each other. Clear examples of this kind of tension one finds in the best observable instance of growth: in the human life cycle. Up to the age at which the human individual is able to decide for himself, life is growing at the cost of stages of relative integration. More than that: growth leads away from security, and into responsibility for one's own life.

By now the reader may wonder where I am trying to lead him, but we really have not strayed away very far. The point is that we may find the same kind of tension at the basis of man's religious life, that the problem of life and the problem of living are to be viewed in a similar perspective. And I think they should. Moreover, I am sure that with this approach we can throw considerable light on the modern problem of God.

If we try to understand what both tendencies lead to in the realm of religion we will see definite connections between certain religious attitudes and elements of religious systems and a primacy of one or the other of the two ways of asking the question of meaning. The problem of life seems to lead to magic, to use of the sacred for human purposes, to a man-centered kind of religion in which certainty and security are predominant, to a religion of consolation and comfort. The problem of living approach leads to a more open, courageous kind of religion, to an attitude of service and love, to a God-centered attitude, a religion of devotion and commitment. On another level, the level of conceptualization we will find the first attitude linked up with closed systems of ideas, with dogmatic thinking, with devotionalism; the second with a searching mind, with openness to new ideas and discussions, with self-critical thought. These are, of course, very rough and unrefined characterizations which need to be worked out, but the general tendencies are clear. In religious life we find indeed a continuation of the distinctions we made earlier. There is a kind of religious life which centers around man's attempt to make himself at home in this world and which consists in filling the gaps of natural existence with supernatural elements. There is also a kind of religious life that finds living a sacred duty, a holy adventure, a god-given challenge. And these two kinds of religious attitudes are in constant tension with each other, the latter breaking down the former as growing breaks down integration.

Now, in this perspective we can, I think, understand some of the most salient features of modern atheism.

Two Kinds of God

Atheism is, this should be clear at the outset, a negative sort of thing. It does not in itself consist in a positive affirmation. It is either a negation of God's existence or the absence of an affirmation of God's existence. There may be a very positive affirmation behind it, such as the conviction that man should be willing to live his life by his own powers, or that this world is sufficient to itself. But, then, this is not atheism yet, for atheism is a consequence or an implication which has no meaning except in the discussion with theism. The word itself has no significance but in the face of the possibility of an affirmation of God. It may be the case that in fact the atheism of a thinker is very much on the outskirts of his thought, and does not really play a role in the development of his thinking. Yet, he would be called an atheist only in confrontation with the question of God's existence.

This consideration leads to an interesting implication. Atheism apparently implies an idea of God. Just as the proofs for God's existence presuppose a certain conception of God, so does the denial of God's existence. And thus we are always justified in asking what kind of God it is whose existence is being denied, or is not affirmed. Most likely the real differences occur on this level of the pre-rational definition of the God we are talking about. Most probably the modern theist, someone like Bishop Robinson, does not believe in the God the modern atheist rejects. Therefore traditional theists have called him an atheist. But the discussion is idle and void. The question lies on another level, the level of what kind of God the talk is about.

It is on precisely this level that the distinction made in this article between the problem of life and the problem of living seems to play an important role. This distinction, to be sure, is between forms of human self-experience in this world, not conceptions of God, but the two seem to be very closely connected. It does make a difference whether one feels at home in this world and is ready to work on it, or feels threatened and anguished. The kind of God one needs must be quite different too: a God who gives man his blessing and lets him work out his problems himself, or a God who is ever ready to help man in his needful existence.

For, whatever God be in his absolute being in himself, what we feel and think about him is related to the way we think and feel about ourselves. This is not to say, with Feuerbach, that all the talk about God is about man and about man alone, but it *is* about man too. And this phase of the argument interests us most.

I am aware of the dangers of bringing history into theoretical schemes. Yet, I would like to suggest that, very, very roughly, there is in human history a pattern of growth in human selfhood, man coming into his own, and that this pattern of growth reflects itself in the religious history of man. If this be granted—the space available here does not permit arguing the point—then we can indeed say that the development has been away from a problem of life attitude and toward a problem of living attitude. And in the line of the earlier discussion of these concepts we are justified in appreciating this development as a growth into maturity—which does not imply that we are at the end of the line! The processes involved here can be indicated very quickly.

The God of Precarious Life

Anyone who has some acquaintance with primitive religion—either among actually "primitive" people or among people living in this modern age—knows that it is marked by a high degree of concreteness and of a mainly magical approach to the sacred. The world of these people is filled with Sacred Presences, and qualities of the sacred inhere in almost everything. There is probably nothing in this world which has not, at some time and at some place, been considered as Holy. Trees, lakes, rivers; animals of all sorts, people of distinctive quality or social status, places and times, even human excrements, have been bearers of sacred power. Primitive man is surrounded, his whole life is ordered by these Sacred Presences. On the other hand, much of his religious behavior is an attempt at dominating these sacred powers, at putting them to his own use. He tries to get the powers to give him rain, to bless his marriage with offspring, to heal the sick. To most of us, moderns, this world of the primitive is rather far off and almost unintelligible, but it *is* a human world, a human way of life, a possibility within the range of human conduct and self-understanding. So it should be possible to enter into it and this might help us to see better where we are ourselves.

What then characterizes this primitive man? Perhaps the best way to approach him is to say that he really does not know, does not understand, the world he is living in, that is: the world of his concrete everyday life. He gives the impression of being bewildered most of the time, of not finding his way, of not being able to control his life. Life itself is very much a mystery to him, and not knowing, e.g. how to locate the parts of the body, the meaning of blood, the function of the heart, he loads them with a mysterious meaning related to the mystery of life itself. Trees, lakes, rivers, delineate the world he lives in, and are related to the powers that brought him to live this life. Not understanding causal connections he links things together which we now know don't belong together. In all sorts of rituals he expresses his will to live and to control his destiny at the same time as his powerlessness to do so effectively. His lack of understanding and control makes him feel subject to the powers that rule his life. And these powers are very concrete: famine, lack of rain, the river, the fish in the lake, the animals in the forest. The primitive lives by the grace of his surroundings. And in his effort to see meaning in it all, to create some order, he "dreams" it together into some sort of mysterious universe in which at least he can feel at ease.

Thus, it would seem primitive man is very much engaged in the task of living and in overcoming the anxieties that beset life. And there is a primary concern with life's security. It's not that the problem of living itself is not present, but it is like a hidden motive behind it all, an instinctive will to live that leads to efforts to come to terms with life's precariousness. It is out of this insecurity, this anxiety, this being subject to uncontrollable powers, that primitive religion grows. It is the need of human existence that makes man reach out to, and, in his magic, try to master these powers beyond his control, powers that he fears and wants to keep friendly, powers that in their mightiness fill him with awe, powers that are mysterious but visible, powers he has to come to terms with if he is going to live. Primitive religion, therefore, can be described rather closely in terms of the immediate experience of life's precariousness. I'm not willing to explain it fully as a projection of man's needy situation, but very definitely the forms it takes, the sort of symbols it uses, the concretizations of the sacred that characterize it, are to be seen in close relation to the experience of existential need.

The God of the Challenge of Living

Modern man looks quite different. Here we have to do with a type of man who knows fairly well how to cope with life's immediate problems, whose life is, if not fully, at any rate to a large extent secure. Perhaps it's difficult to be actually aware of some of these things since we have grown too accustomed to most of the ordinary amenities of life to see them as real accomplishments. But the food supply is not a basic problem any more, ill-health is not such a threat any more, and so on. The most important thing about it, however, is not that modern man has all these things and will have more, but that he is aware of making them himself. If anything, modern man is master over nature and in control over his life. Life's precariousness is not an everyday problem and man knows it to be his own task to make it less of a problem. Nature is not a great mystery surrounding us, but a reality which in principle is open to man's understanding and control. We may perhaps be vaguely aware that somewhere deep down it is really a mystery, and at some peculiar moments we may actually undergo a very lively experience of this mystery, but it does not enter into our everyday lives. It's not concrete, not omnipresent, not continually threatening or awe-inspiring. In fact, modern man feels quite at home in this world and he knows his way around in it. The mystery of life and nature is pushed back to the fringes of life, and disquieting facts like death and incurable illness really do not enter into the scheme of day-to-day living. Even such phenomena as guilt feelings are often successfully dealt with in psychotherapy without explicit reference to the brokenness of man's existence. Life, indeed, seems to be less precarious.

These characteristics of modern man are commonly known and do not need any further elaboration. What I would like to point out, though, is that the developments which have led up to this modern way of life are to be seen in terms of what I called earlier the challenge of the problem of living. Modern times have not come about all by themselves. Behind it all is the will of man to grow, to expand, to develop himself. The historical process that lies between the primitive situation and our own days is a process in which man has gained control over nature, in which, gradually, he has overcome his fears and anxieties and dared to go new ways by leaving the old syntheses behind. In this process, at every point of importance, man has preferred living courageously to living securely. His tendency to grow has prevailed over his tendency to seek safety.

In the realm of religion too this has been a dramatic process in which systems of belief have been broken down in order to free man to live out his own life and to follow new insights and new possibilities. The relative security of the observation of certain tabus had to be given up in order to inquire into their real nature, sacred customs had to be violated, cherished beliefs to be undermined, sacred usages to be sacrificed. For wherever a religious system tends to be closed it really stands in the way of those who vaguely see a reality beyond the system, another way to explain this world. It is the man who dares give up this relative security, who brings about the possibility of a new stage of growth.

In fact, this process has meant a steady desacralization of this world. The sacred, omnipresent, and realistically concrete in the primitive world had to be removed so that this world could become man's world. The sacred animal had to become plain food, the sacred tree had to be sacrificed to a new road, the confidence in magic ritual had to make room for more rational or, later, scientific devices to further the fertility of the land. The sacred had to become more abstract, less concrete. It had to be redefined so it would not hamper man in his efforts to make human life secure in this world. And, in fact, we see, in the history of man's religious life, a gradual spiritualization of the sacred, the emergence of an ever higher and more spiritual conception of the powers beyond, culminating in the monotheistic conception of the one God, or the removal of all sacred realities except the one God, Creator of Heaven and Earth, who is not part of this world but beyond it.

Hand in hand with the process of desacralization goes another development: the decrease of magical elements in religious attitudes and practices. That is to say, that, on the one hand, the higher conception of the sacred, leads to an attitude of awe and service rather than to attempts at using the sacred, and, on the other, the very growth in understanding and control over the world one lives in leads to a sort of self-reliance and self-confidence rather than to reliance on attempts to control ineffectively uncontrollable powers. To the extent that man learns to live in this world, he becomes more at ease in it, feels better at home in it, and learns, indeed, to live himself, to rely on his own work and effort. And where he begins to understand the practical working of things, where he gets a glimpse of the laws of nature, the mystery of the uncontrollable might falls away. The sacred loses therefore more and more of its concreteness and omnipresence, it is located differently, and, most of all, it is not so much the frightening power that constricts and threatens man by holding him in a rather arbitrary dependence, but slowly becomes the Father who blesses man in his efforts to live. And then, less and less, man turns to the sacred for help in concrete emergencies or tries to put the mysterious power to his use, but relies on his own power: the power of reason and technical skill.

The System and the Heretic

The struggle which we indicate here, is, this should be clear, a struggle between integration and growth, between relative security and the will to live better and more intensely. On the religious level this becomes the struggle between established religious systems and the religious duty to live out human possibilities—between a sacred order of life and a sacred order to live—in which the latter carries the day. We should be quite honest about this. Where religion, historically, has furthered human progress, it was by breaking down earlier established forms—and it helped only as long as it had not become a system itself. Every religious innovator of importance has been a heretic in the system he denied. Socrates was ordered to kill himself on the charge of atheism, and Jesus too was the victim of late Judaism in its introverted systematized form. And, whether founded explicitly on a religious basis or not, we find in every creative movement in history some of the elements of a religious devotion to a great cause. It is commonly accepted now that Marxism in its prime was, and still is a quasi-religious movement. The kind of dedication it asks and is able to evoke, the enthusiasm of its devotees and their willingness to suffer for its ideals have often been noticed as being basically religious in nature. We can hardly deny either that in fact it has been a very progressive movement which has changed Western society rather deeply and for the better. Would the injustices of the capitalist system have been overcome without it? It would be hard to prove that the most significant parts of modern social legislation are not related to the Marxist protest. And it would be sheer intellectual dishonesty if we did not evaluate this Marxist initiative as a real contribution to human progress.

One may have the feeling that at this point I am leading the reader astray. Marxism clearly is an explicitly atheist movement and should not be called a religion. I agree, no orthodox Marxist would accept the epithet. But there is in the Marxist movement, and in other atheist movements for that matter, a strong motivation that, at any rate, looks very religious. And we should acknowledge that they are appealing to value apprehensions that are basic to the Christian movement too. Their atheism looks very much like a protest against a belief in a God who stands in the way of real human progress—which is progress in the Christian view also: the furtherance of social justice in the community of man. We have a right, I think, to interpret this particular social movement and, more generally, a good deal of modern atheism as a religiously inspired protest against an established form of religion, i.e. the Christian Church, at a time when the Church really stood in the way of human progress, of the growth of man into maturity, which was experienced as a sacred duty.

To explain this further we have to go back again to the distinction we made earlier between the problem of life and the problem of living, or between the problem of man's insecurity and of man's task of living. The few remarks we made about primitive and modern man pointed to an important historical fact: in the course of history man has indeed managed to conquer a great deal of his insecurity, and this was because he accepted the task of living. The implication for man's religious life is that one of the basic problems on which it builds is of less and less importance. The security-pole in the subjective motivation to believe in a supernatural reality which sustains man has, if not fallen away, lost much of its force. It is the other pole, the call to commitment and courageous acceptance of the challenge of living that has gained. And this change, basic to the understanding of modern man, has made necessary a full reconsideration of the problem of man's religion and of the conception of God. A reconsideration which, in the Christian churches, is only now getting on its way.

Of course, it would be too much of an overstatement to say that modern man has fully conquered his insecurity. Life is precarious, death is a fact, and the brokenness of man's life and existence, the discrepancy between his ideals and his actual living, his guilt problem, are there to stay. But there is something in this modern type of man that refuses to take an easy way out. He would rather face the reality of his death than take refuge in the expectation of a life after death. He would rather learn to live with his brokenness than believe in some mysterious healing grace that does work apart from his own efforts. There is a great deal of honesty and realism in this man who does not want to be anything more than he is: a mortal man, who knows that he has to build his own world, his own life, to die his own death. And thus life's insecurity and precariousness are not a reason to believe in another, a larger world, but a challenge to live notwithstandnig these last limits which, as we remarked already, are not as central to day-to-day life as they were to premodern man.

Part of this attitude is due to the structure of modern man's rationality. First of all, most of this man's thinking capacity goes into the actual organization of life itself, is practical and highly rational, and deals much less with mysterious realities than with very concrete and technical problems. But, also, modern man's mind does not stand still before the mystery where he meets it. The unknown is a challenge, the universe is open to his imaginative mind and he has learned to live with the expectation that some new discovery will open up even further perspectives, even farther reaching possibilities. He does not live in a closed universe, does not even want to close his view on it, to round it off. He does not need to fill the gaps in his understanding. Something might be discovered which would solve the problem and in principle there is no limit to his understanding. He may be vaguely aware of limits, but he is fairly sure we have not reached them yet. He has seen too many victories over nature to believe that he cannot solve some of the riddles that seem to go beyond his power at the present time. To bind himself to a God who would fill the gaps of his knowledge would be counter to his experience that these gaps could be filled otherwise.

Doing Without God

Even more incisive perhaps than these two characteristics of modern rationality is the insight man has gained into his own being. Philosophy, psychology, sociology have brought him to distrust his own thoughts. He is aware of his basic irrational nature and of the danger that his affirmations, if not controlled by serious self-criticism, might be just projections of his deeper wishes. Believing in God might be a father-projection or an hypostatization of society. He has seen and studied the history of man's religious life and understood some of the human realities that were objectified in religious symbol systems. It is not impossible; on the contrary, it is most likely that some of man's religious ideas and beliefs are in fact sheer projections of man's own frustrations. I have referred to this view earlier in this article and accepted it. But how could one firmly believe in a God if one cannot be sure that he is really there? His existence is not controllable, not a fact. We can never really point to him, say where he is, and it is only too likely that we believe in him because we are not willing to face the real facts of life. We would perhaps like him to exist and be a father to us, but is not this escapism? Does not life itself teach us the hard lessons of illness and death? And once you have accepted these facts and learned to live with them, it is amazing how life can still be exciting and good. It is amazing indeed how well we can do without God. We do, most of the time, all of us. This world is man's world, and we can and should be at peace in it.

All of this really comes down to denying, one way or another, man's need for God, for a God to fill the gaps. I think that this is what Bonhoeffer meant when he said that in a world come of age, in a world that can do without the god-hypothesis, we should live as if there were no God. God is not there any more where he was necessary to round off this world: the by definition inexplicable Being that was brought in to explain the inexplicable, the comforter who would take away the edge of life's harshness, the refuge that would make life seem less serious than it is. This God man does not need because he has become aware of himself and would rather be just what he is: man, man in this world. That is also what Nietzsche felt: this God prevented man from being really himself, and man won by killing God. God is dead, so man can live. It is the God who was said not to allow medical treatment of children, and the God who was said to have declared that the sun turned around the earth, and the God who had created all people equal except the Negroes and the Jews and the working class, and the God who made evolutionary evidence a lie. It was, in one word, the God who urged man to accept his life and made it unnecessary to work for its betterment.

It may seem that I am overstating the case in this way. And, in a way, indeed I am. The picture is indeed more complicated. Not all atheism is a real fight against this God. Much of it, statistically perhaps most of it, is rather simply not asking the question. But, apart from the fact that this might be true of much traditional theism too, it should not be forgotten that this widely spread atheism is, in fact, the consequence of not needing this God any more, of lives whose security is ascertained in a world that seems to be able to cope with its own problems. This atheism appears often as a system as closed as the religious systems against which the protest was directed. And there is also an atheism that suffers under itself, an atheism that is not triumphant at all, for which human existence is indeed absurd and tragic but that cannot overcome intellectual doubts and cannot arrive at faith. But here we have to do with an atheism for which God is the one we characterized, for which God is the miracle worker who has become unbelievable or a refuge unworthy of man, and which does ask the question, more basic than ever, of the problem of living but does not arrive at an answer, does not dare to arrive at an answer. And lastly, there are theists for whom God is not the kind of God I characterized above, for whom God is not an easy refuge or an inhibition on man's growth, or well-defined key to the problems of the universe we live in. It is of these I want to speak now.

He Who Orders Man to Be Man

All through this article runs the distinction between man's need to see meaning in his life as a given situation and man's need to find a motive to live out his life, to grow. I have tried to argue that modern atheism is linked up with the conflict between these two in the sense that where religious conceptions, and the conception of God, are too much bound up with the first side of the dichotomy, they are likely to be the victim of man's growth. I've maintained also that this process of growth itself is or can be a religious event. I should show now what conception of God would be at the basis of this religious orientation.

If the "God of security is dead" (as Verhoeven expresses it) it does not mean that God is dead. God may enter a life by way of making it into a sacred duty. God may be conceived of as the Commissioner, as the Creator who by making man able to carry responsibility, calls him into responsibility. God may be the one who puts man in charge and orders him to be man. God may be the one who demands justice and love in this world and who orders man to explore the universe and to conquer it. God may be the answer not to the quest for wholeness and security, but to the question why I should go on and live this life. The Creator may be not the one who structured the universe so that man might live happily, but who gives the universe to man to live in and who is now creating with man. God may be the one who pushes me on, who plagues my conscience when humanity is violated, who gives me that thirst after justice and righteousness, who needs man to make this world into his kingdom of peace and justice and love. God may be the one whom we see behind all those who really could take up their lives courageously and die for their fellows' sake or go beyond their peaceful lives to consecrate themselves to their fellows' salvation. God may be that mysterious power that we see at work in human history which makes for growth, strength, maturity, courage, love, justice, righteousness, greatness, self-sacrifice, endurance, wisdom, freedom, honesty.

It is, of course, a dangerous course, and a methodologically false one at that, to try and build a conception of God which would fit modern man's mind. We cannot create the convictions we want to live by. Convictions grow out of our essential experiences, our realistic thinking, our lives. And realistic thinking is not to construct a world I would like to live in, but to take account of real experiences, to order them and to bring them into some sort of relationship. Talking about God also means separating out some experiences and naming them and recognizing their special meaning. Talking about God means: to say *when* God is, what kind of experiences we have in mind when we say that God is. God is but a name, a name which has no meaning if it is not related to a reality which enters into man's life. And what we mean by the name of God is that sort of presence that is not really our own presence to ourselves, but a presence that is greater than we are, a presence which transcends us and takes us up into being more ourselves that we are by ourselves. And thus we should be able to enter into our own lives and discover what we can, really, mean by God, and by daring to name him, we would give more importance to what makes us better and more human, we would focus our lives on what is best in us. In this way we are not constructing a concept of God that would fit modern man, but trying to take account of how God is still with us in a modern world in which we have learned to live without magic, without a God who would give rain and health and a good business deal and cheap forgiveness, without a God who would not take man seriously.

This does not solve all the problems. It does not pretend to. But it is a way into a more open thinking about God and modern atheism. It is a way of finding God in the center, at the very base of life, and not at its fringes. It is a way to make faith a living reality and not a Sunday affair. And if one objects that I am not really talking about God, I can only say that when you take the Bible and read the scriptures again in this light, you may make some very curious discoveries. The God of Abraham, Isaac and Jacob, the God who sent his prophets to Israel to protest against the injustices of the social order, the God and Father of Jesus Christ, is very much the

God who calls man into obedience and responsibility, who challenges man to go into all the depths of his own being, to meet face to face with the ugliness of sin, with the hypocrisy of a religion that turned God into a handyman and had domesticated the Lord of Creation, with death in all its terror. Jesus is the one who on the Mount held before us a moral code which still is a challenge we have hardly tried to meet but which still appeals to the very best in us.

Does God exist? Or is God dead? What does it matter if it does not make any difference in this world? It is important that God is dead when he really is the one who justifies pettiness and injustice, who hampers human freedom and honesty, who kills the just and saves the unjust, who keeps alive ecclesiastical bodies that do not really help man to live a better and more beautiful life. It is important that he lives if he is the one who calls man to make this world more human, who prevents it from closing upon itself, from stifling into self-sufficiency, who makes himself felt in the conviction of a sacred duty to live this life as best we can, who calls us into service, service of God and of man in the realization of this world's destiny.

But this latter God, does he exist? Can we prove that he is, can we prove it sufficiently and convincingly? Can we say who he is or what he is? Can we reach so far beyond ourselves and this world, beyond the limits of our experience and understanding that we can claim to know him? Can we dare to assert the reality of someone who by definition is not part of this world and beyond our comprehension? I think the best moments of our lives are when we do not feel closed upon ourselves, or concerned about ourselves and when we see this life as a task before us, when we are aware that self-concern hampers honesty. These are the moments when we know that life is good, embedded in a mystery of goodness and love, and that we have to make our own lives such messages of goodness and love.

But then we also know that life can be different, that it is precarious also in this respect, in its moral quality. There is a mystery beyond our own mystery, a mystery that is not a mixture of love and hate, but that is love and brings love and calls for love, a mystery before which we want to keep silence because it judges us and puts us to shame, but at the same time summons us to start anew. It is a mirror of identity before which we all stand and that tells us what we are and should be, before which we are not really free to choose but that intrudes upon our lives forcefully, as a Socratic demon, yet at the same time, gives us strength to try and be honest and truthful. Perhaps we cannot say much more about it without running the risk of defining too closely and again domesticating it, but it says that at the limits of our existence there is a mystery of love that is turned toward us, giving life and the commission to live, to live in love, in creative love. I call this mystery God.

And thus, finally, we can go back to the main question we asked in these pages: what is wrong with God? And the answer is, very shortly, that man has used God until he was of no use any more. But God is never only a solution to man's problems. At the point where man's problems are answered, God is the one to ask the new questions. And the less we need God the more he asks. We have learned to know him better now that he is not hiding behind man's little needs. But knowing him better means that he appears to be calling to deeper honesty and better service. And thus we have to end with another question: will modern man grow up to serve God?

The Secular and the Sacred

Robert Farrar Capon

Robert F. Capon, an Episcopal priest, is Dean and Professor of Dogmatic Theology at George Mercer School of Theology in Garden City, New York, a seminary for training men of late vocations. He holds an M.A. degree from Columbia University and B.D. and S.T.D. degrees from Seabury Western Theological Seminary in Evanston, Illinois. He is author of *Bed and Board* and *An Offering of Uncles*.

If there is a unique work to be undertaken by theology in our time, it will not, I think, be much expedited by further attention to the "death of God." Whatever meanings the phrase had (and apparently it is susceptible of a whole barrelful of them) have been advanced about as much as they can be by the mere repetition of the incantation. I believe it is time to get on with the real work to which it has pointed all along. And that work is the overhauling of our theology of the secular and of its relation to the sacred.

This is, of course, no more than what the best death of God people have been saying all along. We live in an age, they have assured us, in which the old definitions and conceptions of the sacred cut no mustard outside the Church—and very little inside it. They note that it was, as a matter of fact, *secular* idealism that fired the civil rights movement; that it is secular morality that more and more governs our attitude toward marriage and divorce, abortion and euthanasia; and that it is the secular cleavage of conservative-liberal that is the overriding intellectual force of the day. The Roman Catholic Birchite

Reprinted from *America,* The National Catholic Weekly Review, March 4, 1967 (New York), pp. 307–12, with the permission of the publisher.

feels himself far safer with a good Mississippi sheriff than with some of his own co-religionists—freedom-marching nuns, for example. The world is very much with us.

To be sure, we have always known that. In recent centuries, as well as at assorted times throughout history, Christians have been ready with an excessively fast answer to it all. It consisted of screaming: "Secularism!" "Worldliness!" "Profanity!" at the top of one's theological voice, and then of recommending a speedy, if not panicky, return to true spirituality. It comes as a bit of a jolt, therefore, that when this response is offered in our time the world turns a deaf ear, and even Christians find it hard to swallow. We know that the world is a mess, but somehow we feel that it deserves something better than relegation to the trash heap; and we all know that God is our hope and strength, but we seem to find the spiritualities of the recent past (God help us) a little too godly for our tastes.

And thus we are in a bind. The humble among us simply mope around with a bad conscience about not being able to take the old advice and get on with the job; while the arrogant jump up and down with glee and roundly condemn either the sacred or the secular. Neither of them have any solution, however. Guilty breast-beating no more solves our problems than does choosing up sides and yelling that God is (or isn't) dead. On the one hand, the relationship of the sacred to the secular is our own problem: we invented it, therefore we have to solve it—gloom, doom and depression notwithstanding. On the other hand, our own problem is precisely the relationship of the sacred to the secular; therefore the premature dumping of one in favor of the other (no matter how cleverly it is done) solves nothing.

Our real work, then, is to pick up all the pieces and start plying our rightful trade as Christians. While we have been out on our psychological, sociological and anthropological larks, while we have been wandering down the pleasant paths of Hist. Relig. 14 and Lit. Crit. 23, theology has been waiting for us. And when they have all run their course, it will still be there. The dogmatic enterprise and the ascetic pursuit do not go away when we do. My proposal, therefore, is that we get back to them with all deliberate speed. What I give you herewith is a small valise for the return journey.

Let me try to put a few sections of the current picture in perspective.

Where did we acquire our penchant for divorcing the sacred and the secular? What did we do to the theological mayonnaise that caused it to separate so badly?

Mayonnaise! The analogy is more apt than it is startling. It suggests that the fault lies not in the ingredients, but in the handling of them. Mayonnaise is a paradox: oil, eggs and vinegar are an unlikely combination; it takes a good cook to bring it off. Ditto for a sound theology of God and the world.

Let us list the ingredients, then. First, there is God, eternal and uncreated. Second, there is creation, temporal and unnecessary. Did we forget anything? Ah! yes. The seasoning. The salt and mustard of theology: the *goodness* that gives both God and the world their *taste.* They are both *good:* God, necessarily good, and the world, unnecessarily good. God, good just because He *is;* but the world, good because the eternal and creative Word continually and effectively pronounces it so—because, on each successive day of creation, from the beginning to the end, God looks at it and says: "Good." Good. Great. Marvelous. Terrific. *Tov. Tov meod.* Very, very good.

The world exists by virtue of the divine *applause,* by means of the intimate and immediate delight that God has in the sons of men, and in the being of everything that is. It does not exist because long ago He overproduced Himself and is now stuck with a burdensome inventory of creatures. It *is* because He *likes* it—because He shouts an ever-present *bravo* to the *bravura* of its continuous being. More, each thing exists because He likes *it.* The world is no forgotten stamp collection locked away in God's albums for rainy-day attention; it is a gleaming brass washer, a gorgeous beach pebble, a bright ball bearing that God carries in His vest pocket. He keeps it *on His person,* because He will not get its delight out of His system.

Very well, then. Excellent ingredients. The makings of a mayonnaise of surpassing quality. How did we contrive to produce the curdled mixture we have come up with?

Well, first we forgot that God's presence in the created order was *mysterious,* not simple. He made a world utterly dependent on Himself, which, oddly, was capable of standing on its own two feet as if it owed nothing to anybody. He left it up to the rabbits to make more rabbits, to the mushrooms to take care of their own multiplication, and to man to wipe his own nose and write his own letters to the editor. God was intimately present in creative delight, but He was continually self-effacing, because His delight was wholly in the beloved creature.

Once we had forgotten that, the mistakes grew easier. Everyone took to asserting half-truths. The pious said that God was really doing everything even though it didn't look like it, and the profane insisted He was really doing nothing, even though that made no sense. The one abandoned the independence of the world for the sovereignty of God, and the other abandoned the mystery of the divine support of creation for a world that was supposed to be self-caused. The one lost the creation, the other, the Creator; and both proceeded to anathematize each other.

In due time, the world-deniers developed a version of Christianity that was too spiritual to be true. Redemption consisted of unloading the nasty old world as quickly as possible and flying off to a distant heaven. The good news of Jesus Christ was proclaimed to be the promise of an eventual sacred lollipop to make up for the loss of a secular toy. They elaborated diagrammatic Oriental theologies, and anti-material asceticisms, they filled the world with Gnosticisms and Manicheisms of all sorts, and they had their perfect work in the standard cartoon picture of heaven: a lonely figure in a white sheet with two useless wings, a hopelessly inadequate harp and nothing better than a cloud to sit on. They explained heaven, you see, at the cost of earth. They made man's eternal home a monumental irrelevancy in which no sane man would willingly spend five minutes. They gave him a theological mayonnaise of insufferable blandness, all eggs and oil, and no vinegar at all.

On the other hand, the godless world-affirmers did no better. Neat secularity makes no better sauce than neat sacredness. When the world ceases to be the gift of the delight of God, it has only two ways to go: it will become either a curse or an idol. Consider it first as a curse.

When the world is all we have, it quickly turns into a philosophical albatross around our necks. Its past performances take a lot of explaining. (Remember that no matter how we praise the secular city, it is, in fact, the secular city that killed the prophets, incinerated the Jews and is currently stumbling along into something less than the best of all possible worlds.) The utter secularists, of course, urge us to proclaim the death of God with gladsome sound and get on with the business of committing our ship to the winds of the secular sea. I think, though, that we may all be excused if we choose to keep one hand on the rudder.

Only the bright-eyed social optimists of the late 19th and early

20th century ever thought that the kingdom was on the way in, here and now, and they arrived at that conclusion by including a little divine or deterministic jimmying in their scheme of things. The utter secularists have inherited their optimism without inheriting their theology. And without that, it is hard to see (on the basis of the record thus far) that the world is going to turn into an eschatological unmixed blessing in our day. We can talk all we want about man come of age, and throw all the stones we like at the gloom of orthodoxy and neo-orthodoxy, but by George, we are still building ghettoes and we are still learning rather effectively how to hate one another. The world needs loving, to be sure, but it is not *ipso facto* the first thing in which to put our trust.

Consider the world next as an idol. If God is indeed dead, and the world *as it is* is seen as the curse that it constantly threatens to become, the only thing left to do is to deal with it *as it isn't.* Man will always trust something, until he takes the gas pipe. Accordingly, if he cannot make much sense out of what things *are,* he will take refuge in what they can be made to *mean.* When the children of Israel gave up trying to deal with the wilderness as it was, they took to idolatry. They made a calf in Horeb; thus they turned their glory into the similitude of a calf that eats hay.

But idolatry is a two-edged sword. It is not only an insult to God; it involves an implicit despising of the world. Whatever grace of metal, whatever loveliness of line, was in the golden calf went begging on the day they decided *it* was their savior out of Egypt. Once the world is turned into an idol—once man shifts his delight from what it *is* to what it *means*—he loses his grip on the real world altogether. His much touted world-affirming secularity becomes only another marcher in the dismal procession of world-missing secularisms that have in the past so dependably destroyed whatever balm there might have been in Gilead.

In any case, therefore, the result is the same. Affirm God without the world and you lose the world. Affirm the world without God and you lose it just the same. And all the while you still have to live on in it, stumped, lost and lone, with nothing but a dish of curdled mayonnaise for your comfort. Surely the members of the Mystical Body—the sharers of the priesthood of the incarnate Lord—can do better than that.

But before trying to make positive suggestions about a viable Christian asceticism in a secular age, I want to put down a few additional notes about the current emphasis on the secular. Its appearance in connection with the announcement of the death of God has not been entirely convenient.

First, a relatively kind word. If the radical theology was indeed necessary to redirect us to the secular, let us be duly grateful. No merely heavenly Christianity will ever do justice to the Incarnation. If it took all this fuss and feathers to wake us up to that fact, then three cheers for our discomfiture. Only let us remember that whatever the radical theology has done for our sense of the importance of the world, it hasn't given us too much information about the role of the Church in the world. And since God has not yet reneged on the Church—since the Church is still Jesus in His members—that means that the bulk of our work is still before us.

Second, a caution. In our new-found insistence on the importance of the secular, we should bear in mind that we are not the first and only age to give it its due. Those who will not study history are doomed to repeat it. The world has been loved, and loved marvelously, by Christians before us. Aquinas spent a lot of energy on it, and so did Francis of Assisi. And in my own tradition lie some of the loveliest lovers of all. Go and read George Herbert and Traherne before you lift a snobbish, death of God nose at the failure of Christendom to do the world justice. Our age did not invent mayonnaise, you know. We have been preceded by cooks whom we shall be lucky if we equal.

Protestantism has been cursed for lo these many years with what I call the German Academic fallacy. This consists in equating the pursuit of truth with the destruction of your predecessor's doctrines. It makes for masterly Ph.D. theses, no doubt, but it plays hob with history. It produces shortsighted men who seem to believe that it is up to them to discover, in this age, what no one so far has ever gotten right. It saddles us all with a cult of the contemporaneous, with a penchant for being theological fashion plates—which is the cause of endless mischief. No age is safe until it knows its roots in all other ages. We need old books.

Third, a criticism. *Secularity* as a corrective to the old high-and-dry concept of secularism is an excellent contribution to the theological enterprise. But secularity alone, secularity without a working doctrine of God—secularity pursued while the doctrine of creation is left in abeyance—is bound to come a cropper. It will turn into a distinction without a difference.

How do you tell the real world from the fake? Only by asking a true lover of it what it really is. You cannot decide how fat a man should be by looking at a chart. You must make your inquiries of those who look on him with delight. The chart will give you a prescribed weight to pare him down to, but only at the price of violating the man himself. "Poor old Otto. The doctors may be happy with him, but his skin doesn't fit him any more. He just doesn't look like Otto." So with the world. If you turn it over to the secularists, if you trust them to handle it properly, you run the risk of having it dieted into a low-budget monstrosity.

The world, by and large, fears the world, abstracts the world or idolizes the world. It does not love it for itself with sufficient regularity to inspire confidence. Poor old matter takes a terrible drubbing. We have lost the two sexes, for example, in a diagrammatic blizzard of Sex; we have misplaced good things to eat somewhere in a mental labyrinth called nourishment; and we have buried our cities under the mistaken notion that real things can be equated with abstract space.

What we need is to look at the world again with the eyes of a great delight. And only God's eyes will do for that. God's eyes, and ours, in His image, looking out gladly on the goodness of being. Matter *matters* before it *means*. Its *being* must be loved before its *use* can be discovered. Omit the delight of God from creation and the world will soon look as if it had been left in the custody of a pack of trolls. Soon? It does already.

The distinction between art and trash, between food and garbage, between a *soufflé au point* and a postprandial disaster—and, above all, the distinction between the Heavenly Jerusalem and the City of Hell—depends on the presence or absence of the loving eye. The world cannot be loved well without an active, conscious and deep love of Him who is the source of its amiabilities. Secularity in the presence of a dead God, or even of a temporarily suspended ascesticism is a gone goose. It will vanish in a flurry of uncritical absorptions; in the end no one will love even an onion. The world of the loveless diagrams ends neither with a bang nor a whimper. It sits down to a perpetual banquet of canned chow mein.

Fourth, an accusation. How did we lose our grip on all these delectabilities? Where did our theologies lose sight of goodness and then of God? It happened partly, I think, because we forsook our proper trade—the chewing of the cud of revelation—for browsing in fields of flowers. Sociology and comparative religion are honorable subjects, to be sure, but cows need grass or they don't give good milk. I realize that dogmatic theology is a dirty word. But without something awfully like it, we shall continue to wonder why we have so little cream to treat the world to.

That, however, is not the whole story. We have lost our grip on our treasures not simply because other pastures were more inviting, but because of spooks and goblins in our own attic. Chief among them is historical skepticism. Ever since the 19th century, and especially—with a vengeance—since Schweitzer, we have been scared out of any possibility of seeing the work of God in history. Most notably of all, we have been utterly conned out of seeing anything historical in the Scriptures.

The result has been a prodigious theological reconstruction in which the obvious heart of the matter has been renounced, and fearful and wonderful formulations have been offered for what is left. We have had incarnational theologies, for example, that find the Incarnation in the present, or that find it everywhere, or nowhere, or that locate it in the eschatological future and assign it a mystical property by which it works backward into the now. In short, we have Incarnation everywhere but where the eternal Word was conceived by the Holy Ghost and born of the Virgin Mary.

It is all a bit odd. Not from the point of view of orthodoxy, mind you. (Most of it has been put forward before.) It is just odd as a system for handling a subject. It has a Ptolemaic ring to it. Ptolemy succeeded in explaining the motions of the heavenly bodies even though he took the earth as central. Having gotten the heart of the matter wrong, however, he bequeathed to his followers a system that required inexhaustible resourcefulness to keep it going. If a planet didn't fit, it was necessary to add three new cycles and five new epicycles to the already creaking heavenly machinery. The work was kept up with great ingenuity, and by means of brilliant improvisation—until Copernicus came along and pointed out that if you put the sun in the center, you didn't need all that fancy gear.

So, too, theology in our day. We have multiplied sociological cycles and Oriental-style epicycles until the mind grows dizzy with admiration. But all the while, what we are really waiting for is a Copernican revolution that will put the system back in the real world of revealed theology. If the orthodox among us will only put their house in order, we will find that it is possible once again to do the work of the death of God without the danger of the death of God. But it will not happen without exorcizing the spooks. The attic must be dehaunted. All things considered, it has the best view in the whole house. It is time to break out the holy water and reclaim it.

Fifth (and last), an observation. What has happened to theology in our time is that we have attempted a doctrine of redemption without a solid doctrine of creation. If you try to talk about Christianity in the face of a serious belief in the real absence of God, you end up with something that makes no sense at all. After all, God redeems because He likes what He has made and hates to see it flushing itself down the drain. It is precisely the *Creator alme siderum* who comes down *ne perderet quos condidit:* the gracious Word by whom the stars were made became incarnate to prevent the loss of the loveliness He created. To be sure, He saves it by a super-elation, carrying it to a second glory far beyond its first, but He saves *it.* If we will not talk germanely about His first love, we shall hardly understand His second.

As a matter of fact, we shall do worse than that: we shall end up *mis*understanding His second. For the theology of creation will not allow itself to be neglected. If it is not handled for itself, it will horn in on our treatment of salvation and turn that into a covert theory of creation. I have Altizer in mind here. He will not discuss God as Creator. Accordingly, when he comes to discuss Christ as Redeemer, he is forced (by his awe of all the historico-skeptical spooks) to treat redemption in general terms. Incarnation becomes a kind of quasi-Oriental, non-historical coincidence of opposites, which is either a universal condition to be found everywhere or an eschatological truth working backwards from an as yet unattained future. It is, of course, a brilliant synthesis. But it is also a million miles away from the Christian categories of the Son of Mary, the Israel of God, and the priesthood of Christ present in the Holy Catholic Church to draw all men unto Himself. Altizer is not only in another league. He is playing another game.

You cannot generalize, you cannot Orientalize redemption. That is only to act as if its categories were the same as those of creation, and to lose both doctrines in the bargain. It is to slip covertly but surely into the Oriental world of Yin and Yang, where nothing ever really happens and where the last truth of the created order is that it is a front for an omnitolerant All that doesn't give a damn. It is, for all its exaltation of the secular, to lose the secular in the great

Eastern Sacred with a capital S. Gone is the divine exclusivity that chose Abraham, gone are the utterly directional vagaries of the children of Israel, gone is the linear, thrusting drama of the Incarnation and the Catholic Church, gone is the hidden progress of the City of God roaring like an express train through the cuts and tunnels of the created order—gone, above all, is the New Jerusalem as the fulfillment and flowering of this amiable old world we loved and knew. And in their place is only a metaphysical carrousel, which circles perpetually until Buddha awakes from the dream of creation and opens his eyes upon the Nothing that is the last revelation of all.

The wind from the East has already begun to blow. Hold on to your hats. It will be the death of us, for sure, unless we get our theological overcoats out of the Judeo-Christian closet in the attic and put them in wearable condition.

All our needs go back, therefore, to the reclaiming of our attic from the demons who have so long possessed it. We come at last to our rightful subject. The apostles, with all the good will in the world, tried their hand at casting out a few devils. They were amazed at how little effect sincerity has on goblins. Our Lord explained it to them patiently: "This kind goeth not forth but by prayer and fasting." Ascetics has been waiting for us even longer than dogmatics.

This is the weakest point in the whole contemporary theological structure. It is all very well to say that we must wait as men without God, if you are thinking of how best to make your apology to a world that has no use for Him. But if the advice is taken literally, within the household of faith, it cuts the roots of the deepest delight for which we were made. Out of deference to the world's dyspepsia, we may find it propitious to drink water in public; but we have wine at home. To forget the splendor of our cellar is to pretend that our greatest treasure doesn't exist.

Here, however, we must be careful. It is so easy, at this point, to urge a return to spirituality in the old terms—to suggest simply that we get back to seeking God in prayer, and acquiring self-discipline through fasting—and, by every such counsel, to slip back into the overspiritualized asceticism that even we know will not work. What is needed, therefore, is a re-examination of the *basis* on which we pray and fast, a clear enunciation of what it means to be a *Christian* in one's prayer and fasting.

As soon as you attempt that, the picture begins to clear again. For Christian prayer is the prayer of Christ the Incarnate Lord, offered through His Mystical Body, the Church. It is not an individual spiritual exercise, comparable, save for its phrasing, to all the other praying in the world. It is not even the finest, best and chiefest of all such exercises. It is a new exercise—not the prayer of natural man, but of the new man Christ Jesus. It is the prayer of the Second Adam, offered as a vehicle for the praying of the First Adam. It is not my prayer or your prayer, first of all, but the Lord's prayer, the Lord's praying in us and through us.

We miss the point of the sacramental principle when we look on the ordinances of Christ as merely occasional rites. The Lord's Prayer and the Eucharist are precisely *sacramental*—that is, effective signs, not of something odd imported from the outside, but of something abidingly true, continually present on the inside of the Church's life, and effectively manifested in the sacrament. Jesus does not, in the Eucharist, arrive in the midst of a congregation from which He was absent; rather, He makes the sacrament to be a real and effective outcropping of what was there all along: His sacred humanity mystically present in the Church. We do not receive something new we never had. Instead, we are really confirmed in what we already are.

So, too, with prayer. The Lord's Prayer was not given to us as a kind of divine conceptual model from which we could derive an idea of how to pray privately. Rather, it was enjoined upon us because the whole prayer of a Christian is Jesus' prayer, just as his whole life is Jesus' life. In the Lord's Prayer, we have a sacramental outcropping of that principle. We do not simply imitate the Lord's praying when we recite it. We do more. We enter into it. We climb aboard it. It is effective not because it is roughly like the prayer that Jesus once prayed, but because it is exactly the praying that Jesus now does as the great high priest, in and through His Mystical Body.

Any other notion of prayer is too general for Christian purposes. It puts us back in the old morass of comparative asceticism, just as the failure to see the Church as the Body of the Incarnate Word traps us in the bog of comparative religion. The reason why we have had no viable asceticism to offer to a secular age is precisely that we have let slip the utter secularity of Christ's presence in the Church. We have turned the Church into a club of Jesus' admirers, into an association for the propagation of Jesus' teaching—into everything but what it really is: Jesus Himself in us. The Church is not *about* Jesus; it *is* Jesus. He is present in all too earthen vessels, to be sure; but Chateau Latour 1945 in a coffee cup is still Chateau Latour 1945.

The acts of the Christian religion, therefore, have no *proper* effectiveness as religious acts. Recent theologians who have harped on the notion that Christianity is not religion have had a point. So have the reformers who pointed out that we are not heard for much praying—or much anything else. But the followers of both of them wandered from the truth of those insights when they concluded that therefore the Christian may safely sit loose to *religious acts.* The motions of Christian piety are so many entrances into the praying, the fasting, the obedience of Jesus. As the Lord's Prayer is my door into *His* converse with the Father, so my fasts are roads into His passion, my crosses gateways to His death and resurrection. Christianity still uses the *forms* of religion; but as accesses to a new and perfect *substance,* not as availing in themselves.

The realization of that truth is salutary several ways. First, it restores to us the sanity of the Reformation, without depriving us of the practices that we sometimes foolishly abandoned, or else used with a questioning conscience. But second, it liberates us from the terrible burden of thinking that unless we can come up with a red-hot prayer life of our own, we cannot present ourselves to the world as pray-ers at all. Let us be honest: we don't, by and large, pray very much or very well; but it doesn't matter all that much so long as we pray in obedience. The prayer of the Church is the prayer of Jesus. It is already going on full tilt. It is not up to us to invent it, but only to join it, to enter it, by whatever sacramental acts of prayer we can offer.

There, if you will, is the greatest ascetical blunder of the God is dead theology. *It isn't all up to us. Any* obedience will make an entrance into the high-priestly intercession of Jesus. If we can't come up with a de luxe version intelligible to our age, we can still use the old ways until we think of something better. But even if we could come up tonight with the clearest, most communicative expression of prayer in a secular age, it would still, in itself, have no *proper* efficacy; it would be only a better and more intelligible door into the endless praying of Jesus Himself. We are free to pray badly, you see. The only thing we are not free to do is not pray at all.

I shall not dwell much on the point here, but all of this leads to the absolute necessity of the rediscovery of the Eucharist as the central prayer of the Church. If all prayers are sacraments and all sacraments are doors into His praying, then the Great Sacrament is the greatest door of all, the main portal of the ascetical life. The Eucharist is the principal, signal outcropping of the nature of the whole Church. It is the evident diagram, the effective form, of what we are as the body of Christ. Until it is central once again, we shall continue to see our face in a glass and straightway forget what manner of man we are.

For it is the Eucharist that is the choicest vehicle for the recovering of our sense of the priesthood of the Church as the true point of contact which we have with the secular age. It is in the Eucharist that the Church once again sees itself as the Body of Him who came to lift, to offer the secular order, and who, by His lifting, draws all men to Himself. Only the Eucharist is sufficiently secular to be recognized by this age as meaningful prayer; but alas, we have hid our light under a vast assortment of bushels and excuses. We have omitted, in a dozen ways, the clear proclamation of the one act by which the world might see our asceticism as something other than a flight from the secular.

What our age needs is a vision of the Mystical Body of Christ again at work gathering the world into the sacred humanity of the New Adam, a vision of the Church once more concerned with the world, and not simply with religion misconceived as mere godliness. If there is any act of prayer that is readily available to us, it is intercession. And if there is any age in which the Church is ideally situated to intercede, this is it.

The pioneer on his farm met the world—the city—once a week when he went to market, or once a day if someone came down his road with a piece of news. Man in our day meets the world a dozen times an hour. The city is never absent from him. He lives in the midst of it: he breathes its air, mouths its slogans, thinks its thoughts, and, by a hundred technological intimacies, is the familiar of all its goods and all its evils. Accordingly, the Christian in our day—the Church in our day—draws the world willy-nilly into the intercession of Jesus unceasingly present in His Mystical Body. All we need is to act out what we already are.

We are the sacrament of the world within the priesthood of Christ; and we are the sacrament of that priesthood within the world. Do you understand it correctly? We *are*. Not should be, may be, could be, shall be. We *are*. Both of them. The only disaster that could befall us would be to try to play one off against the other—to leave one alone until we get the other straightened out.

Forget style. Forget success. Forget the temptation to wait for a neat synthesis. Act. Act in the world. Delight in it. Build it. Love it. Pity it. Heal it, if you can. Curse it, if you must. But act. And act in the Church. Enter the high-priestly intercession of Jesus by prayer and fasting. Go in by any pieties you can manage, modern or antique. *They* may not be germane, but *you* are and *He* is, and that is enough for any present. He did not rise from the dead to have His work fail now. . . .

A Spirituality for a Time of Uncertainty

José-María González-Ruiz

José-María González-Ruiz, a priest of the diocese of Málaga, Spain, studied at the Gregorian University and the Institut Biblique, both in Rome, earning his doctorate in theology in 1940 and a degree in Sacred Scripture in 1953. He was Professor of the New Testament at both the seminary in Málaga and the University of Salamanca. His published works include a number of books on St. Paul and numerous articles for theological journals and biblical encyclopedias.

The free circulation and expansion of a dynamic and historicist spirituality, such as the deepest vision of the bible postulates, has up to now been prevented by the enormous weight of the old Hellenic tradition.

The great "metaphysics" of the West—those of Plato, Aristotle, Augustine and Malebranche, for example—display coordinated constants of this spirituality of "preestablished transcendence." According to them, morality does not have to be developed; it exists prior to the thinker's reflection, and all he has to do is discover it. It is the sum total of laws derived in logical progression from the characteristics of the universe and the place man occupies in it.

The concept of preestablished morality has come under attack today from Marxist and existentialist humanism. "Man makes himself," says Sartre; "he is not something already made; he makes

Reprinted from "A Spirituality for a Time of Uncertainty," by José-María González Ruiz, in *Spirituality in the Secular City, Concilium,* Vol. XIX (Glen Rock, N.J.: Paulist Press, 1966), 59–72, with the permission of the publisher.

himself by choosing his morality, and pressure of circumstances is such that he has no choice but to choose one." [1]

The Czechoslovakian Marxist philosopher Karel Kosík asks likewise: "What does man work out in history? The design of providence? The march of necessity? The progress of liberty? In history man works himself out. The meaning of history is to be found in history itself; in history man explains himself to himself, and this historical explanation—the equivalent of the creation of man and of humanity—is the only meaning of history." [2] Kosík himself attributes this revolutionary anti-theological concept of history to none other than Cardinal Nicholas of Cusa who wrote, "*Non ergo activae creationis humanitatis alius extat finis quam humanitas*"—the active creation of humanity has no other end than humanity.

We must frankly acknowledge that, in the moral tradition that sociologically passes for Christian, the aspect of the "ready-made model," seen as the only possible basis for a valid moral order, has been overemphasized. This concept reduces the moral life of man to the mere carrying out of transcendent concrete laws, valid *a priori* and unchangeable in time and space. Basically, this anthropological vision implies a negation of history. Men would have no more bonds between them than a series of lines converging on one preestablished point; the human adventure would have no meaning. In the place of history it puts a gigantic bureaucratic system of the order of some preexisting absolute value, which can be God or Progress or Reason or any other illusion of the human mind written with a capital letter.

Those who refuse to accept this purely executive sense of man's creative activity do not claim that individual action is an absolute initiative in history, disconnected from the sum total of previous achievements or outside human confines. "If the first basic premise of history," Kosík continues, "is the fact that it is *made by man*, the second and equally basic premise is the need for *continuity* to exist in this making. History is possible only insofar as man is not always beginning anew and for the first time, but is continually linking himself to the work and results achieved by preceding generations." [3]

There is no space here for a detailed analysis of the failures—and achievements—of this "morality of the preestablished order" over the course of nearly 2,000 years of Christian tradition. I simply

1 *L'existentialisme est un humanisme* (Paris, 1965), p. 78.
2 *Dialektika konkrétního;* It. tr.: *Dialettica del concreto* (Milan, 1965), p. 260.
3 *Ibid.*, p. 261.

propose to go back to the fountainhead, to start from the historical sense of the spirituality of the bible itself. The religion of the bible differs radically from all other historical religions through its particular concept of "spirituality." While in other religions "spirituality"—man's relationship with God—is obtained at the price of a greater or lesser renunciation of the task of building up the human world, in the bible man is bound to God—"the image and likeness of God"—by virtue of his responsibility for the transformation of the cosmos in which he lives and has his being (Gen. 1, 26).

Now this task of "creating history" is imposed on man with all the consequences entailed by his creative autonomy. In fact, for the Semites, to "name" something was the equivalent of having the power to transform that thing. So in the story of the six days of creation God "names" what we could term the previous objective conditions of history: light, darkness, the firmament, the dry land, the waters, the sun, the moon. But the animals—the first object of man's intervention—he leaves unnamed. The God of the bible adopts a paradoxical attitude of expectancy toward man's transforming activity, ". . . to see what he would call them" (Gen. 2, 19).

In the context of world religions, as H. Duméry has clearly pointed out,[4] a further absolute novelty in the bible is that it presents history as revealing God; to whatever extent man is made responsible for the making of his own history, a God who presents man with a ready-made model for him to copy purely and simply is inconceivable within the framework of the biblical viewpoint. Neglect of man's creative responsibility in forming himself has tinged Christian spirituality with security and stability, very far from the true nomadic character of the great believers and prophets described in the bible.

I

Christian Spirituality Is a Bond with a Transcendent and Gratuitous God

To speak of a transcendent God with whom man forms spiritual links is to oppose transcendence to immanence, but not to "incarnation." The strict monotheism of the bible continually emphasizes the transcendence of God, conceived as a radical resistance to the intra-creatural reductibility of divinity. God always has to remain outside the intrinsic web of human and worldly dynamism. There is no

[4] *Phénoménologie et religion* (Paris: P.U.F., 1962), p. 9.

reason to consider God as an immanent explanation of the enigmas of the human mind or an intrinsic cog in the mesh of reality created in evolution.

Throughout the whole bible there appears, time after time, the anguished cry of the just man who meets with failure, constantly asking God why he has departed from him and left him at the mercy of the internal rhythm of history. Not even the greatest of the just who fail is exempt from this cry of interrogation. Jesus himself died repeating in anguish the lament of the psalmists and the prophets: "My God, my God, why hast thou forsaken me?"

The temptation to immanentize God so as to manipulate him to the tune of an ordered sequence of events is described in the bible as belonging to the very infra-structure of human history: in the middle of the Garden of Eden stands the tree of universal knowledge ("of good and evil"), and the tempter assures man that just by stretching out his hand and eating the fruit of the tree he will immediately obtain what would otherwise be the end result of a long and difficult process of elaboration (Gen. 2, 17; 3, 2–4). Man commits the sin of "magic"; he uses a device to hasten the process and abuses religion so as to free himself from the charge laid upon him of building up history with the resources given him.

Religion becomes a force of "alienation" to the degree that the believer abandons the uncomfortable position of being bound to the absolutely transcendent. Men try to scale God down so as to fit him into a pattern of immediate utility and offer him the place of honor on the boards of all great human enterprises.

Now this being bound to the absolutely transcendent has to be achieved in a dialectical rhythm, a difficult rhythm to which human laziness often refuses to adjust. The biblical God, the "utterly other," is not absent from the dynamics of human history; on the contrary, he constantly impinges on it and involves himself in the affairs of men without ever coming to belong to them. The transcendent God of the bible is the God of Abraham, Isaac and Jacob. "Yet he is not far from each one of us, for 'in him we live and move and have our being'" (Acts 17, 27–28; cf. Is. 55, 6; Ps. 145, 18; Rom. 1, 19).

But his presence is completely gratuitous. There is nothing in the intrinsic mechanism of the cosmos or the course of history that needs God as the immanent explanation of being or becoming. In the bible we constantly find God described as the one who is coming—God is *ho erchómenos*—knocking at the door of human consciousness when least expected, coming like a thief in the night (Mt. 24, 43; Lk. 12, 39; 1 Thess. 5, 2; 2 Pet. 3, 10; Apoc. 3, 3; 16, 15). The biblical God is a "thief-God" whose presence cannot be taken into account in the daily run of domestic economy.

This dialectical tension between transcendence and incarnation can be broken by an undue emphasis on one aspect or another. In the first place, there is a sort of sin of excessive emphasis on transcendence: God, being utterly other, requires of those who adore him a complete or at least partial estrangement from their spatio-temporal context. Religion then retreats into "places of worship"; these form federations and become hallowed precincts within whose walls a life of evasion and flight is carried on. The religious man becomes someone literally "set apart," someone who organizes the administration of his life within the confines of a *sacra civitas*.

In the history of Christian spirituality this pole of evasion and estrangement can easily be recognized in religious orders and various schools of perfection. They give the impression that man lives in an autonomous religious universe, somewhere beyond which dwells the profane sphere, and a heavy entrance fee is normally demanded at the frontiers of the religious universe.

An inevitable consequence of this excess is an over-valuation of grace. The possession of grace becomes a key to human fulfillment, which in some way dispenses its owner from the need to use other instruments of progress and advancement. The option for "the one thing necessary" is constantly preached. It is this that Marxist humanism is criticizing in its stricture on religion as "the opium of the people."

This "transcendentalist" excess of Christian spirituality has its hidden psychological motivation in a desperate search for security. The Polish Marxist philosopher Hans Schaff has made a subtle analysis of this *embourgoisement* of religion:

> For a believer the question is very simple: life always has a meaning—i.e., it is worth living, under any conditions—since even suffering, pain and death are in conformity with the designs of the superior being who will compensate for the sufferings of this life in the after-life or who has decided to inflict these terrestrial punishments for sins committed. Let us admit that in many circumstances—and in this case too—it is very comfortable to be a believer; the most difficult questions become excessively simple. But the price paid for this comfort is a crushing one: the renunciation of all scientific enquiry.

> Precisely for this reason it seems continually more difficult to allow oneself the luxury of such "comforts" and simplifications.[5]

In its attempts to avoid this transcendentalist excess, Christian spirituality shows, over its nearly 2,000 years of history, numerous examples of the opposite extreme: an excess of "incarnationalism." The hermit emerges brusquely from his cell and at one fell swoop sets himself to control the destinies of the secular *civitas.* An attempt at "reconciliation" with the "world" is made, but this is accompanied by an attitude of more or less barefaced paternalism toward it.

This process of "incarnational extremism" got off to a flying start with the Peace of Constantine and reached its apogee in the grandiose structure of medieval Christendom. When secular values started their struggle to free themselves from the yoke of religion in the 14th century, a long process of secularization was begun, which has still not fully worked itself out. The remains of this subjugation of the secular field to the religious can be seen in the sectarian attitudes that still affect important areas of economic, social and political life.

The *Pastoral Constitution on the Church in the Modern World* is a difficult and painful attempt to rid Christian spirituality of this unreasonable pretension; however, we must remember that "the world" will need abundant evidence of a change of heart before it is convinced that this is not just a piece of tactical opportunism designed to enable the Church to overcome the crisis of secularization. This "opening-up" of the Church is still regarded as a flirtation with the adversary aimed at obtaining a truce. This is how the Soviet philosopher F. V. Konstantinov sees it:

> In our day, religion and the Church are still the implacable enemies of science, which does not prevent the Vatican and other religious institutions from flirting with it and trying to "reconcile" scientific discoveries with religious dogmas. . . . The Catholic Church is a powerful political organization, with endless ramifications and a wealth of capital, property and other assets. Its center, the Vatican, is a corporation looking for spiritual take-over bids and the social exploitation of many nations. It supported the Fascist regimes and today is the ally of every sort of reaction. It supports reactionary plots. The Vatican uses Christian or Catholic political parties and other Catholic organizations to put its reactionary policies into force. In order to strengthen its influence over the workers and in-

[5] *Filosofia czlowieka;* Sp. trans.: *La filosofía del hombre* (Buenos Aires, 1964), p. 74.

tensify its fight against communism, the Church puts forth the false notion of so-called "Christian socialism," makes extensive use of demagogy and in fact acts as a spiritual stranglehold in the hands of the exploiting classes.[6]

Whatever elements of truth this view may contain, it must be recognized that in Vatican Council II the Catholic Church has clearly defined the principles of its "temporal incarnation" and roundly condemned those incarnational excesses that largely justify criticisms such as the above.

Above all, it roundly condemns "clerical domination" of the political actions of Catholics: laymen must "realize that their pastors will not always be so expert as to have a ready answer to every problem (even every grave problem) that arises; this is not the role of the clergy. . . . They ought to remember that in those cases no one is permitted to identify the authority of the Church exclusively with his own opinion." [7] At the same time, the Church states that it is not its role to produce technical solutions to problems of social structure, but to limit itself humbly and religiously to witnessing "the birth of a new humanism, where man is defined first of all by his responsibility toward his brothers and at the court of history." [8]

As Catholics we cannot but lament the gulf that still yawns between these forthright official declarations of the Church and the actions of so many of our most representative institutions. The word "Catholic," or even "Christian," is still strongly associated with numerous institutional forms of reaction in economic, social, cultural and political fields. Most lamentable of all is that the spirit of clerical domination, which still survives among us, imposes and propagates a spirituality based on bourgeois and neo-capitalist securities, and even offers them a transcendental justification.

Both tendencies—toward transcendentalist or incarnationalist excesses—are frequently united in a hidden infra-structure on which they ultimately rest. As so often happens, extremes meet. And the common element that brings them together is, without doubt, the desperate search for spiritual security. Man has a tendency to set himself once and for all in a fixed and secure position, and to rebel against the only possible stance which the true believer must main-

[6] *Fundamentos de la filosofía marxista* (Mexico, [2]1965) pp. 585ff.
[7] *Pastoral Constitution on the Church in the Modern World,* n. 43.
[8] *Ibid.,* n. 55.

tain every day and almost every minute: that of dialectical tension between transcendence and incarnation.

The more religious a man is, the more human will his basic attitude to life be; but he will never use his religion as an instrument of dominion or monopoly in the marketplace of different social, economic or political techniques.

II

Christian "Religiosity" Is Primarily Anthropo-Central

A common error of perspective in the world of Christian spirituality is to place the foreground of the believer's ethical and mystical impulses in God, and only through God in the world and in man.

This has led atheistic humanism, both Marxist and existentialist, to reproach Christianity with nothing less than destroying love of one's neighbor. In effect, if I love my neighbor simply and exclusively because he is an incarnation and representation of God it is not man that I am loving, but God in man. Man fades away before the image of God; he becomes no more than a peg on which to hang the only interesting reality, God. My neighbor will feel humiliated and degraded, sensing that he as a person is of no interest to me, except as a sort of "recommendation" from a superior being.

This misdirection of focus in love of one's neighbor can be seen in the practice of many religious institutions that are dedicated by their statutes precisely to love of neighbor. The "neighbor," the object of the cares and solicitudes of "professional do-gooders," is shown, explicitly or implicitly, that his concrete human reality counts for nothing: all that counts is his transparency that allows the divinity to shine through the fragility of his existence.

This can easily lead to a real lack of interest in the tragedy of man, the professed object of the charity. He is frequently made to feel that if it were not for the fact that he represents God, he would not deserve any attention whatsoever. This explains the "angelism" of many so-called Christian attitudes toward human reality. We boast about not knowing the tragedies of our neighbors, because in fact all that concerns us is this misunderstood presence of God in our neighbor.

And yet, throughout the whole of the bible, the opposite view is constantly in evidence. God himself interests himself in man precisely on account of his reality as man. There is a prophetic current running through the bible which continually reproaches men for trying to find a direct short cut to God without passing through love of neighbor.

It is easy for the believer to succumb to the temptation to establish a direct link with the divinity without treading the high road of contact with his neighbor. And so, a spirituality of pure transcendence grows up, taking refuge in the temple as a place of complete security. This is the spirituality of "liturgical security" which the prophet Jeremiah described in such vigorous terms (Jer. 7, 1–7). Jeremiah roundly states that *before* going into the temple, you must proceed along the only possible route of effective attention to your neighbor. This involves a recognition that God is found through one's neighbor, and not one's neighbor through God. The neighbor is considered as something with a prior existence of his own and worthy of being valued for himself.

It is interesting to note that this "theocentrism" condemned by the prophet is clearly tied to a spirituality of certitude and security: "Will you steal, murder, commit adultery, swear falsely, burn incense to Baal, and go after other gods that you have not known, and then come and stand before me in this house, which is called by my name, and say: 'We are delivered!'—only to go on doing all these abominations?" (Jer. 7, 9–10).

The neighbor is considered so autonomous in biblical spirituality that the route passing through him is held to be sufficient for eschatological salvation itself, even when it does not explicitly lead to the high road to God. In Matthew 25, 31–46, the Son of Man will recognize as his all those who serve their neighbors, even when they have not expressly recognized him in them. This is the only way to explain the question that the "good" will ask in surprise: "Lord, when was it that we saw thee hungry, and fed thee, or thirsty, and gave thee drink?" (Mt. 25, 37).

Having rid ourselves of this gross error, we must not allow ourselves to forget that our "neighbor," as an object of Christian love, is precisely a representation of God, an authentic incarnation of God. This is why the "neighbor" participates in the gratuitousness and transcendence of God, dialectically combined with his incarnation.

Our neighbor in the Christian sense is, in the first place, somehow gratuitous and transcendent. Love of our neighbor does not compete with the corresponding techniques of hominization which jostle each other in the marketplace of the different forms of humanism. It would be a mistake to imagine love of one's neighbor as a sort of universal panacea, dispensing man from his task of individual and collective auto-creation. Christian love goes beyond all human presuppositions without thereby invalidating them.

The concept of neighbor transcends the bonds of flesh, geography, race, culture and politics. The neighbor bursts into everyone's life, outside the bounds of all provisions and beyond the scope of all planning. The great novelty of the Christian message is the duty to "prove oneself a neighbor" to others—the parable of the Good Samaritan. Neighbors cannot be chosen, but they are accepted at even the most inopportune moments.

The transcendence and gratuitousness of the neighbor should show itself in a sort of allergy to institutionalization. In the same way that throughout the history of Christian spirituality men have tried to immanentize God, belittling him and trying to fit him into the framework of human comprehension, so they have tried to reduce love of one's neighbor to a set of minutely detailed rules that remove the element of surprise and insecurity from life.

This produces the not infrequent case of religious institutions, created to mold this love of neighbor into shape, which have come to the point when they plan every act of love in such detail that they leave no room for the real neighbor, who by definition transcends all calculations and provisions.

At a time like the present, when fortunately many of the causes of human insecurity are disappearing, "love of one's neighbor" is even more useful than ever. The tangled web of coordinated securities—which wrap man up to such an extent that spontaneous action becomes impossible—can only be broken in the name of absolute fortuitousness and transcendence.

However, love of one's neighbor, though resistant to immanentism, is not something abstract and distant either, but must, on the contrary, become incarnate by acting on concrete and immediate reality. We Christians have to love human beings in their unpredictable and concrete reality.

The first thing this "incarnate" love requires is to be completely in tune with men of our time and with our surroundings. An "angelist" spirituality—by making man lose his sense of history, sending him chasing, like Don Quixote, after ways of life and ages long dead and gone—seriously fails in this task of making Christian love incarnate.

This means that many of our monastic, religious and even lay institutions that seek a sort of "spiritual" security through abstracting themselves from contemporary events, will have to be revised. The absolute ban on the reading of newspapers in some religious houses, for example, can easily prevent the members from carrying out their inescapable duty of being in tune with the times, which is absolutely necessary for genuine love of one's neighbor.

Here we have to face the very real question of "compromising with the times" which is such a burning problem today for the best of active Christians. At one moment full of fight for the advancement of humanity, the next moment they find themselves drawing back for fear of "compromising" their essentially Christian identity by involvement in the immediate present, and in doing so appear to others as an equivocal and evasive witness in the search for new and more just historical orientations. In fact, love of one's neighbor as a typically Christian product requires for its realization a sort of dialectical tension between transcendence and incarnation.

The parable of the Good Samaritan (Lk. 10, 25–37) gives an excellent outline for the understanding of this dialectical equilibrium. On the one hand, the "neighbor" was something unforeseen and unforeseeable; the priest and the Levite passed him by because they could not see in their liturgical agenda any place for this unforeseen demand for help. They thereby renounced the transcendence of love of one's neighbor. At the same time, the samaritan did not try to comply with the normal demands of the Welfare State by the money he gave the innkeeper; he was not organizing a fund for those found wounded by the wayside; on the contrary, he understood that to "show himself a neighbor" he had to come close to a particular individual in a particular situation.

III

Conclusion

This brief survey has shown that Christian spirituality is essentially a spirituality of insecurity, even in times of certainty, which ours most certainly is not. In a time of uncertainty like ours this inevitable dialectical tension between transcendence and incarnation, which characterizes genuine Christian spirituality, needs to be stressed.

In the *Pastoral Constitution on the Church in the Modern World,* the need for this continuous process of setting up and taking down the very fabric of our religious universe is explicitly recognized: "The accelerated pace of history is such that one can scarcely keep abreast of it. Hitherto the destiny of mankind as a whole consisted of the fragmentary annals of various peoples: now it merges into a complete whole. And so mankind substitutes a dynamic and more evolutionary concept of nature for a static one and the result is an immense series of new problems calling for a new endeavor of analysis and synthesis."[9]

The new efforts of analysis and synthesis required are bound to entail a painful effort. Perhaps the resistance we put up to setting out on this dialectical road is due in large part to the undoubted entrenchment of the Church in bourgeois forms and modes of life.

I think this is the moment to shake the consciences of Christians out of this, the moment for them to set out on the true road that all real believers have trod in the wake of the father of them all, Abraham, who, when God called him to seek the land he was to receive as his inheritance, set out *without knowing where he was going.*

[9] *Ibid.*, n. 5.

The Liturgy and a Theology of the Secular

Gabriel Moran, F.S.C.

Gabriel Moran, F.S.C., is Assistant Professor of Theology at Manhattan College in New York. In 1958 he received his B.A. degree in philosophy from the Catholic University of America; he also holds M.A. and Ph.D. degrees in religious education. Among his published works are *Scripture and Tradition, Catechesis of Revelation,* and *Theology of Revelation.* He has contributed articles to such journals as *America, Catholic World, National Catholic Reporter,* and *Theological Studies.*

The world was at first considered to be the place of the gods. Ancient man did not begin by setting aside an offering from the world of the profane in order to make it holy for the gods. On the contrary, the primary word that was spoken was holy. It was only gradually that man removed a sector from the temple to make it his work-a-day world. Man discovered his own initiative and his ability to change the world. Thus there appeared man's world, a world distinct from the divine.

For a long time this world of the profane was judged to be next to nothing. The real world of ultimate truth was the archetypal world of the gods. Man was allowed a profane existence only on the condition that he continually re-establish contact with the primal reality through the divinely revealed rituals and divinely designated things. Certain provinces of nature seemed to ancient man

Reprinted from "The Theology of Secularity: What Happens to Worship?" by Gabriel Moran, F.S.C., in *Worship in the City of Man* (Washington, D.C.: The Liturgical Conference, 1967), pp. 80–90, with the permission of the publisher.

to be clear manifestations of the divine. The sea, the earth, or the sky might awaken fear, affection, or adoration. In any case, ancient man recognized that there were incomprehensible mysteries that he dared not tamper with.

As we now look back from the present, we can see that there was a long process of gradual change that altered this balance of the profane and the sacred reality. Wherever one might locate the turning point, it is undeniable that the last few centuries of Western civilization have seen the shrinkage of the sphere of the sacred. Today we seem rapidly to be approaching the end of the period of historical bifurcation. Man has taken over the whole of the universe as the province of his inquiry and the material for his work. Not even on the moon is one safe from the eye of the television camera. If there are parts of the universe yet untouched by man, this is traceable not to religious awe before the holy but to the present lack of thrust in our booster rockets.

We have come full circle, therefore, from an original simplicity, through a division into sacred and profane things, and back to a new unity. Until recently, most religious men have bemoaned this development. They have protested in the name of God against the continuing extension of man's profane interests with the consequent reduction of the number of things considered sacred and untouchable. But now other voices are being heard in Christian circles. These people are saying that not only is the process not bad but that it is something to be encouraged and applauded. For many Christians this attitude of their supposed leaders is puzzling, to put it mildly. Does it not appear that these Christian thinkers are trying to play it fast and loose by giving up the battle and saying that we were really on the other side all the time? Many people see this development in theology as the most extreme example of the Church not only baptizing what she once opposed but even claiming that she is the rightful parent.

Faced as we are with this contemporary problem of religion and secular life, it is not enough for us to give cautious approval to worldly concerns. Neither will it be sufficient to talk loudly in favor of this world while pretending that we do not have a past which speaks both positively and negatively on the matter. We spring from an historical tradition for better or worse. It is a tradition that has more to say on this question than might at first be apparent.

I suspect that much of the confusion in terminology in this area is at least partly traceable to the failure to work from any past tradition. Unfortunately, my remarks are not going to contribute much to the clarification of terminology. If I were treating this topic in scholarly fashion, I would have to define my terms carefully and give variations in different people's use of terms such as sacred and profane, secular and religious, natural and supernatural. But just to list the ways in which these words have been used would take more time than is available here. Instead, I will confine myself to describing the process that most people seem to agree is occurring. My use of terms will I hope be consistent and meaningful in the context without any pretension that this is the best or only use of the words.

In this essay I shall deal first, with the meaning of secularity and in particular the Christian view of this as a legitimate development; second, with the dangers that seem to me to be implicit in this process; third, with the implications that this valid but dangerous process has for Catholic liturgy.

The word "secularity" is of recent coinage. The extensive use of the word is still a matter of surprise for many people. When used by Christian writers, secularity is almost always placed in contrast to secularism, a better known word. Secularism connotes an attitude of mind that is closed to the worship of God and to a concern with Christian faith. The word secularity, on the other hand, means simply an attitude that affirms the goodness and relative autonomy of this world and the worldly concerns of men. If that were the whole issue, there would be few disputes about secularity. The problem is that the increased emphasis upon the secular has meant a decreasing concern with areas once thought to be religious. Whether this had to be so and whether this is a good or bad development, the fact of the process is denied by almost no one. My first aim will be to indicate why many Christian theologians think that this secularizing process is not only acceptable but is an inevitable consequence of Christianity.

What we identify as Judaic-Christian revelation came into a world in which a split existed between the realm of the gods and the less than absolute world of passing experience. In Judaic revelation there was implicit from the very beginning a denial of this presupposition of ancient religion. For if Yahweh is creator of the universe, if he sustains all on the basis of his unique gratuitous love, then all wedges that deny the unity of creation are impossible. This does not necessarily mean that there are not grades of perfection in creation and that some modes of experience are not more conducive or appropriate to divine worship. It does mean, however, that all security and coziness in an untouchable sector of the world is gone. No place, no rite, no thing is guaranteed to be the way to God. That is the negative and somewhat frightening part of Judaism-Christianity. The positive side of the same picture is the implication that God is not in the distant past but now, that no place is God's place but that all places can become the place wherein God meets man.

Judaic-Christian revelation has sometimes been described as the triumph of time over space; that is, God reveals himself in history. This is true, but it might be more accurately described as the triumph of presence over non-presence. God is to be met in the here and now. Interestingly enough, the word presence includes the spatial with the temporal. When man hears God speak in the present, then space can be human space and included in the conversation between God and man. On the other hand, when man does not live in the present but in the past, then he is no longer fully a person and space will tend to dehumanize him.

Contrary to other religions that found God in some realm of things outside man's daily, temporal experience, Judaism-Christianity represented the approbation of history, the full acceptance of time. Put in other words it was the acceptance of the secular because secular refers not first to space or world but to time. Not only can God be found in the temporal or secular, Judaism claimed, he can be found nowhere else. The secular comes fully into its own precisely in being seen as the image and likeness of God. God meets man in real experience, and the being of man is to be in time and to be in a world; that is, man is necessarily secular.

What then of the word "religious"? Is there not a place for concern with the other worldly, the divine as opposed to the human, the worship of God as distinct from the work-a-day affairs of man. I think that it is undeniable that some distinction should continue, but the way in which this distinction has perdured has not been in entire accord with the fundamental Judaic-Christian belief. It has been too easy to defend Christianity with unchristian arguments that insist on a realm of religious or revealed things as distinct from ordinary, human things. This is the distinction that has become indefensible today. If Christianity is to be fully itself it must be concerned with the whole of man's life and not just a religious segment of life.

It is for this reason that the word religious, even in Christian writing, often has a pejorative meaning today. Largely through the influence of Barth and Bonhoeffer, an opposition has been drawn between religion and Christianity. It must first be said, of course, that there is a terminological problem here. Where Bonhoeffer speaks of religion in a very negative sense it might be better translated as religiosity rather than religion. Even granted this, however, there remains a fundamental question: whether Christianity is a religion or whether it should be essentially different from the religions of mankind.

It would seem to me that there is a sense in which everyone knows that Judaism-Christianity is a religion or religions, belonging within the world's great religious groups. It would be jejune to think lightly of the disintegration of other religions on the premise that Christianity is not one of these anyway. Christianity cannot escape from the world's religious problems by redefining itself out of its relationship to other religions.

There is, however, a valid sense in which Judaism-Christianity is in fact the opposite of religion. The fulfillment of a process is from one perspective the destruction of the process. In uplifting and transforming the old, the new both perfects and destroys. By being receptive to the aspirations and cultic drives of previous religions, Judaism-Christianity perfected religion. But precisely in its acceptance of God in history Judaic-Christian revelation destroyed forever the distinction between things worthy and unworthy of God. Religion as an aspect of life was superseded by Judaism-Christianity as the fullness of life.

To say that God is not present in an isolated section of life is not to reduce revelation to an undifferentiated or abstract universality. The exact opposite is true. A god of the past or a god of a religious sector is an abstraction or a controllable thing. A god of the present is a person who must meet us in the incarnation of the moment. When God takes to himself a particular moment or a chosen people it is not in order to exclude the rest but in order to take hold of all. Mediation does not mean substitution; it means the giving of grace to all to bring about what God is so clearly accomplishing in the life of the proto-typical reality. Thus Israel and the

Church are not the good people standing opposed to the bad world, but they are the servants of all who reveal what God is doing in the whole of his creation. In this way the whole temporal world is enabled to become more truly itself, the mirror of God's glory.

If there could be any doubt in ancient Israel about the nature of God's choice, the definitive answer was given in Jesus of Nazareth. In him and through him all creation is chosen; his life was given for the sake of the world. In Jesus, the beloved of the Father, there appears the final collapse of the two kinds of reality. With him divine messages come to an end because the Word is now flesh. Through him it becomes clear that the transcendent God is not to be sought apart from human life for he has himself lived a human existence.

Judaic-Christian faith should mean all of these things. Judaic-Christian faith, however, has always been a difficult thing to hold on to because it means holding on to God. And that is all that we can do: hold on but never possess. The God of Israel and the Father of Our Lord Jesus Christ is always to be met anew in the present moment of experience. He cannot be tucked away in the solidified things of the past. "Woe to the man so possessed," writes Martin Buber, "that he thinks he possesses God." The temptation of Christianity has always been to fall back to the security of a religious realm of existence where God is guaranteed. This in consequence leads to a neglect of the temporal, social, and this worldly life of the Christian. It takes a constant faith, a Jewish infused attitude, and a courage in the face of forces to the contrary, to affirm God through affirming the whole of creation in its temporality and materiality.

An example of the kind of subtle error that a false piety has caused for Christianity may be found in the argument over secondary causes in the Middle Ages. Though the words may sound quaint and irrelevant the problem is most apposite to our difficulties today. There was a school of thought in the Middle Ages that wished to deny a causality proper to created things. These Christian thinkers favored a creation in which nothing would be taken from God and all things would simply be signs pointing to God rather than be themselves opaque and autonomous realities. St. Thomas Aquinas, in opposing this pious sounding argument, stressed the basic Christian teaching that creation takes nothing from God and that the more creation is true to itself the more it shows God's glory. Considering the argument that a lack of proper causality in created things would be more resplendent of God, Aquinas flashed out in one of his extremely rare touches of impatience: "This is repugnant to sense, repugnant to reason, and opposed to the goodness of God."

Belief in a realm which has no reality except as the place of the divine would be a denial of God's taking hold of mankind and man's world. It is to posit once again a world of magic. The difference between a magical world and a sacramental world is that in the latter things possess their own autonomy. The greater they are and the more true to themselves they are the more they lead us to God. Either all things are in some sense sacramental or else nothing at all is a sacrament. There can be no choice between a sacramental world and one which has its own ontological density; we have both or we have neither. The other-worldly appears only in the full reality of the this-worldly. The transcendent God draws near to us in the autonomy of creation and most of all in the freedom of Jesus who is called Christ.

The need for a Christian acceptance of the totality of creation is, I think, beyond dispute. It must be pointed out, however, that this apparently simple position has a number of complexities which will endanger the valid affirmation if we are not careful. I will simply mention two possible misinterpretations of secularity.

First, the acceptance of the totality of human history as revelatory of God does not imply that everything that is happening must be approved without qualification. Christianity is called today to support the human and establish the secular in its autonomy; but what is truly humanizing is not always apparent. We must face the possibility of widespread aberrations in a particular historical period. If a theologian says that today people cannot understand anything but the empirical, this may mean that Christianity needs empirical reinterpretation; but it may also mean that there is something wrong with people who think only in this way. Furthermore, it is perilous to make generalizations about modern man or even a single modern man. There is a sense in which each of us must affirm himself against himself. We are all of us many possibilities. This does not mean that we should negate a part of the human. It does mean that we should hesitate to construct a picture of modern man and then cut Christianity to fit it. It is enough to be man, but we must not assume that the final standard of the human is what a few contemporary scientists or college students think it is. The Christian claim is that ultimately we find what it means to be human only before the face of God where we are judged for failing to become as human as God wishes us to be.

There is in the second place a more radical and shocking danger in the full approbation of the secular. To say that this world possesses its own autonomy and that nothing is divine can lead some people to conclude that God therefore is nothing. The reasons which ancient man had for worshiping God have fallen away. We do not need a god to explain lightening and thunder, nor a god for the yearly harvest, nor a god to give birth to life. The only reason we need God is for there to be anything at all. That is not a bad reason; in fact, it is a better reason than men in previous eras have had. Yet so amazing is the idolatrous power of man that he can now decide that he no longer needs God.

This position is understandable if not justifiable by reason of some of the bitter battles fought in recent centuries. Christian apologists, instead of pushing men beyond a superficial atheism that denied all finite gods, have often tried to carve out a little religious area within the secular. Christian theology, instead of centering its attention on man, has generally tried to keep men's eyes fixed on a realm of religious objects. All reality is now focused on man. This means that we have the greatest possibility for either suicidal narcissism or else for a true Christian theology which claims that God has become man. The one burning question today is not whether man and the secular are good, but whether man can be helped to accept his own freedom in a world to be perfected unto God.

With those brief remarks let me turn to the question of worship and liturgy, and ask what is implied by a theology of the secular. First, we may note that Christian liturgy had from the start a most amazing sense of what its general program should be. I have said that the uniqueness of Judaism-Christianity was in the acceptance of time, an acceptance that revoked all previous religious rites by fulfilling their deepest longings. The liturgy rightly took time as its decisive category, bringing all else into a unity within the ascending spiral of man's temporal movement toward God.

The Church in this view becomes what is happening in the lives of people; in every moment the Church is born anew. All of human history is henceforth to be revelational, but precisely in order that each moment can be revelational some moments must be intensely so. The liturgical act extends the mediational principle; in the chosen moment of the liturgy other moments are in some way contained and given meaning.

It should be clearly perceived, however, that in abrogating a separated realm of the sacred the liturgy did not do away with the ritual, symbolism, and myth making power of man's religions. The liturgy subsumed these within time. These elements of the liturgy are not simply left overs that can be done away with in the age of secularity. If there is one thing Catholic liturgy should be able to teach contemporary men, it is that they must retain poetry and symbolism, stories and playfulness, beauty and compassion. These are human and they cannot be lost without man being lost. The liturgy can be brutally realistic about time, history, and evolution; this realism excludes a nostalgic romanticism. It does not exclude a style of thought and life that may seem unreal to some people today. The liturgy is not to be reduced to the lowest common denominator to please all such people. On the contrary, the liturgy should be a primary force in resisting the trivialization of life in the contemporary world. One of the most serious questions in America today is not whether teenagers can grow up into adult society, but whether there is an adult society for them to grow into. If the music or clothing industry finds its greatest profit in appealing to the bad taste of thirteen year olds, this is all the more reason for the liturgy to raise the level of its appeal. Not to meet men where they are would be bad, but to confirm people in their own worst tastes by holding out nothing better would be inexcusable.

My second point is that a theology of the secular means that no structure is unchangeable and no place is of itself sacred. The Christian temptation, I have said, is to reinstate the spatial over the temporal, the objective structure over the human process. From the time that Abraham was told to leave his place and found a people, there has always been the tendency to build new temples for permanently housing the gods. Surely from the time of Christ it should have been clear that the temple of the Spirit is the body of the Christian, that God is not in the building but in the community of love. This does not mean that there is no place for a church building; on the contrary, the God of history always meets us in the incarnated moment of space and time. The decisive difference here is that a place does not have holiness in being set aside but in its being a place where human care and concern occur.

Sacred space is humanizing space; it is there that the Church happens. For this purpose the storefront may or may not be a better place than a gothic cathedral. The test is whether the space is for man and whether it is a place where a thoroughly secularized world can be itself. Beauty and style, elegance and simplicity, are never to be disregarded in the humanizing of God's world. Beautiful buildings are not a luxury, they are a desperate necessity. On the other hand, pouring enormous amounts of money into enormous rock piles that look like what churches are supposed to look like is hardly the great need of our day.

I take the church building as the most obvious example of the structures in Christianity that must be in constant change. It is not possible to live always in the present but it is possible to live continually in the past where life is well organized and where Christianity is a set of beliefs, precepts, rituals, and buildings. But to live with a past revelation and unchanging forms of worship is to destroy the unique character of Judaic-Christian faith. The liturgy must meet men where they are most themselves, where they express themselves freely, and experience their real joys and sorrows. There must be in the Church and in her liturgy an openness without *a priori* limits, a readiness to break and reshape any human structure that acts as a haze of fiction between the simple lives of people and the lives they bring to church.

A third area not far removed from the previous two is a concern for the autonomy and integrity of everything used in the worship of God. I have said that in a sacramental world, as opposed to a world of magic, things most truly symbolize God by being themselves. This demand, inherent to Christianity from the beginning, has become one of absolute necessity in a world of secularity. It may once have been possible to insert pious messages into literature or place holy visions into paintings, but this kind of artificial selling will no longer be effective.

The Christian who desires to love and worship with the whole of his life intuitively grasps that art is not to teach us things about God, but that by being art it will be the revelation of the beauty and terror of existence which leads to God. If we really believe that God is creator of this world and that man fully alive is the glory of God, then we can relax in the singing of a hymn which may or may not carry an obvious religious message. We can experience the joy of simply being with our fellow men without immediately introducing God through a trap door. We can delight in all works of art because we know that all things are for man and man is for God.

As a kind of corollary to this point I would cite the implications which this has for preaching. I think that it is still widely assumed that the good preacher today should try merely to imitate the great sermons of the Middle Ages, the patristic age, or best of all the apostolic age. Perhaps this is essentially true, but I think that the age of secularity requires a quite radical change in the form which preaching has taken over the centuries. The time for elaborate exposition of texts and for persuasive urgings from the pulpit is over. If preaching is to play any role today it can only be as a pointer to what is going on in the world, an attempt by the preacher to cast some light of intelligibility on what we are experiencing in our lives.

Preaching cannot be subtle persuasion; anyone who watches an hour of television each week knows how to turn off his attention from such urgings. The preacher's role is to search for the truth with his hearers and let this truth take hold of their lives. Eventually, I think, this must involve an exchange between preacher and listeners, a dialogue in which the congregation can contribute to the growth in understanding. For the present, preaching must at least include a dialogic attitude on the part of the preacher. If preaching begins to take on this character there will probably be fewer words spoken but that would not be so bad. The important thing is that the words emerge from the human experience of men today and deepen that awareness of the human to the extent that God will emerge at the center of life.

This is the note on which I would like to conclude: that worship as a separate section of man's life has been destroyed, that religion as a set of things encasing and protecting man is becoming an indefensible burden. But all of this only means that man discovering man in the nakedness of finite freedom must come to a deeper form of divine worship. For after all the paeans in praise of man have been sung the question of Dostoyevsky's Karamazov will remain: "Whom will man love, to whom will he be thankful, to whom will he sing the song?" There is no way to go back to past ages supposedly more religious than our own. God cannot be reintroduced as one object of concern among others. "The God who withdrew behind the heavens," wrote Rilke, "must reappear out of the center of the earth." God is nearer than ancient man could ever have imagined. It is up to us to pronounce a total amen to creation, and he will be found in the love of the earth, the freedom of my brother, and the song of joy in worship.

The Secularity of Christian Worship

Daniel J. O'Hanlon, S.J.

Daniel J. O'Hanlon, S.J., is Professor of Fundamental Theology at Alma College in Los Gatos, California. He received his doctorate in theology in 1957 from the Gregorian University in Rome. During the Second Vatican Council he was an interpreter for English-speaking observers. Coeditor of *Christianity Divided,* he has written extensively on ecumenical subjects in such journals as *Theological Studies, America, Commonweal, Worship,* and *Concilium.*

In trying to put some apparent order into the real confusion of ideas which I bring before you today, I have somewhat arbitrarily arranged them under two main headings. I hope that as I move along, the descriptions of the two areas I want to discuss will become somewhat clearer. The first part I call "The Internal Secularization of Christian Worship"; the second, "The Outward Secularization of Christian Worship." I deliberately speak of *secularization* rather than secularity or secularism to make it clear that in the world in which we live we are faced not just with an existing fact or mind-set but rather a development, a growing process. Subtitles for these two main headings could be: (1) Liturgy and Time and (2) Liturgy and the World.

I

The Internal Secularization of Christian Worship

I plan to develop the first half of my paper in this order: (1) a description, perhaps almost a caricature, of the starting point from

Reprinted from *Worship in the City of Man* (Washington, D.C.: The Liturgical Conference, 1966), pp. 16–27, with the permission of the publisher.

which this process of internal secularization of Christian worship departs; (2) an account of what secularization is and how it has happened; (3) some of the problems it has raised; (4) the possibilities this process of secularization has created for more authentic Christian worship; (5) a few concrete remarks about reform and renewal in Christian worship.

1. Let us begin with the starting point from which this process of the internal secularization of Christian worship is taking place: it is liturgy and Church conceived as a refuge from the world of change and movement into the eternal realm of the really real of the *ontos on*. This view of worship, not unknown among those who call themselves Christians has affinities with the nature religions which surrounded the people of Israel in Old Testament times. They were closely tied to the eternal cycles of nature which always repeat themselves. In religion of this kind, the ideal is to achieve harmony by becoming attuned to the impersonal laws of nature. But Yahweh called his people from these religions of the ever-recurring cycle into the onward-moving line of history, of a time which was going somewhere.

To come closer to our own experience, I think that we Christians, in a way admittedly different from these nature religions, have put too exclusive emphasis on the timeless and eternal. One consequence of this has been the consecration of a form of worship which has put such stress on these elements that the forms and even the language of worship have seemed to want to escape the reality of time. One had the impression that time was something the Christian should flee, not the place in which God could be found. In this view, which I am caricaturing somewhat, bible, ritual, and story become a series of parables or symbols meant to help man to rise above time into communion with a world of hidden, changeless, timeless essences. One is very strongly reminded of Plato's Cave and his world of ideas.

2. Well, then, what has the process of secularization done to this view of Christian worship? What new directions or modifications has it suggested? In this first part of the paper, I take the word "secularization" as coming from the word "*saeculum*," and with Harvey Cox I take this to be a time word: "*saeculum*" refers to this age. The process of secularization then, is one which brings the dimension of forward-moving time into our lives whether we like it or not. I would also agree with Cox that this process helps

us to recover an understanding of the God of Israel, and the God who manifested himself in the event of Jesus Christ. He is a God of history, who does not speak his decisive word through the fixed cycles of nature, but rather in a personal call which is above these patterns and free from them. Nature is no longer a god, as Cox has pointed out. Nature is no longer something to be taken with total awe as a dwelling place of gods who determine our existence. Nature has been disenchanted and the Lord of history, who personally calls us, becomes the center and focus of our attention. Now this way of thinking, which had its Christian parallel in the Platonic retreat from linear time has, I think, had a healthy corrective from the growing awareness of the evolutionary process in time and a more and more conscious acceptance of it by everyone, Christians included. Time and the evolutionary process is thought of more and more not as an enemy from whom we run and try to escape, but as a positive dimension of all that is best in man's fulfillment (Teilhard de Chardin). Through the process of urbanization man has been freed more and more from the constructions of narrow tribal and rural life. The more open and anonymous life of the city has created possibilities of personal freedom and forward-moving change which cannot help having an impact on all aspects of his life, worship included.

3. What are some of the problems that have been created by this development? One of the problems is an over-reaction by which we fall back into a more extreme version of what I described at the beginning. The sheer frustration of excessive mobility and change may tempt us to make worship even more of a refuge from all of this buzzing, bewildering confusion of mobility and time.

A problem of another kind is that when we are given movement and freedom, we are given more possibilities of mature personal response, but by the same token there exists the possibility of irresponsible and destructive use of this freedom, and of all the new slaveries which can emerge from this misuse. We must face this problem very honestly. Earlier this year I took part in a two-day discussion of the work of Teilhard de Chardin. The principal criticism which this largely Protestant group leveled at his vision of man was that he seemed to accept as too easily inevitable the movement of evolution toward better and better things. It missed an awareness of the demonic possibilities which lie in freedom and evolution.

I have heard students of Teilhard de Chardin say that such a criticism of his views is not justified. In any case, the facile presumption that freedom inevitably moves toward the good is a temptation to which we may very well be open.

As we accept more positively the reality of time, history, and the person, another danger must be avoided, that of undercutting too completely their basis in nature. Nature, after all, comes from the same God as history and persons. There is no such thing as the free-floating person, or history which is not rooted in nature. Any effort to set persons and history free from their context in nature is bound to fail. Both covenant and nature are from the same God. Furthermore, in the incarnation God has joined himself to nature too. There is a personal encounter—indeed, I think this is primary—but it is in the context of nature, and that is something we must never forget. God is certainly the absolute personal demand to which we must respond from moment to moment, but this does not wipe out entirely the specific patterns which are built into nature. They are the vehicles of our response.

Another problem: since the transcendence of timeless eternal truths in a changeless God has no longer been left as the center of attention, there is the danger that all transcendence will be threatened; man will seem to be at the mercy of unpredictable chaos. There is danger of uncritical immersion in what is immanent. If we remove an imperfect scaffolding too soon, we may leave man not with God, but with nothingness. I suppose that a pastoral judgment has to be made in dealing with such cases. How far and how fast should one go in demolishing an inadequate view of God? When is such a procedure healthy purification, and when does it become irresponsible overkill?

4. Let us move on to a more positive consideration. How does this process of secularization create the possibility of more authentic Christian worship? The Council's Constitution on the Church in the Modern World invites us to ponder and respond to the signs of the times, to see the work of the Holy Spirit in areas where perhaps we had not expected him to turn up. In this sense, secularization brings us back to what we have forgotten: Christianity is distinctively a religion of time, and the Christian God is a God of history. Our faith in him is the answer to an historically singular event and not simply the dramatically-clothed objectification of a timeless, metaphysical self-consciousness. Christian worship then is a response to the God who manifests himself primarily in history

rather than in nature or the philosopher's meditation on nature. The Christian as Christian must be thoroughly involved in the course of history. He must give himself unreservedly to man and his temporal existence, and, as Daniel Callahan reminds us, if he fails to do this it is hard to see how he will ever live in the present, much less speak to the present.[1]

Time, then, must become for us Christians a dimension of life which is friendly and familiar. We must embrace it with warmth and enthusiasm. Another consequence of this approach is that as Christians, we should be led mainly by the personal call of God to specific tasks in the here and now, not just by impersonal timeless laws of whatever kind, not principally by human philosophies or myths no matter how profound or good these philosophies may be in themselves. Worship then, it seems to me, is precisely that act which expresses, shapes, and directs the free personal response of the community at this moment of time. Authentic Christian worship is the actualization of this present moment of salvation history. It is, as it were, the crest of the wave of God's history actualized by the Father's here-and-now invitation through his Son in the Holy Spirit. Worship bears a great responsibility for this present moment of freedom, a freedom whose potentialities have been expanded and deepened by the processs of urbanization and secularization. Worship is not an automatic process, but a mode of opening our freedom to the Holy Spirit in a situation pregnant with possibilities for fulfillment or destruction. At this moment, when we have fewer and fewer norms which are seen as eternal and precisely applicable, the personal invitation and guidance of the Holy Spirit becomes a decisive guide. It is only within the worshiping community together with our fellow Christians, listening with humble sensitivity to God's word, that we can expect to be led safely into God's new future. The "discretion of spirits" must be undertaken not just as an exceptional thing, but more and more as a normal part of our Christian lives. Since we are not being led around a clear, fully-charted cycle in which things always repeat themselves, but along a non-circular road which moves into a really new future, as Christians we will often have no other *decisive* norm but the lead of the Holy Spirit here and now in this situation. Worship must have a shape and a style which takes all this into account.

[1] *Commonweal,* Sept. 17, 1965, p. 662.

This way of thinking about God and our life of worship carries with it, it seems to me, the recovery of what could be called incarnational transcendence. If we keep firmly in our minds the fact of the incarnation and the sending of the Spirit on the Church, God's transcendence is not best understood by using models of distance, or changeless independence of the present moment of history. For us Christians the key to grasping God's transcendence must be the *absolute freedom* of his intimate presence. When time and history really become the central locus of God's action and man's response, then the unity of his immanence and transcendence can be understood more profoundly. Transcendence is the deep built-in spur to freely and creatively "go beyond," following the lead of God who in his freedom is always beyond and always calling us in faith to that hidden future which he has freely chosen for us and into which we freely move. This kind of transcendence is fully compatible with our status as friends of God, truly his friends. We know that the more deeply one friend is accepted by another, the more this other person becomes himself, the more radically is he free in his own possibilities for the future. The astounding friendship with himself into which God has drawn us is, then, no barrier at all to his transcendence. His intimate presence is one which he has freely chosen, and freely maintains.

5. Finally, a few practical remarks about the concrete significance of all of this for reform and renewal of Christian worship. It seems to me that what I have been saying, if it is at all acceptable, highlights the crucial importance of the homily. In each celebration, it is the homily which bears major responsibility for raising to the level of consciousness all those things of which we have spoken. The homily must make every effort to bring God's personal call to bear on this community at this particular moment. In small group celebrations the use of group meditation on the scripture readings might at times serve this purpose even more effectively than a homily from the celebrant alone.

Secondly, in the style of worship which I have tried to describe, it would seem desirable that wherever it can be done, the celebrant and homilist should prepare the celebration ahead of time with the worshiping community, so that it will as far as possible touch this community at this present moment of time in this particular place.

Thirdly, the choice of the prayers of the faithful should be such as to deepen the awareness of the present moment and the future as the normal milieu of Christian life and concern.

Finally, serious thought has to be given to the style and the structure of the whole of our celebration and to the cycle of the liturgical year. They must create a sense of involvement in time and history and avoid, or, where they exist, eliminate any style, pattern, or symbols which invite us to retreat from time and history.

Perhaps it is clearer now why I have called the first half of this paper "The Internal Secularization of Christian Worship." The key word is "time," and secularization of worship is seen as the restoration of time to its proper place as an internal dimension of all Christian worship.

II

The Outward Secularization of Christian Worship

In speaking of the outward secularization of Christian worship I am thinking of the relation of the worshiping community to what we loosely call the *world* and so in this section the key word is "world." A subtitle for this section might be: "Liturgy and the World."

1. That means we begin with a description of the starting point away from which the process of secularization, in the second sense, moves us. Once again, the point of departure may be overdrawn almost to the point of caricature to bring out the contrast with what follows.

We begin from a dualistic understanding of Church and world, of the sacred and profane, of the religious and the secular. These are thought of as distinct, separate, even opposed areas. What of this statement of Thomas Clarke, for instance?

> The distinction between the sacred and secular is beyond question. There is an area of man's life that is necessarily withdrawn (though not isolated) from his temporal concerns. In heaven the distinction will cease. . . . But as long as he is in this life, Christian man will need to express and confirm his transcendence of the temporal and the worldly by creating a realm of the sacred. Liturgy, or to use Josef Pieper's term, "celebration," is the heart of the realm of the sacred.[2]

Over the centuries, recent centuries at least, the Church has regarded the worldly and the secular with suspicion. There is no

[2] *America*, May 29, 1965, p. 802.

doubt that a chasm grew up between what we roughly label "Church" and "world." The question of the Church and the world was not even on the agenda of Vatican II when it began, which suggests the chasm which had grown to separate the two. But almost all of the work in the last session was devoted to a struggle with the issue, which suggests that a beginning, at least, has been made toward bridging this gulf. Fr. Metz remarks that "the misfortune is not the secularization of the world, but the manner in which we Christians have regarded it, mistaking or disowning our own offspring so that he early ran away and now views us with hostility." [3]

I think we see a virulent and extreme form of this kind of dualism in the anger of those persons or groups whose property interests or national pride are affected when they hear homilies on racial justice or the duties of Christians toward international peace. I think there is no doubt that it was precisely this gap between a formalistic, irrelevant, escapist kind of worship and the crying human needs of the worker for justice and decency which led Communism to label religion the opiate of the people. It is very significant, I think, and a kind of warning to us, that the only kind of religion that is tolerated in Russia today is a religion and forms of worship which are not permitted to speak of man's human need for justice or social issues in the world. Shrewdly enough, those who work for the annihilation of religion will tolerate only that style of religion which they can point to as irrelevant.

Fr. Berrigan, a little closer to home, writes at one stage of his recent tour of Latin America:

> Consider the lag in conscience of one who first of all is "most exact in religious observance," for whom "the Mass is everything," and yet whose public actions are marked by unawakened resolve or by positive injustice. One would be horrified at the suggestion of sacrilege at the altar; at the same time one is ready for sacrilege against his neighbor. Indeed, the possibility of the second does not occur to such a man under the sign of danger of sin. . . . Today we cry "Church! Church!" somewhat as the men of our Lord's time cried out "Lord! Lord!" But the cries are equally unavailing when a man's works are dead.[4]

[3] *Theology Digest,* Summer, 1965, p. 98.
[4] *Jubilee,* July, 1966, p. 15.

There is nothing really terribly new about this divorce between worship and man's life in the world. We have the words of Isaiah with which you are all familiar. Because they are appropriate for our discussion today, let me remind you of them:

> What care I for the number of your sacrifices? says the Lord. I have had enough of whole burnt rams and fat of fatlings. . . . Bring no more worthless offerings; your incense is loathsome to me. New moon and sabbath, calling of assemblies, octaves with wickedness; these I cannot bear. . . . Put away your misdeeds from before my eyes; cease doing evil; learn to do good. Make justice your aim: redress the wronged, hear the orphan's plea, defend the widow. [Is. 1:11, 13, 16–17.]

And a little earlier, the brooding shepherd, Amos:

> I hate, I spurn your feasts; [speaking in the name of the Lord] I take no pleasure in your solemnities; your cereal offerings I will not accept, nor consider your stall-fed peace offerings. Away with your noisy songs! I will not listen to the melodies of your harps. But if you would offer me holocausts, then let justice surge like water, and goodness like an unfailing stream. [Amos 5:21–24.]

2. These are various attempts to describe the starting point away from which some movement might take place in the outward secularization of Christian worship. Now let us look again at the forces which have driven our attention to this kind of a problem. How has the process of secularization—and here I take the word "secularization" not so much from "*saeculum*" as a time word but as a word referring to the world at large—forced our attention once more to this problem? First of all by the well-known reaction of Communism, to which I have already referred, against a purely cultic Christianity in which the priest and the "good Christian" pass by the man who is robbed and left dying by the roadside. The dedication even of atheists to the cause of human brotherhood gives us pause. Indeed, it is not at all unlikely that if our Lord were telling that parable today, the Samaritan who actually went out to help the wounded traveler might very well be a Communist.

Another "secular" development which compels us to re-examine our style of worship is the convergent drive of the whole human family, aided by the secular facts of technology and mass-communication, toward unity of some kind, toward a growing sense of community. This becomes visible more and more in "secular" structures like the United Nations, the Red Cross, the World Health Organization and many, many others. We must also take note of the great human compassion and dedication to the cause of justice, civil rights and international peace which are often totally outside the Churches. Our conscience should be touched by the fact that many of these dedicated people are not religious; some are even non-believing or anti-religious. Now what does this say to us about our Church and our worship? It compels us to be honest, asks us about the relation between Church and world, and hence, inevitably and immediately, the relationship between worship and world. We are forced to recognize, if we have forgotten it, that God's interest is the *whole* human family, and that the Church is false to its calling if it is not an instrument of God's purposes for the *whole* world. If the Church is turned in on itself, if it is totally churchy, if it spends most of its time praying just for the Church, then it has missed God's point.

We must also recognize in the depths of each man's being the anonymous presence of grace, of God's invitation to the fundamental option of openness and love for others. There are very profound and insufficiently explored truths implied in Matthew's account of the last judgment. (Mt. 25:31–46.) This scene tells us who really respond to the grace of Christ, and they were mostly the people who did not know they were doing it. (I will not go into the problem now for lack of time, but will mention only the so-called supernatural existential, Rahner's way of talking about a kind of built-in Christic potential which is there even before the active grace of Christ arrives.)

In his article commenting on Harvey Cox's book, to which we have already referred, Daniel Callahan warns us that ". . . even the freshest Catholic theology has the same mark of irrelevance as did its forerunners. It is essentially turned in upon itself, and nowhere more obviously than when it tries to talk about 'the world' exclusively in the language of philosophy." We run the very real danger of failing to acknowledge God's work outside the formal structures of the Church. This action of God's is, as you know, acknowledged in the second chapter of the Constitution on the Church which deals with the various ways in which people belong to the Church. Vatican II provides an opening there which needs a great deal more development, but even what is there would have seemed bold to the textbook ecclesiologist of a few years ago.

Finally, it seems to me that the sacred must not really be separate from the secular, but must rather be that point within the secular, within God's world, where the deepest meaning which is hidden in its depths is brought to the level of consciousness and made known. In the incarnation of the Word, in the light of the community which lives in the power of the Spirit, the Father wishes to manifest the deepest meaning of this world which from the start was "Christic"—to use Father Thomas Clarke's phrase. He writes:

> By the incarnation, by the cross and resurrection [and I myself would add—by the original design of the Father who fashioned the created universe intending Christ as its head], the world is already Christic and ecclesial in its dynamic orientation. Its Christianity is, in Rahner's now famous term, *anonymous,* but it is real.[5]

This same kind of relationship between Church and world is expressed in a somewhat different way by Fr. Schillebeeckx:

> In the plan of salvation, the concrete world, by definition, is an *implicit Christianity;* it is an objective, non-sacral but saintly and sanctified expression of mankind's communion with the living God; whereas the Church *qua* institution of salvation, with her explicit creed, her worship and sacraments, is the direct and sacral expression of that identical communion.[6]

3. Before concluding with some practical reflections which grow out of these thoughts on liturgy and the world, let us take note of a couple of problems they raise.

I think we are sometimes tempted to be embarrassed about the specific and unique quality of being Christian. I am sure you have heard this many times, perhaps you have said it yourself. In a seminar I took part in . . . , a very eminent Catholic sociologist spoke with some anger of the annoyance and revulsion he felt when he heard the phrase "People of God," especially with a capital "P." This struck him as presumptuous and arrogant and he did not want to be identified with anything of the sort. It seems to me that what seems at first sight to be humility, might well be an abdication of responsibility. The fear of seeming to make oneself better than anyone else is certainly commendable as long as it is genuinely that. But

[5] *America,* May 29, 1965, p. 802.
[6] Cited by Clarke, *loc. cit.*

an inclination to blur the lines between Church and mankind too completely might grow out of other motives. If we remember that the Christian and the Christian community are chosen as God's people, not because of any original merit of their own, and that the real meaning of this choice is that they are called to die for others, arrogance is no more appropriate than it was for the suffering servant to whose Church we belong. Arrogance will disappear only if the Christian worshiping community sees its mission to the whole world as truly one of service. Now this is a very difficult thing to bring off. It is easy enough to call yourself the "servant of the servants of God," but just using that phrase does not automatically bring about everything that the phrase calls for. All of us proclaim that our ideal is one of service but it is a very, very tricky business. I am reminded of what happens sometimes at a concelebration where the sacred ministers (minister, you know, means servant) are gathered around the altar. Perhaps a dozen priests are concelebrating, but when there is something to be done that demands a bit of practical service, a couple of unordained "non-ministers," altar boys, are put to work. I do not want to make a large issue of this example, but it may suggest to us that the real notion of service is a very hard thing to maintain in the Church. It must involve a genuine respect for all men, including those whose response to Christ's grace is anonymous; not an artificial respect, being nice to people in spite of the fact that they really do not deserve it, but a respect for the real work of the grace of Christ in these people who have never heard of him. This response is often more profound and dedicated than what we find in ourselves. Only if the Christian community dedicates itself in this spirit to true peace and justice for the whole human family may it be able to redeem itself of arrogance.

Another problem which would have to be raised in any complete discussion of Church and world is the meaning of "the world" in the pejorative sense, as St. John speaks of it. Perhaps the simplest thing to say is that it equals all of those forces, in Christians as well as in others, in the Church as well as elsewhere, which are turned in upon the self, closed to the beckoning of God's grace which invites us to open ourselves in love to God and to other persons.

For completeness, the question of the sin of the world, of original sin, of the demonic forces in the world would have to be considered but I have no time now to do more than mention these problems.

4. Much of what was said about practical renewal of worship at

the conclusion of the first half of the paper is also applicable here, with a slight shift of emphasis. We must make every effort, it seems to me, to establish continuity between our liturgical celebrations and the ways in which human community and unselfish dedication are celebrated. We must look around very openly and with great imagination to find out how this can be done. What are the liturgical possibilities of what has become a normal part of the secular drive for justice: the march? What about *agape* meals? Liturgy, which grows out of what we might call "worldly situations," which releases a full awareness of their meaning, an awareness of their full meaning in Christ, and sends the worshipers back with a deeper realization of what life is about when they are not at worship, seems to me to be some kind of an ideal. We should see worship not as a movement away from life in the world but a deepening of insight which helps us to understand the meaning of everything that goes on in the world.

Let me say that in a slightly different way, and end without peroration. Worship must use as its material those human experiences and symbols which contain hidden in them somehow the deepest meaning of human existence, and it must illuminate them with the light which God has shed through Christ: through his incarnation, life, death and resurrection and through the sending of the Spirit at Pentecost. This is light which has been shed on man's life in a world already Christic in some sense from the Father's original plan.

The Witness Only the Layman Can Give

Thomas S. Klise

Thomas S. Klise, Catholic layman, graduated from St. Ambrose College in Davenport, Iowa in 1948; he then undertook graduate studies at Notre Dame University until 1950. He is president of the T. S. Klise Co. of Peoria, Illinois, producers of filmstrips and recordings for religious education. The filmstrips concentrate on the social implications of faith and are used by Catholic and Protestant catechetical groups. Klise was editor of *Scope* and *Junior Scope* magazines, and he is a frequent lecturer at catechetical and liturgical institutes.

One of the major discoveries of my adult life is that on the religious principle alone, it is impossible to divide mankind into the Good Guys and the Bad Guys. I would be ashamed to tell you how old I was when I found this out but I will drop the hint that I was well past eighteen before it dawned on me that the only reason Jesus was in that tabernacle was to *not* be in it. I can't blame my prolonged religious adolescence on my training because the name of the high school was *Mystici Corporis* and college was a place called *Mediator Dei.* In other words, I should have known better.

I don't know which generation I belong to, Cogley's or Callahan's, but if any identification is necessary we were the group who one year were reading Father Daniel Lord and the next, Cardinal Suhard. Instant sophistication. We thought we were fortunate at twenty to have Maritain and Gilson, *The Catholic Worker* and *Integrity,* the first French worker priests, the Little Brothers of Charles Foucauld.

Reprinted from *Jesus Christ Reforms His Church* (Washington, D.C.: The Liturgical Conference, 1966), pp. 148–57, with the permission of the publisher.

We *were* fortunate. And yet one's enthusiasms in those days wore an air of marked restraint. The distance between the ideal and the real did not seem bridgeable by what we now call commitment. At least no one had to disprove for us the Socratic dictum that knowledge is virtue. Even under the accelerated conditions of a wartime summer school, that fallacy was self-evident.

I can point to the place, the day and even the hour I got the first glimmer of understanding into the meaning of the Christian mystery. The enlightening instrument was Guardini's *The Church and the Catholic,* and I remember when I finished it, I burst into the room of a classmate to tell him what I had found. He wasn't interested in what I had found and after thirty seconds, neither was I. An excited announcer on the radio was going on about a superbomb an American plane had just dropped on Hiroshima.

I don't apologize for this more than slightly Hollywood touch; it belongs here. This whole script deals with the struggle between the cops and the robbers, the cowboys and the Indians, or, as I said in the beginning, the Good Guys and the Bad Guys. And the simple confession I am making is that having sat through the film more than thirty-five years now, I continue to be astonished at the turns in plot. I think I know how the story ends—which doesn't at all lessen my surprise when a Bad Guy acts like a saint and a Good Guy like a heel.

Permit me a sweeping generalization. *When it comes to applying the gospel message of justice and mercy to the problems of the contemporary social order, Catholics show no more sense of mission than anyone else.* The Good Guy in America today might be a Catholic but he is just as likely to be—atheist, for instance. Let me put it another way. That notorious "sociological Catholic" of the first century, James the Less, once defined religion pure and undefiled as taking care of widows and orphans and keeping oneself unspotted from the world. If for widows and orphans we read the American Negro, the American migrant worker, the American slum dweller, the American poor, the American old person—and if for care, we read personal involvement in secular programs that have the aim of aiding these victims of the American dream, the Catholic community of this country is no different in behavior from any random gathering of forty-five million people. In fact, to sweep the generalization even further, if there be such a thing as a typical Catholic, his typical preoccupation is not in caring for the widows and orphans but in keeping himself unspotted from the world.

Sweeping generalizations are no fun if you have to prove them, but this one is no fun at all because no one expects you to prove it. Documentation is unnecessary; we are in the dreary world of well known fact. The situation doesn't even qualify as a scandal because the necessary ingredients of news and the disappointment of an onlooker who had come to expect more, are missing. And if you try to argue out of the charge by pointing to the work of specialized Catholic organizations—this movement, that "apostolate"—you only support the case because you are admitting that if there is a broad Christian witness being given by this generation of Catholics, you cannot arrive at it by consulting the conscience of the community; you have to go to specialists. And this leads nowhere anyway because for every Catholic specialist you give me, I will give you a Unitarian specialist, a Jewish specialist, an agnostic specialist, and I think I could show that my specialists are proclaiming the objective gospel message of justice and mercy as well as your Catholic, and maybe even better.

How do we explain this continuing phenomenon of American Catholic life? That is the question that has to be answered if the title of this paper has any meaning at all. To my mind, to ask "What witness can the layman give?" does not mean what witness does he have the right to give but what witness is he morally capable of giving? And at a certain point, even that question must give way and we have to ask: Taking the creature as we know him, as we understand his cut of mind and his temper and his habit and his past history, what witness is he willing to give—what witness is he *going* to give? And that is the same as asking: "This Constitution on the Church—is it really going to motivate the Catholic laity of this country to give full and effective witness to the gospel of charity and justice?"

Now when you begin speculating about this question of why supposed Good Guys fail to do good deeds, you bump into many a curious thing and just when you think you have the answer you find that all you really have is one more description of the problem. In the first place, the Kierkegaard approach, though appealing, will get you nowhere. You know the Kierkegaard approach: you simply accuse the whole community of spiritual corruption. You say that the Church has sold out on the gospel of justice and charity and then you say the Catholic layman is just like everybody else, he's only interested in making money, and somewhere along the line you work in "bourgeois mentality," and throw in hypocrisy for good measure. As I say, it's an appealing approach—indignation is a basic human need—but in the end it raises more questions than it answers. To mention just a single item: If you want to score the Catholic on grounds of greed and selfishness, how do you explain his readiness to part with the dollar to build almost anything asked of him, even when, in his heart of hearts, he thinks much of the building ill-advised? For that matter, how do you explain that deeper, nobler thing that enables parents to give up children and children to give up parents that the gospel be carried, often in difficult ways, across the earth? Hardly the characteristics of a radical spiritual corruption.

There is always the nice, straight anti-clerical answer to the problem. It goes like this: *You can't get people interested in the social question if the priests and bishops aren't interested. When did you last hear a sermon on race or poverty or anti-Semitism? The clergy are too busy operating the machinery of the institutional Church to even notice what is going on in the world at large.* Now, I am the first to applaud pastorals and sermons that deal with the human problems we have in our society, and I wish we had a lot more of them, and I mean to get no one off the hook. But I am always a little baffled when a man of forty, a Catholic college graduate, comes up to me in great consternation and says: "When is Father So-and-So going to get with it on the colored situation?" And then I say to him: "Let's you and I form a neighborhood group and integrate the subdivision." And then he says to me: "Bye, Charley."—I reserve the right to be as anti-clerical as the next man but I do not care for the implication that I cannot see injustice unless Father points it out to me nor act to foster justice unless through bishop's mandate. The point is, what if there *aren't* any pastorals and any sermons, what if Father *is* out of it on the social question, where does that leave me? Am *I* then completely off the hook? Another thing. Suppose the name of your pastor is Father Larry Liberal and one fine morning Father Liberal really opens up on race in his pure white suburban parish. What happens then? I will tell you what has been known to happen: Father Larry Liberal finds out from the janitor that the boys in the men's club wonder if Father doesn't need a vacation. Father is beginning to worry about things that have nothing to do with our fine parish. Why, there isn't a colored person living within miles of our church. What's more, shouldn't Father stick to religious subjects in the pulpit and not get off on controversial political tangents?—

One last point. Even if I concede you the argument, how much does it explain? You tell me Father will not preach social justice, he opposes parish groups that want to act, he won't allow *The Commonweal* in the rectory—how do you account for Father? What makes *him* tick? In a strange, roundabout but sure way, this will lead you back to the beginning question. What is there in the American Catholic character, lay or clerical, that makes the person slow to respond to the gospel demands in the social order?

And so by quick and crude and over-simplified process of elimination, we come to what we all knew to be the villain of the piece in the first place. *Religious education.* What a feast we have here! The food for diatribe is so plentiful we don't know what to serve up first. Here's an appetizer: The morality taught in the schools is not the morality of the beatitudes but a check-list of do's and don'ts which ground the whole response of man to God on obedience. Here's the salad: The system presents the charity of the gospels in such an abstract way that it comes to mean nothing but a diffuse good will toward mankind in general coupled with this ounce of responsibility toward mankind in particular persons: you don't talk about them behind their backs. Here's the fish course: The religion of the textbooks is so busy spinning out someone's version of Thomas Aquinas, someone's definition of nature, someone's opinion about purgatory, there isn't any time for Jesus the Lord. Here's the rare steak: The new catechetics (which is really the oldest catechetics) represents a great step forward but unless the people teaching the new catechetics make us behold the blind man and the exile and the leper who stand in our own midst, then it will be wonderful bible history—and nothing more. And here now is the heady wine: From the time we are small children, we are told that the only really important thing we have to do in this life is save our souls. After so many years of What does it profit a man? and Seek first the kingdom of God, the impression is gained that the whole idea of being in this vale of tears is to get out of it safely. The result is not an incarnational Christian but a Manichee, who thinks of this world as his natural enemy, who is distrustful of secular man and his achievements, who tends to cultivate in the name of piety a resolute detachment from the very things that ought to be his natural and most important concerns. And this vice of other-worldliness is so entrenched that even when witness becomes evident moral imperative, instinct will betray it and habit confound it, and the frazzled prophet—what will he do? He will found a study club.

You will tell me this is caricature, and I will say of course it is caricature. But aren't there a few recognizable portraits around the table? I think there are. In fact I think one of them is mine. Else, why am I surprised that the Bad Guy should be good? Why am I startled when I see the sign of the Lamb glowing on the brow of the agnostic social worker? Why am I scandalized that the peacemaker should be unbelieving, the lover of the poor without everlasting hope? (Why should the holiness of the apparent sinner so stab the heart?) Because I hold the world in low regard. Because I forget that the sun in the sky is Christ Jesus not Satan. Because I forget that all men—repeat, all men—are victims of the benign fallout bearing in certain inconspicuous ways some of the radiance of the ever-present Word.

What says Vatican II of this? Can The Constitution on the Church tell us why instead of caring for widows and orphans we pursue our careers of unspottedness? Is there anything in this chapter on the laity, Chapter IV, that might embolden us to move in new directions with regard to the witness of the gospel in the social order?

First, honesty requires that we admit that we have here no blueprint for social action. That, of course, is not the purpose of the Constitution. At the same time, it is interesting to take up Chapter IV as a magnifying glass and through it read the blueprints we already possess in *Mater et Magistra* and *Pacem in Terris*. That can get to be a very lively party.

I suppose for the record we ought to say that there are words of encouragement here for the Catholic Actionist; there are words of guidance for the intra-Church critic and opinion builder; there are words of esteem for all those worthy bearers of mandate who teach and minister and heal in the name of a higher office. For the record, we ought to say these things. And then we ought to say that the great achievement of the Council where the layman is concerned lies elsewhere. To my ordinary eyes, the real breakthrough of Chapter IV, its distinctive genius, lies in the principle of *Christian secularity*.

I wish I could define that in twenty-five words or less but after twenty-five attempts, I gladly surrender the job to Father Rahner. If you think defining a Christian is tough, try secularity; and then try to splice the two together. But that difficult thing is exactly what this Council did in the Constitution: it took Christian and it took secular and it spliced them together. And the result is called: the primary and fundamental witness of the Christian layman. Let me summarize a bit.

The Council was not afraid to state the obvious when it was the obvious that needed stating. It had the courage to say that the first thing, the main thing, the really important thing to remark about the layman is his secular nature itself. In and by and through his secular state itself, the layman seeks the kingdom of God and gives witness to the divine plan. He mediates and he reconciles and he leavens "by engaging in temporal affairs . . . in all of the secular professions and occupations . . . in the ordinary circumstances of family and social life." He works "for the sanctification of the world from within as a leaven." In the very program of his secular life, he proclaims the Lord and his "evangelization takes on a specific quality and a special force in that it is carried out in the ordinary surroundings of the world." And this mission of his, this witness, is not merely "inspirational" or "exemplary"; it is charged with salvific power. It sanctifies, it redeems; it makes the Church "present and operative"; it causes the yeast to rise; it flavors the earth. So secularity is no handicap to the mission; indeed, secularity is its pride and its glory, its distinctive and characteristic note. Secularity is to this common witness of the laity what bread is to the Eucharist; it is necessary for validity.

Behold, therefore, the layman. His engagement with the secular: *there* is his priesthood. His preoccupation with the profane: *there* is his prophecy. The very act by which he encounters the world around him—in work, in civic concern, in political and social commitment: *there* is his first and obligatory apostolate. And what does all that come down to but the ungrudging declaration that the layman is a worldly creature, full of earthly concerns, secular and glad of it, in the world—and let us say it—*of* the world, immersed in time and time's affairs and happy in the state, devoted to temple but not detached from city, pledged to gospel and for that very reason wedded to world.

That is a way of summing it up, forcing it a little maybe, but then a little forcing never hurt an official document in the least. Two things, I think, ought to be noted in the idea of the summary. The first is that the definitive worldliness of the kind of witness we're talking about makes it the special, not to say exclusive, possession of the layman. Obviously, there are areas of shared responsibility but generally speaking when one role abandons its post to take up the cudgels for another role, there is the danger of confusing the functions proper to each. This would not hold true in the case of moral crisis where certain offices by the very unfamiliarity of their presence in the secular world perform a valuable teaching function. In other words, it was nice to see the priests and the sisters down in Selma.

The second point has to do with the business about the layman making the Church "present and operative" in certain "places and circumstances." I think we ought to imagine neither far off jungle missions here nor any of the things that come to mind when we say "institutional Church." The places and circumstances the Council is talking about take in the whole profane order of life. And making the Church present and operative may simply mean voting in conformity with a gospel conscience, joining the Urban League, working with the United Fund. How so? Because this world already belongs to Christ and every good happening in it is a kind of Epiphany, a step toward total reconciliation, a tiny unfolding of the bud, a bringing to light of the Christianity that has been implicit in the world since the incarnation. Where a true Christian is present and operating, Christ and the Church are present and operating.

Can it be put this way?—*Before the layman can reconcile the world to God, he must first reconcile himself to the world.* Is that the gift of Chapter IV? I believe it is; I believe the breakthrough is right there. For we have known for years that the layman, through baptism and confirmation, shared in the priesthood of the Lord. And where did that lead us? That led us into the blind alley of imitating the only priests we knew, the ones we saw on Sunday. That led us to the whole futile business of trying to define the lay role in terms of the cleric's role; and that was a betrayal of ourselves. We have known for years that every Christian has an obligation to conduct himself in such a way as to give good example. And that led many to try the dizzying feat of standing outside the temporal order and from that point in outer space, coax and cajole the worldlings to virtuous deportment; and that was a betrayal of the worldlings, who weren't watching anyway. We have always known that every Christian has the duty to do what he can to spread the gospel. But how often that became one or another form of proselytizing, where one forgot the person to save the soul. The Council does not talk that language at all. In telling us that the fundamental task of the layman consists in temporal engagement, the Council is saying that the best witness consists in an incorruptible *truthfulness to the world*.

Truthfulness to the world implies many things. It implies that the Christian never conceive his mission to be that of the religious imperialist or the crusader or the image-maker or the public relations artist. He will never become the apostolic equivalent of the Don Juan, the man for whom persons are only things. He will have more respect for the world than to treat it merely as a fairly good place to build a new church. He will love and revere the world's own immanent values and will devote himself to cultivating those values not just because, in the cultivating, he might snag a convert here or there but because the values of the world are worth cultivating in their own right. He will work for social justice not just to score points for faith and not just because, if he doesn't, the presumed Bad Guy (the Communist) will win—but because both faith and world tell him that social justice is the human good and must be sought for its own sake. (And here I think of all the breast-beating that has gone on in the Catholic community these past few years about the lateness of our entry into the racial struggle and how shabby our tardiness has made us look. We *have* looked shabby, we *still* look shabby—but if our reason for joining the fight now is merely to look good before our colored brothers, then we are as wrong-headed in our present action as we were in our earlier silence; we are still failing to see the Negro as a person, still failing to see his freedom as a good to be sought for its own sake.)

But most of all, where the witness of the gospel in the social order is concerned, truthfulness to world means *truthfulness of method*. What import this has for the widows and orphans! For if I am going to be true to them as persons and true to their actual needs in this life, then I must choose among many possible methods the one best suited to aid their condition. I must ask myself not, what means are the most Catholic, the most spiritual, the most edifying—but, preserving morality, what means will work? What means will give them shelter and food? And until this good pragmatism is accepted across the board in the Christian community, then we will continue to insult the orphan and the widow with our impotent compassion, our spoonsful of pity, our mere prayers.

Truthfulness of method: This will raise some painful personal decisions. It may mean leaving the Catholic Interracial Council for the

NAACP. It may mean quitting the Legion of Mary for the nonsectarian settlement house in the ghetto. It may mean resigning from the men's club in order to serve on the city planning board, whose decisions will determine whether in the years to come the Son of Man will have a place to lay his head. It may mean reaching the conclusion that to witness the gospel you will have to clear out of every church-related organization you now belong to.

But won't this lead inevitably to mere liberalism? Won't this reverse exodus, this fooling around in the desert, sooner or later invite idolatry? Won't secularity dilute the potion of faith, produce in the end a sociological Christianity that has lost its soul? You hear this fear expressed from time to time, as I too hear it expressed. And frankly, I can't trust myself on the subject anymore, having passed, in my reactions, through practically all shades of the emotional spectrum from rage through amusement to tears. So recognizing my own tendency to hysteria on the point, I shall only say that with forty million Americans under the poverty line, it is no time to worry about activism. With the economists and demographers now calmly predicting mass starvation for half the globe within ten years, it is not exactly the moment to fret about a merely sociological Christianity. With the Jew locked out and the *bracero* exploited and the mental patient forgotten and the alcoholic shunned and the black man murdered and the red man reserved and the Latin homeless and the nations at war and the bomb ever-present—"laicization of the heart" might be learnedly discussed somewhere; but not in my house.

In my house henceforth, the book will ever be open at Matthew 25. Attend to them or not, live by them or not, the words will be there for me and any visitor to read.

> When the Son of Man returns in his glory, and escorted by all the angels, he will seat himself on a throne befitting his glory. All the nations will assemble in his presence, and he will part mankind into two groups just as a shepherd parts the sheep from the goats. The sheep he will range at his right, and the goats to his left.
>
> Then the King will say to those at his right: "Come, the elect of my Father! Take possession of the kingdom prepared for you at the beginning of the world. For I was hungry, and you gave me to eat; I was thirsty, and you gave me to drink; I was a stranger, and you took me into your homes; I was naked, and you covered me; I was sick, and you visited me; I was in prison, and you came to see me!"

Then the saints will be surprised and say to him: "Lord, when did we see you hungry and feed you? or thirsty and give you to drink? And when did we see you a stranger and take you into our homes? or naked and cover you? When did we see you sick or in prison, and come to visit you?" And in explanation the King will say to them: "I tell you the plain truth, inasmuch as you did this to one of these least brethren of mine, you did it to me."

Selected Bibliography

Altizer, Thomas J. J., *Mircea Eliade and the Dialectic of the Sacred*. Philadelphia: The Westminster Press, 1963.

Armbruster, Carl J., *The Vision of Paul Tillich*. New York: Sheed & Ward, 1967.

Auer, Alfons, *Open to the World*. Baltimore: Helicon Press, Inc., 1966.

Balthasar, Hans Urs von, *Church and World*. New York: Herder & Herder, Inc., 1967.

———, *A Theology of History*. New York: Sheed & Ward, 1963.

Bonhoeffer, Dietrich, *The Cost of Discipleship*. New York: The Macmillan Co., 1963.

———, *Ethics*. New York: The Macmillan Co., 1955.

———, *Letters and Papers from Prison*. New York: The Macmillan Co., 1962.

Brungs, Robert A., *Building the City*. New York: Sheed & Ward, 1967.

Callahan, Daniel, ed., *The Secular City Debate*. New York: The Macmillan Co., 1966.

The Christian and the World, Readings in Theology. New York: P. J. Kenedy & Sons, 1965. Includes essays on Christian secluarity by W. Dürig, L. Scheffczyk, H. R. Schlette, H. Schlier, and others.

Cox, Harvey, *The Secular City*. New York: The Macmillan Co., 1965.

Davis, Charles, *God's Grace in History*. New York: Sheed & Ward, 1967.

de Blank, Joost, *The Return of the Sacred*. New York: Morehouse-Barlow, 1968.

Dewart, Leslie, *The Future of Belief*. New York: Herder & Herder, Inc., 1966.

Duquoc, Christian, ed., *Spirituality in the Secular City*. (*Concilium*, Vol. XIX.) Glen Rock, N.J.: Paulist Press, 1966.

Ebeling, Gerhard. *Word and Faith*. Philadelphia: Fortress Press, 1963.

Eliade, Mircea, *Patterns in Comparative Religion*. New York: Sheed & Ward, 1958.

———, *The Sacred and the Profane*. New York: Harcourt, Brace & World, Inc., 1959.

Faricy, Robert L., *Teilhard de Chardin's Theology of the Christian in the World*. New York: Sheed & Ward, 1967.

Ferré, Nels, *Christianity and Society*. New York: Harper & Brothers, 1950.

Gogarten, Friedrich, *Demythologizing and History*. New York: Charles Scribner's Sons, 1955.

———, *Der Mensch zwischen Gott und Welt*. Stuttgart: Friedrich Vorwerk Verlag, 1956.

Gogarten, Friedrich, *Jesus Christus, Wende der Welt*. Tübingen: J. C. B. Mohr, 1966.
———, *The Reality of Faith*. Philadelphia: The Westminster Press, 1959.
———, *Verhängnis und Hoffnung der Neuzeit*. Stuttgart: Friedrich Vorwerk Verlag, 1953.
Guardini, Romano, *The End of the Modern World*. New York: Sheed & Ward, 1956.
Heuvel, Albert van den, *The Humiliation of the Church*. Philadelphia: The Westminster Press, 1966.
Jenkins, Daniel, *Beyond Religion*. Philadelphia: The Westminster Press, 1962.
Johann, Robert O., *The Pragmatic Meaning of God*. Milwaukee: Marquette University Press, 1966.
Leeuwen, Arend van, *Christianity in World History*. New York: Charles Scribner's Sons, 1966.
Loen, Arnold, *Secularization*. London: SCM Press, Ltd., 1967.
Löwith, Karl, *Meaning in History*. Chicago: University of Chicago Press, 1957.
Lumiere et Vie, Vol. XIV, No. 73, 1965. Entire issue deals with the theme of the Church and the world.
Mascall, Eric L., *The Secularization of Christianity*. New York: Holt, Rinehart and Winston, 1966.
Meland, Bernard E., *The Secularization of Modern Cultures*. New York: Oxford University Press, 1966.
Metz, Johannes B., ed., *The Church and the World*. (*Concilium*, Vol. VI.) Glen Rock, N.J.: Paulist Press, 1965.
———, ed., *The Evolving World and Theology*. (*Concilium*, Vol. XXVI.) Glen Rock, N.J.: Paulist Press, 1967.
———, ed., *Is God Dead?* (*Concilium*, Vol. XVI.) Glen Rock, N.J.: Paulist Press, 1966.
Michalson, Carl, *Worldly Theology*. New York: Charles Scribner's Sons, 1967.
Micklem, Philip A., *The Secular and the Sacred*. London: Hodder & Stoughton, Ltd., 1948.
Montague, George T., *The Biblical Theology of the Secular*. Milwaukee: Bruce Publishing Company, 1968.
Munby, Denys L., *The Idea of a Secular Society and Its Significance for Christians*. New York: Oxford University Press, 1963.
Newbigin, Lesslie, *Honest Religion for Secular Man*. London: SCM Press, Ltd., 1966.
Ong, Walter J., *In the Human Grain*. New York: The Macmillan Co., 1967.
Otto, Rudolph, *The Idea of the Holy*. New York: Galaxy Books, Oxford University Press, 1958.
Pieper, Josef, *In Tune with the World; towards a Theory of Festivity*. New York: Harcourt, Brace & World, Inc., 1965.
———, *Leisure, the Basis of Culture*. New York: Pantheon Books, Inc., 1964.

Rahner, Karl and Edward Schillebeeckx, eds., *The Church and Mankind.* (*Concilium,* Vol. I.) Glen Rock, N.J.: Paulist Press, 1965.

Richard, Robert L., *Secularization Theology*. New York: Herder & Herder, 1967.

Richardson, Alan, *History Sacred and Profane*. Philadelphia: The Westminster Press, 1964.

Robinson, John A. T., *Honest to God.* London: SCM Press, Ltd., 1963.

Schall, James V., *Redeeming the Time*. New York: Sheed & Ward, 1968.

Schilling, S. Paul, "Friedrich Gogarten," *Contemporary Continental Theologians.* Nashville, Tenn.: Abingdon Press, 1966, pp. 102–19.

Shiner, Larry, *The Secularization of History; an Introduction to the Theology of Friedrich Gogarten.* Nashville, Tenn.: Abingdon Press, 1966.

Smith, Ronald G., *Secular Christianity*. New York: Harper & Row, Publishers, 1966.

Student World, Vol. LVI, No. 1. Geneva: World Student Christian Federation, 1963. Entire issue deals with secularization.

Teilhard de Chardin, Pierre, *Building the Earth*. New York: Dimension Books, 1967.

Vahanian, Gabriel, *The Death of God.* New York: George Braziller, Inc., 1961.

———, *Wait without Idols*. New York: George Braziller, Inc., 1964.

Van Buren, Paul, *The Secular Meaning of the Gospel.* New York: The Macmillan Co., 1966.

Vincent, John J., *Secular Christ*. Nashville: Abingdon Press, 1968.

Weizsäcker, Carl F., *The Relevance of Science*. New York: Harper & Row, Publishers, 1965.

Wicker, Brian, *Toward a Contemporary Christianity*. Notre Dame, Ind.: University of Notre Dame Press, 1967.

Williams, Colin W., *Faith in a Secular Age*. New York: Harper & Row, 1966.

Winter, Gibson, *The New Creation as Metropolis.* New York: The Macmillan Co., 1963.